OUR GANG

THE MODERN JEWISH EXPERIENCE

Paula Hyman and Deborah Dash Moore, *editors*

OUR GANG

JEWISH CRIME AND THE NEW YORK JEWISH COMMUNITY, 1900-1940

Jenna Weissman Joselit

INDIANA UNIVERSITY PRESS
BLOOMINGTON

The author would like to thank Thomas E. Dewey, Jr., for permission to quote from "Reminiscences of Thomas E. Dewey"; Paul O'Dwyer for permission to quote from "Reminiscences of William O'Dwyer"; and Henoch Mendelsund for permission to quote from the ILGWU Oral History Interview with Charles Zimmerman. The oral history memoir of Jonah J. Goldstein is copyrighted by The Trustees of Columbia University in the City of New York and is used with their permission.

First Midland Book Edition 1983

Manufactured in the United States of America

Library of Congress Cataloging in Publication Data

Joselit, Jenna Weissman.
Our gang.

(The Modern Jewish experience)
Includes bibliographical references and index.
1. Jews—New York (N.Y.)—Social conditions.
2. Jewish criminals—New York (N.Y.) 3. Crime and criminals—New York (N.Y.) 4. New York (N.Y.)—Social conditions. I. Title. II. Series: Modern Jewish experience (Indiana University Press)
F128.9.J5J67   1983   305.8'924'07471   82-49287
ISBN 0-253-15845-1
ISBN 0-253-20314-7 (pbk.)
2 3 4 5 87 86 85 84

for JOZ

Most Jews are entirely ignorant of the
fact that there is a problem of this nature
confronting them. They apparently rest
secure in their notions of the traditional
reputation of the Jewish race. Few Jews
have the remotest notion of the extent to
which this thing has taken hold and is
undermining the best traditions of the race.

HARRY W. NEWBERGER, 1916

Contents

Acknowledgments

Comments the Midrash: "We should be grateful to those from whom we profit." In the course of writing this book, I have profited from many people—and am duly grateful. Sigmund Diamond first suggested the possibilities of writing on Jews and crime, for which I thank him. Walter P. Metzger saw me through the various stages of research and writing of my dissertation; I learned a great deal from his keen sense of style and acute historical sensibility and hope that this book is one of which he can be proud. Herbert Gans, Marvin Herzog, Paula Hyman, and David Rothman read an earlier version of this study and their incisive comments helped me to sharpen my focus, as did Jeffrey Gurock's reading of a subsequent draft. Deborah Dash Moore's interest in and encouragement of my work was of enormous value to me as were several conversations with Arthur Goren. The research for this book was funded by generous grants from the Memorial Foundation for Jewish Culture and the National Foundation for Jewish Culture; I thank them both for their support. I am additionally grateful to the National Foundation for Jewish Culture for its special grant toward reproduction of the photographs used in this book.

I owe a great deal to the staffs of the various archives and libraries with whom I consulted. I am particularly indebted to Idilio Gracia Peña and Kenneth R. Cobb, Director and Assistant Director respectively of the New York City Municipal Archives, for helping me to find my way through the maze that is New York City's criminal justice records; their assistance went far beyond the call of duty. Henoch Mendelsund and Robert Lazar of the ILGWU Archives were most helpful, as were the staffs of the American Jewish Archives, American Jewish Historical Society, Central Archives for the History of the Jewish People (Hebrew University), Columbia University libraries, Yivo, and the Jewish Division of the New York Public Library.

xi

I am deeply obliged to Ivan Karp for his generous and friendly interest in my work, to Joan Kaplan for her expertise as a photographer, and to Ari Goldman for his cheerfully rendered assistance.

My greatest thanks I reserve for my family—especially my parents—whose love and warmth sustained me through many rough moments. Finally, I dedicate this, my first, book to my husband, Joz, for sharing his wife and his home with the members of Our Gang—no mean task but one which he bore always with grace, patience, and love.

OUR GANG

INTRODUCTION

"Black Sheep in New York Israel"?

Throughout their long residence in North America, a residence which dated back to the mid-seventeenth century, Jews had a reputation for being among the more law-abiding and peaceful of the nation's citizenry. In New York of the eighteenth and nineteenth centuries, police officials often commended the city's Jews for keeping their neighborhoods free of crime, noting that in the Jewish quarter "there is less crime . . . than in any other . . . ." In the nation's capital, Jews were singled out for praise by the *Washington Sentinel*, which found them to be "among our best citizens. This ancient race can boast that there are fewer paupers and fewer criminals among them than any other race can exhibit." "Proof of the high moral standing of the Hebrews," related a third contemporary source, the popular *Century* magazine, "is that only two murderers have sprung from their ranks in two hundred and fifty years." Now and then, Jews were criticized for their "excessive" fondness for money—and their purported zeal in acquiring it. Images of the crafty Jewish peddler and the wily Jewish businessman were common features of American folklore and Jewish "monetary malfeasance" a familiar theme of mid–nineteenth century plays and dimestore novels. Yet, to engage in sharp business practices was one thing; it was quite another to commit an actual crime. In this respect, most Americans believed the Jews were exceptional. "If we enter a penitentiary or prison of any description," commented a nineteenth-century journalist, "the marked face of the Israelite is rarely to be seen within its walls," while the Philadelphia *Evening Telegram* observed that "no other element in the community is so orderly in character and so observant of the law. A Jew," the paper added, "is seldom or never seen in our courts on a criminal charge."[1]

1

Americans accounted for the impressive morality of their fellow Jewish citizens in a variety of ways. Some attributed the paucity of Jewish prisoners and paupers to a kind of Darwinian struggle of the fittest; they believed that by successfully weathering centuries of persecution the Jews had emerged hardier and less inclined to fall into criminal ways. Others held that obedience to the precepts of Judaism was a deterrent to the pursuit of illegal activities; still others suggested that by inheritance, somehow, Jews "possess a certain moral stamina," as one Boston economist put it. Whatever the reason, Americans believed that Jewish malefactors were "almost unknown" in the years preceding the great waves of immigration.[2]

American Jewry could hardly agree more with these evaluations of its character. "The crown of the Jewish people," boasted Jewish civic leader Isidore Strauss, "is the purity of its home." Social worker Morris Weinstein, writing in the pages of the *American Hebrew*, concurred: "The moral fiber of the Jewish race has been its greatest pride for centuries." Attributing this admirable record to their being God's Chosen People, a nation among whom "the roots of morality are firmly planted," Jews felt bound to a higher moral standard than that of other nations and governed their lives accordingly; their sense of themselves as a "holy nation, a nation of priests" did not allow easily for lapses from that standard. Jews maintained, almost as an article of faith, that "THERE OUGHT TO BE NO JEWISH CRIMINALS AT ALL." When it came to crime, exceptionality was not simply a part of the Jews' traditional belief in the Chosen People notion or merely a source of ethnic pride; it was also a weapon, a tool of survival. In addition to their well-ingrained habit of presenting their best face to the outside world, a habit assiduously cultivated over the centuries, Jews understood all too well that being linked to burgeoning crime rates in America could spell disaster. As nativism or anti-immigrant, and sometime anti-Semitic, sentiment began to sweep the country toward the latter part of the nineteenth century, American Jewry's long-standing belief in its own moral probity became a practical matter as well, serving as a bid for special exemption from mounting nativist pressures. "The member of our faith who lives through illicit gain," explained one anxious Jew during the pre–World War I era, the heyday of nativism in this country, "is not only a disgrace to us but a dangerous foe to the liberty we Jews now enjoy in America. To continue liberal immigration," he added, "Jews must live pure lives."[3]

The importance of living a "pure life" was not a new concern of America's Jews; nor, for that matter, was anti-immigrant sentiment. For much of American history, Americans fastened on the immigrant as the source of the nation's criminals. During the colonial and federal periods, Americans blamed the growing crime problem on England's practice of transporting convicts and sometimes even the unemployed to the New World. In later years, as German and Irish newcomers arrived in great numbers, the native-born American worried lest his country be "infested by hordes of foreign wretches, pickpockets, thieves, robbers, forgers etc." Determined to prevent America from becoming the "penal colony" of the world, anti-immigrant partisans, or nativists, as they were called, formed political parties to press for the restriction of immigration from abroad. Despite the prevalence of nativist sentiment in the United States, efforts to enact federal legislation institutionalizing nativism were largely unsuccessful. Not until the very end of the nineteenth century did restrictive or anti-immigrant legislation campaigns actually take hold. Arguing that "if the colored and foreign born elements were eliminated this country would almost realize a golden dream of freedom from crime," the nation's most ardent nativists in 1894 organized a lobby group, the Immigration Restriction League (IRL), to crusade for a national policy of restrictive immigration.[4]

Composed largely of Boston Brahmins, the IRL preyed on the fears of many Americans that the moral fabric of American society was being undermined by the country's open immigration policy. The immigrant served as a foil by which dissatisfied Americans, entering the twentieth century, could grapple with the twin ills of modernity and urbanization. Cities were bewildering; newspapers and magazines were constantly reporting that crime was on the upsurge; the economy appeared to be unstable and the country at large incapable of accommodating the millions of immigrants seeking admission. Who other than the foreigner was responsible for these ostensible symptoms of disorder? If at the same time that crime was increasing, the foreign born were inundating the United States, might there not be some connection between the two? To comprehend the processes of modernization and to make them more manageable, Americans, observed one sociologist, tend "to person[ify] the cause for all crime in the figure of a man with a foreign sounding name . . . ." Placing responsibility for the alleged crime wave on the foreigner not only made sense, it also carried with it a large measure of psychological comfort by removing responsibility from the native-born American. Thus, the immigrant became a scapegoat for the ills of modernity. To IRL members E. A. Ross, a leading University of Wisconsin sociologist, and Boston blue-blood DeCourcey Ward, the new immigrants—those hailing from Southern and Eastern Europe—were likely to become a "menace" to America's health and morals; IRL lobbyists, writes John Higham, "fixed upon the new immigration as a major source of current disorders." To their "practiced eye," the Jews were decidedly inferior, "moral cripples" who "because of their lack of reverence for the law break any ordinance they find in their way." Furthermore, suggesting that there was something inherently corrupt and wily about the Jews, the nativists maintained that even Jewish *children* were guilty of malfeasance; Jewish youngsters, Ross complained, were "importunate" about having their grades changed! Convinced of the moral inferiority of the new immigrants, the IRL campaigned energetically for the imposition of quotas on immigrants from Eastern and Southern Europe. Seasoned enough politically not to rely solely on the impressions of their "practiced eye," IRL lobbyists buttressed their pleas for a closed immigration policy with seemingly irrefutable and "scientific" statistics. With little regard for such mitigating factors as age or percentage of population, they drew on prison and court statistics to show that in the aggregate, the foreign-born population included far more ne'er-do-wells than the native-born.[5]

As pressure for immigration restriction grew apace, crime rates became targets of legislative inquiry; ultimately, criminal statistics provided the factual groundwork on which proposals to limit immigration or to compel repatriation rested. The Dillingham Commission, for example, was the first of many federally sponsored investigations of the impact of immigration upon the culture, economy, health, and moral well-being of the nation at large. Established in 1907, it labored for three years, at a cost of over one million dollars, examining virtually every aspect of the immigrant experience. After closely inspecting all sorts of data on American criminal activity, ranging from published United States census material to the unpublished reports of local workhouses and jails, the commission's researchers concluded that "no satisfactory evidence has yet been produced to show that immigration has resulted in an increase in crime disproportionate to the increase in adult population." Though the Commission's findings appeared to exonerate the new immigrants of the charge that, as a group, they were inherently criminal, the association between them and crime persisted. A decade after the Dillingham Commission, the first quota, closing the open door policy and sharply delimiting the flow of Jews and other disfavored groups into America, was on the books. Perhaps not many Jews on the Lower East Side actually read the Dillingham Commission reports or the publications of the IRL. But the findings which highlighted the alleged moral inferiority of the new immigrants were freely disseminated through the Jewish and the metropolitan press and undoubtedly became the subject of many heated discussions on the "Jewish street." There was no mistaking the climate of the pre–World War I era: the Dillingham Commission notwithstanding, belief in the criminality of the foreign born was widespread.[6]

Given the popularity of that view, Jews were forced to sit up and take notice of it. What is more, reports of pronounced Jewish criminal activity in New York, home to America's largest concentration of Jews, were beginning to emanate at the turn of the century from circles far less jaundiced and far more objective than the IRL. The Lexow Committee report of 1894, an investigation into municipal corruption in the Empire City, was one such document. Publicly disclosing, for perhaps the first time, the existence of a sizable Jewish criminal element on Manhattan's Lower East Side, the over-ten-thousand-page report startled the New York Jewish community. Acting on information provided by the crime-fighting Reverend Charles Parkhurst and his Society for the Prevention of Vice, the seven-member committee charged that the New York Police Department had actively protected gamblers and prostitutes and that Tammany Hall had tacitly sponsored such activities. Dozens of Jewish prostitutes took the stand and testified to having paid hundreds of dollars in protection money to greedy policemen; residents of the Lower East Side, victims of extortion schemes, told of being bamboozled out of their savings by a corrupt ring of Essex Market Court lawyers, policemen, and bail bondsmen like Charles "Silver Dollar" Solomon and Max Hochstim.[7]

In the years following the publication of the Lexow Committee report, Jews increasingly appeared as members-in-full of the city's underworld. The Mazet Committee investigations of 1896, a second inquiry into municipal corruption, covered much of the same ground as its predecessor, and it too reported evidence of active Jewish participation in prostitution, extortion, and petty crime. A year later, perhaps the most damning description to date of Jewish criminality appeared. Entitled *The American Metropolis*, the three-volume work was written by Frank Moss, a patrician civic reformer and former chief counsel to the Mazet Committee, and described various aspects of the urban experience in the greatest of American metropolises, New York; among Moss's themes was the Jewish underworld. Moss depicted "Old Israel"— the German-Jewish community—as respectable citizens, in contrast to "New Israel"—the Eastern European Jewish community—whose people lived lives of unbridled license. On the narrow, dirt-encrusted streets of the Lower East Side with their "babel of symphonic and dissonant sounds," Jews could be found everywhere "addicted to vice." Many Jewish women, Moss observed, "know no other occupation than prostitution," while "a large number of worthies, some of them pimps, gamblers, thugs, fighters and dive-keepers represent undoubtedly the ruling power of the great district . . . ." The Lower East Side, the civic reformer concluded, "is a distinct center of crime . . . and the criminal instincts that are so often found naturally in Russian and Polish Jews come to the surface here in such ways as to warrant the opinion that these people are *the worst element in the entire make-up of New York life*."[8]

Accounts like Moss's, purporting to show the extent and nature of Jewish criminality, shocked and frightened most New York Jews, blackening their reputation and threatening their security. More importantly still, it forced many to grapple with the very real, if distasteful, possibility that their once vaunted self-image as a "holy people" was now to be replaced by that of "merchants of vice." "It was not to be supposed that there were no black sheep in New York Israel," commented the *Jewish Messenger*, an Anglo-Jewish middle-class weekly, "but that there should be so many is . . . an unpleasant revelation." Jewish crime, lamented another Jewish New Yorker at the turn of the century, was a "black spot" on the Jewish community's hitherto unassailable reputation. Still another contemporary complained bitterly that the existence of a Jewish underworld "will be our disgrace . . . the evil will be laid at our doors." For its part, the immigrant or downtown community was equally if not more disturbed. Perhaps the existence of a Jewish underworld in the New World did not come as a total shock to the Yiddish-speaking residents of the Lower East Side, but their concern was real enough. These revelations of Jewish criminality were symptomatic of an uneasy future. To be sure, Jewish criminality in the Old World was far from rare. The *betteljuden* of the medieval and early modern period, bands of wandering beggar Jews who often turned to crime to support themselves; the Jewish fences and pick-pockets of eighteenth-century England; and the Odessa *voil yungen* of the late nineteenth century—"young sports and toughs . . . dabbling in prostitution and blackmail"—suggest the extent to which crime was a constant feature of the European Jewish experience. Yet, perhaps in this instance, as in so many others, immigrants wanted to believe there existed a radical break between life in the Old and in the New Worlds; what was tolerated in Europe was not to be tolerated in America. If Jewish crime in the old country, the immigrants reasoned, was a func-tion of centuries of oppression and therefore easily understandable, how was one to understand the existence of a Jewish criminal element in a land where, presumably, oppression was conspicuously absent?[9]

Even as they pondered the future of Jewish life in New York, both German and Eastern European Jews were reluctant to take any action to curb the growth of the Jewish underworld. Embarrassed by the existence of Jewish criminals, they were far more willing to "cast them off" than to effect their rehabilitation or eliminate the sources of vice and crime in the Jewish quarter of the city. There was one small or-ganization, known as the Jewish Prisoners Association, that ministered to the tiny number of Jewish inmates in the state's prisons; the com-munity treated it with indifference. Founded in January 1891 by the Board of Jewish Ministers, an association of local New York rabbis who were troubled by the lack of "moral considerations" which Chris-tian chaplains were giving to the Jewish inmates of Sing Sing and Auburn prisons, and with Adolph Radin, a young Polish-born rabbi with a degree from the University of Berlin, as its chaplain, the Jewish Prisoners Association regularly visited the Jewish prisoners, attending to their spiritual needs. Perhaps an even stronger incentive to the for-mation of the Association was the need to combat Christian missionary efforts in the state's penal system. Contending that Christian missionaries visiting the jails would "steal our boys" by giving them sympathy and understanding where the Jewish community, embarrassed by their existence, ignored them, the Jewish Prisoners Association hoped that Radin's presence would serve as a deterrent to Christian "missionary wiles." Despite the priority the community had generally placed on anti-missionary work, the Jewish Prisoners Association fared poorly; between 1891 and 1893, it lived from hand to mouth, barely able to meet expenses. New York Jewry's collective reluctance to admit to the existence of Jewish criminality apparently overshadowed whatever dismay it may have felt at Christian missionary activity.[10]

The organization gave every indication of closing. Fortuitously enough, in March 1893, Jacob H. Schiff and Rabbi Gustav Gottheil, rabbi of the prestigious Temple Emanu-El, stepped in and took over the financially strapped organization, reconstituting it as the Society to Aid the Jewish Prisoner (SAJP). Contending that no matter how steep, the price for indulging in "the luxury of revelation" had to be paid, and with fifty-five Jewish men incarcerated in the state's prisons, Schiff and others insisted that the community take steps to prevent future outbreaks of Jewish criminal activity. "We dare not close our eyes as we have done in the past," the SAJP Board explained. "Knowing the existing evil, we must face it and do our best to mitigate its dire consequences." With a virtual monopoly of Jewish civic leadership and in the habit of addressing difficult social problems, of which crime was one, German Jews like Schiff took the lead in sponsoring and building institutions to "mitigate the dire consequences" of Jewish criminality. German Jewish leaders also knew that, because of mounting nativism, they could neither escape nor ignore the problem of Jewish crime by emphasizing the ethnic difference between themselves and the Eastern European Jews. The outside world, they realized all too well, classified the two groups as one. Like their non-Jewish counterparts, Schiff and his colleagues built a series of institutions, beginning with the SAJP and culminating years later in the Hawthorne School, designed to prevent the future emergence of Jewish criminals on the one hand and, on the other, to rehabilitate those who had already lapsed. By the tail end of the nineteenth century, uptown's Jews had developed an institutional framework in which to address the problem of Jewish criminality.[11]

The Society to Aid the Jewish Prisoner was the cornerstone of New York Jewry's efforts to eliminate Jewish criminality. With a membership of approximately two hundred persons, virtually all of them German Jews, the society was concerned more with rehabilitating Jewish prisoners than with combating missionaries. Retaining Radin as its primary chaplain and eventually hiring several additional clergymen as well, the SAJP attempted to ensure that every Jewish inmate of a correctional facility receive the financial and spiritual care necessary to effect his rehabilitation. It extended material aid to the families of men imprisoned and granted small stipends, ranging from a few dollars to fifty dollars, to released Jewish convicts. While in prison, Jewish inmates were asked by the society to attend weekly religious services and to seek out the counsel of Radin and his men. Instilling spiritual piety in the prisoner through the medium of religious instruction and counseling, SAJP members believed, was an effective agent of moral reform.[12]

Using as its motto, "Though fallen from grace, he remains, as God's child, your brother still," the leadership of the SAJP campaigned ardently among the members of the uptown community for financial and moral support. Yet it seems they made little headway. Some Jews ignored the pleas of the SAJP hoping that Jewish criminality was temporary; others felt the establishment of a Jewish society to deal publicly with Jewish offenders was dangerous and a poor reflection upon the good name of the community at large, "We grant this is so," replied the officers of the SAJP to such rejections. "But is not the frightful *horde* [!] of them [Jewish prisoners] . . . an abundant reason for us to make every proper effort to reduce their numbers?" Not until 1907, with the establishment of the Hawthorne School, America's first all-Jewish reformatory, did uptown Jews finally overcome their deep-seated reluctance to acknowledge publicly that Jewish criminality was a very real social problem.[13]

In the intervening years, Schiff and his fellow SAJP board members continued their efforts to win support for the Society to Aid the Jewish Prisoner. Not surprisingly, few if any Eastern European Jews were consulted or even asked to participate in the society's fund-raising drives. Perhaps had they been asked to do so, their attitude to Jewish criminality might have been altogether different. As it turned out, downtown Jewry took far longer than its uptown counterpart in recognizing and combating Jewish crime. It was, of course, hard for residents of the Lower East Side not to be aware of Jewish prostitution, thievery, or pickpocketing; as one observer put it, Lower East Side Jews "rubbed up" against the Jewish criminal element almost daily. Jewish women lined Allen and Rivington Streets calling out to passersby while thieves and strikebreakers loafed brazenly outside of any number of Second Avenue restaurants and cafes. The East Side, noted Abe Shoenfeld, a keen-eyed detective who spent much of the pre–World War I era intently observing the activities of the Jewish underworld and whose first-hand accounts of Jewish crime on the Lower East Side

are an unparalleled source of crime history, "is sullied by these things—
pool parlors, illegitimate saloons, hangouts, street corner conditions,
and what not." Not only was the city's densest Jewish quarter "sullied"
by the presence of criminals and criminal haunts but it was also integrally linked to the Jewish criminal enterprise: Jewish criminals drew
much of their sustenance from the neighborhood's businesses; the Lower
East Side molded the criminal activities of its more deviant residents.[14]

Yet only when the outside world pointed an accusatory finger at
them did the immigrant members of New York Jewry take steps to
eradicate Jewish criminality. As stories of wholesale Jewish wrongdoing figured more and more prominently in the English-language
metropolitan press and as Jews increasingly became objects of public
review, the Eastern European community could no longer remain
"dimly conscious" of the dimensions of Jewish criminality. By World
War I it had come openly to recognize Jewish crime as a serious social
problem and to work in concert with uptown Jews to ferret out
Jewish criminals in its own neighborhood. Anxious lest immigration
restrictionists compel repatriation or, worse still, shut the doors to
future immigration from abroad, the immigrant community joined
forces with its uptown coreligionists and formed a Jewish detective
agency. Known as the Bureau of Social Morals and sponsored by the
Kehillah, New York Jewry's much-heralded umbrella organization,
this "Jewish police station" worked for five years, from 1912 until
1917, surveying the activities of local Jewish criminals and then reporting their whereabouts to the police.

Through it all, the members of the pre–World War I Jewish community wondered what had gone awry. Startled, embarrassed, and
frightened by the seeming explosion in Jewish criminal activity, prewar
Jews gingerly engaged in a series of ongoing internal reviews of New
York Jewish life to help them comprehend the uprooting of their
"firmly planted morality." Examining the community's social, religious,
cultural, and economic institutions, New York Jews came to the sorry
conclusion that these institutions were woefully lacking, inadequate
to the task of successfully introducing the immigrants to the bewildering texture of the New York Jewish experience. They also belatedly
realized that their earlier reluctance to confront Jewish criminality
head-on, a reluctance which predated the massive upswing in Jewish
crime, fostered conditions in which a Jewish underworld could take
root and flourish.

Though distressed by the emergence of such a large Jewish criminal element, Jewish communal leaders and social workers remained guardedly optimistic that Jewish crime was a transient phenomenon, destined to fade away as immigrant Jews became more Americanized, more sure-footed in the ways of American life. Jewish crime, they insisted, was a consequence of the immigrant experience and not the result of some genetic, built-in defect. Eliminate the social and environmental causes of criminality, reasoned New York Jewry's moral custodians, and the underworld would disappear as a matter of course.

Ultimately these expectations were fulfilled. Jewish crime, for the most part, remained an immigrant phenomenon, the malaise of one generation of transplanted European Jews and their children. In succeeding decades, the number of Jewish criminals declined markedly, so much so that one contemporary, surveying criminal statistics in the 1930s, reported that the Jewish underworld was rapidly "sinking." But, though a shadow of its former self, the Jewish underworld of the interwar years did not disappear altogether: this was the period which witnessed the rise of Arnold Rothstein and Lepke Buchalter, a period when savvy graduates of New York's street gangs became sophisticated bootleggers. Nevertheless, in both absolute and relative terms, Jewish criminality had ceased to be a Jewish social problem by the outbreak of World War II. Then, too, over the years, Jewish criminality had become an enterprise increasingly divorced from its Jewish context. In contrast to the highly visible and distinctly Jewish flavor of the prewar Jewish underworld, tightly bound up with the Lower East Side and neighborhoods like it, the postwar Jewish underworld was both less visibly Jewish and less distinctly tied to the Jewish ethnic economy.

Reflecting these changes in the Jewish underworld experience, New York Jews of the interwar generation were far more relaxed and accepting of Jewish criminality than their parents had been. Though, like their mothers and fathers, New York Jews of the 1920s and 1930s were never fully able to read about a Jewish criminal without experiencing a twinge or two of anxiety, though never able to acknowledge the existence of a Jewish underworld in a wholly dispassionate fashion, New York Jews of the interwar generation—of the second generation—consistently failed to exhibit the fear and angst which had characterized the attitude of their parents' generation toward Jewish criminality. For a host of reasons which will be explored, Jewish criminality did not connote for them (as it had for an earlier generation) the failure of the American Jewish experience. Where immigrant Jews had viewed Jewish crime with unqualified alarm, as a development which threatened their stake in American society, their children came to see it as a natural part of the American landscape, a phenomenon that in no way colored or impinged on their own growing sense of security as Americans.

The history of Jewish criminal activity in New York over a forty-year period and the response of the organized New York Jewish community to that phenomenon lies at the heart of this study. Opening with a description of the Hawthorne School, New York Jewry's ambitious attempt to rehabilitate Jewish delinquents, this volume continues with a portrait of the Jewish underworld of the pre–World War I era. That, in turn, is succeeded by a detailed analysis of New York Jewry's response to crime in general and to the Bingham and Rosenthal affairs of 1908 and 1912 in particular. The chapters that follow deal with such crucial aspects of the Jewish underworld's history as Prohibition, racketeering, and the careers of the "businessmen" of crime, Arnold Rothstein, Lepke Buchalter, and the Murder Inc. gang members. The book closes with an analysis of the interwar Jewish community's response to each of these developments. Ultimately, though, this study is not so much concerned with the history of the Jewish underworld, fascinating as it may be, but rather with the changing self-perceptions and self-images of the New York Jewish community over time. This work suggests that the attitude of both first- and second-generation New York Jews toward crime provides a wonderful handle with which to explore the identity of that community. The issue of crime, like the Emancipation debates of the nineteenth and early twentieth centuries, served to emphasize and to delineate the identity of the modern European Jew. In the period of Jewish Emancipation in Central and Western Europe, prolonged and heated national debates over the civic and political rights of the Jews gave the Jews a clear sense of what was expected of them by the host society. Living in a post-Emancipatory society where, from the very outset, the granting of civic and political rights to the Jews was a built-in condition of their existence (and not something subject to debate), America's Jews had little, if any, insight into what others thought of them; Americans at large, by the same token, had little notion of who or what the American Jew was. But crime, a problem that engaged the attention of the New York Jewish community and, in turn, that of the larger New York population as well for close to four decades, served to highlight New York Jewry's understanding

of itself even as it shaped the outside world's view of its Jewish neighbors. The continuous controversy that raged between the authorities
and Jewish communal leaders over Jewish criminality, a controversy
that extended well into the 1930s, spilling over to such diverse areas of
American life as immigration restriction, Prohibition, and the unionization of American labor, sharpened each side's perception of the other.
Moreover, like little else in American Jewish history, crime forced New
York's Jews into evaluating their communal institutions and ultimately
into addressing the central issue of the New York Jewish experience:
the shape and future of New York Jewish life.[15]

"A SPLENDID INSTITUTION"

The Hawthorne School

On a bright spring day in May 1907, several hundred
of New York's most socially prominent Jews—among them
the Schiffs, the Loebs, and the Mayers—gathered at Grand
Central Station in preparation for a trip upstate. In five specially rented coaches, they traveled for nearly two hours until they
reached the small Westchester town of Hawthorne. Upon arriving,
the travelers were then transported by a caravan of forty carriages
"along a steep, rocky and tortuous road" (as a somewhat nervous member of the party later recalled) until they arrived at their destination:
a 260-acre site atop a mountain ridge. An ordinary spring get-together
for the members of "Our Crowd"? Though it certainly had all the
earmarks of a holiday jaunt in the country, this was no routine social
gathering: these guests had come to dedicate America's first all-Jewish
reformatory: the Hawthorne School.[1]

Calling the dedication a "happy moment" in Jewish history, Henry
Solomon, chairman of the building committee, officially opened the
day's celebration by presenting a detailed account of New York Jewry's
recent efforts at eliminating Jewish crime. Explaining that it was an
"absolutely new problem," Solomon described how ill prepared most
New York Jews were to recognize its seriousness. Though reports of
significant Jewish criminal activity had appeared in the metropolitan
press as early as the 1890s and been privately discussed by concerned
New York Jews at that time, it was not until 1900 that the SAJP board
"seriously considered" establishing a Jewish correctional facility. It
took yet another six years, Solomon reminded his listeners, for New
York Jewry to be "educated into a realization of the tremendous necessity" for a Jewish reformatory. An effective and impassioned speaker,

Solomon in no way exaggerated the difficulties Hawthorne's earliest supporters had had in obtaining support for the project. Generous in committing funds to a Jewish hospital or orphan asylum, many German Jews had balked at building a Jewish reformatory. Their motives were varied. Some felt that Jews as a group had no business establishing a correctional facility; since crime was a social problem, they argued that the state—and not private philanthropy—should assume responsibility for curbing it. "We deprecate an exclusively Jewish movement in this direction," explained the *Jewish Messenger*. "Why not insist on Jewish prisons and Jewish insane asylums? Sectarianism can be carried too far." Others believed that Jewish juvenile delinquency could best be eliminated by placing recalcitrant youth in a vocational school and "training them [to] a useful career." Still others of a more practical cast reasoned that the small Jewish community, already financially overburdened, could ill afford the cost of erecting and maintaining yet another institution. Hovering above all these explanations was the fear that building a Jewish reformatory would call undue attention to Jewish criminality and in turn to New York Jewish life. Many Jews, observed Louis Marshall, feel "it is better that [Jewish offenders] be lost to Israel; they will not redound to the credit of Israel." Yet this view, the civic leader explained, was short-sighted, for when the Jewish criminal was arrested, "discredit attaches to us whether we do or do not recognize him." New York Jews, commented the *Israelite Alliance Review*, "preferred to live in the memory of the past when the ties of home and religion were stronger and our young less beset by temptations. We preferred to let the few transgressors be lost among the greater number belonging to other creeds rather than call attention to our own by a special institution."[2]

Yet over the years the growing number of Jewish "transgressors" simply rendered these objections obsolete. "There have never been as many Jewish children before the courts as there are now," commented social worker David Blaustein in 1904; Jewish children, another contemporary noted, "throng the courts." "It seems as though there were some positive force that is drawing Jewish children into criminal ways," an alarmed *American Hebrew* wrote a year later; more than one-third of the population of the House of Refuge and the New York Juvenile Asylum, two of New York's leading correctional facilities, was then Jewish. Given the "brutality of statistics," concerned Jews could no longer sidestep the need for some organized and preferably institutionalized way of combating Jewish criminality; a Jewish reformatory, cried the *American Hebrew,* was now a "necessity."[3]

Alarmed by what seemed to be a virtual explosion in the number of youthful Jewish offenders yet confident they could eliminate or at least moderate the problem, Jacob H. Schiff and his fellow SAJP board members crusaded energetically among the members of the uptown community for their financial and moral support. Holding special fundraising events and even special Sabbaths devoted to the theme of moral uplift, they eventually overcame the community's deep-seated opposition. After years of "incessant labor" New York Jews raised close to three hundred thousand dollars with which to purchase, build, and operate a Jewish correctional facility.[4]

Located on a magnificent tract of land overlooking the Hudson River, replete with baseball diamond, running track, football field, playgrounds, and individual "garden plots," Hawthorne evoked a deliberately unprisonlike atmosphere. "It has more in common with a country home," remarked one delighted Hawthorne supporter as he surveyed the pleasing surroundings. A central building housed classrooms, workshops, a gymnasium, and a synagogue. Flanking it on both sides were several small cottages which the visitors believed "resembled summer homes." Designed to "duplicate the natural surroundings of the home," each cottage housed thirty youngsters or "waifs," most of whom had thus far spent their lives in shabby and crowded tenements. Contributing to the casual atmosphere was the absence of walls; "there are no iron hands to institutionalize the children," boasted Julius Mayer, Hawthorne's president, while its newly hired superintendent, John Klein, explained that "we try to escape as much as possible from the Protectory idea and to consider and treat our institution at Hawthorne as a school, pure and simple." From the individual garden plots to the euphemistic name, Hawthorne was to be the sort of place where, when asked where he learned his trade, the former inmate "may not hesitate to pronounce [it]." "There is much in a name," commented the *American Hebrew* in connection with the decision to call the Jewish correctional facility the Hawthorne School as opposed to the Hawthorne Protectory or the Jewish Reformatory. "Euphemism has its purposes and here is where it may serve a good purpose."[5]

In calling itself the Hawthorne School—in fact in building the institution as a training school and not as a reformatory—Solomon and his coworkers drew on the most up-to-date notions of penology. During the pre–World War I period, social scientists and prison reformers began gradually to develop new theories of criminal behavior and, in turn, new theories of penology. Favoring an environmental interpretation of crime, they rejected the biological determinism of an earlier generation of penologists and social theorists. During the latter part of the nineteenth century and the early years of the twentieth, theories of the "born criminal" were widely circulated among and favored by the American public. The criminology of Cesare Lombroso, an Italian doctor, was one of the most popular. Lombroso discovered in the 1860s that the cranial structure of one of Italy's most famous outlaws resembled that of a rodent. This discovery, which the doctor called a "revelation," led him to develop an interpretation of crime according to which criminals were distinguishable from noncriminals by a variety of physical characteristics. Enormous jaws, high cheekbones, handle-shaped ears, and flat feet were some of the hallmarks of the "born criminal." At the same time that Lombroso was scrutinizing the population of Italian prisons, American social scientists claimed to have found evidence of the genetic origins of deviancy and social pathology. Tracing the history of the Jukes family, most of whose four hundred members were either mentally unbalanced, physically defective, or criminals, Robert Dugdale sought to show the organic roots of deviancy. Adherents of this particular branch of criminal anthropology received further confirmation of their views with the publication in 1912 of a study by psychologist Henry Goddard. Like Dugdale a generation earlier, Goddard found evidence demonstrating that deviancy could be transmitted from generation to generation in the history of the Kallikaks. Like the Jukes, the approximately five hundred members of the Kallikak family had an essentially unbroken record of social pathology. Using the work of Dugdale and Goddard as their guide, eugenicists subsequently pressed for the sterilization of the unfit and the restriction of immigration. Ultimately, though, biological determinism gave way to a broader and more sociological analysis of criminality. The publication in 1915 of psychiatrist William Healy's *The Individual Delinquent,* for example, encouraged the development of a multi-causal interpretation of crime. Stressing the psychological roots of criminality, the work also showed how poverty, overcrowding, and bad companions contributed to delinquency. Using Healy's work as their guide, many social scientists and prison reformers of the immediate pre–World War

I generation adopted an environmental interpretation of criminality according to which external factors—not genes—shaped or determined criminal behavior.[6]

In their understanding of criminality, Jewish social workers and civic reformers stressed environmental factors over biological ones, social factors over physiological ones. They referred to the then-popular notions of the "born criminal" only to refute them. "New York's preponderance of Jewish criminals," explained the *American Hebrew*, "is not due to inherent qualities—if this were so, one would find Jewish criminals in Hartford, Syracuse, and Albany—but rather to some local condition: congestion. When three thousand people live on one block, how can the decencies of life be maintained? Under conditions in which ten to twelve people of both sexes live together, moral health cannot help but deteriorate." "Heredity," insisted Boris Bogen, a leading Jewish social worker of the prewar generation, "plays a very insignificant part" in the etiology of Jewish criminal behavior; unlike the Jukes or the Kallikaks, the Jews "do not carry the ban of a criminal ancestry." Firmly rejecting biological determinism, Jewish moral custodians believed that the "outcropping" of crime on the Lower East Side was a consequence of the social and economic circumstances of life in the New World. The slum, they argued, was the breeding ground for prostitution and pickpocketing, truancy and desertion. To their minds, when herded into neighborhoods whose average density exceeded that of Bombay or into tenements which accommodated what seemed to be entire villages of people, the immigrants were willy-nilly "attacked in their moral fiber . . . for the natural concomitants of overcrowding are disease, vice and crime." Just as congestion bred TB and consumption, it bred promiscuity and immorality. Social workers Boris Bogen and Charles Bernheimer found the slum to be a metaphor for the frustrations of adjustment to American life or what was poetically called the "vicissitudes of unusual surroundings." Unfamiliar with the economic and social landscape, the immigrant, they explained, all too often jettisoned his traditional habits in order to become more fully integrated. Thus, "religious moorings," commented the *American Hebrew*, are "thrown over here." With little or no religious ballast, Jewish children were "all the time under influences that are NON-JEWISH." Viewing the Jew as little more than a Yiddish-speaking older man with an unkempt beard, the daily continued, Jewish youngsters "know and care nothing for Judaism and JUDAISM IS MORALITY." No wonder, then, it concluded, that criminality on the Lower East Side was growing.[7]

The abandonment of religion was, of course, not the sole factor in the etiology of Jewish criminal behavior; economic pressures, maintained Jewish social reformers, also took their toll. Forced to eke out a livelihood by hawking notions from a peddlar's stand or by toiling over a sewing machine for hours on end, the weary immigrant parent had little time to supervise the activities of his children. Growing up with a modicum of home life, these youngsters, Bernheimer related, "drift to the streets" where they substitute bonfires, pickpocketing, and robbing drunks for the lack of healthy recreational outlets. Unsupervised, the boys of the Lower East Side also spent much of their time in front of the poolrooms and saloons which dotted the neighborhood, hoping to be called upon to perform an errand for one of the regulars. "Standing there," related one long-time resident of the area, "the youngster hears and learns very quickly . . . and the tendencies for criminality are being slowly but surely developed."[8]

Attributing the emergence of Jewish criminality to local and environmental conditions, Jewish moral custodians also rejected the notion, so popular among nativists, that Jewish criminality was a European import. "Not Europe but America," exclaimed one Jewish prison official, "has produced many of the foreign born criminals within its precincts." Admittedly, most Jews listed on the criminal dockets hailed from Europe; according to the New York County District Attorney's office, an estimated three-quarters of Jews brought before it prior to World War I were foreign-born, the majority products of Russia. Nevertheless, few European Jews brought a tradition of illicit enterprise with them to the New World. With the exception of the "Odessa Thieves," a group of Russian-born pickpockets and master thieves whose specialty was robbing guests at Jewish weddings, and a number of white slave traders from much the same region, most Jews then branded as criminals apparently had become so in the New World, not in the Old. "Eighty-five percent of foreign-born criminals," wrote Rabbi Samuel Koch in the annual proceedings of the American Prison Association, "lived here for five years before they went astray. But five years of glorious Americanism proved more than their weak flesh could stand . . . ." Commenting on the charge that Jews were a group with decided criminal instincts, instincts honed from years of experience, Louis Marshall staunchly and unequivocally maintained that

Jewish criminality was "the product of conditions in *this* city and *this* country."[9]

Given the environmental roots of Jewish criminality—the overcrowded tenements, bitter economic conditions, inadequate recreational facilities, and the abandonment of religion—Jewish social workers remained optimistic that crime was a transient phenomenon among New York Jews, a consequence of the immigrant experience and not the result of some collective genetic defect. "I venture to state emphatically," Bernheimer related, "that the result [of Jewish criminality] is not due so much to inherent qualities as to the influences to which they have been subjected." Jewish social workers also knew, even if others did not, that those who made their way by illicit means represented a fraction of the larger Jewish community. "The East Side has its bad side," one contemporary explained, "but this is . . . not so serious and extensive as [is] represented . . . . " Aware that the Lower East Side produced "saints and sinners, philosophers and gunmen," the community's Bogens and Bernheimers believed that under the right conditions Jewish criminality could eventually be eliminated. Like many Progressives, Jewish social reformers held that "the problem [of crime] was manageable: it could be located spatially in the ghetto and it could be solved, given the right programs." The Hawthorne School, uptown's answer to downtown's problem, was New York Jewry's version of the "right program."[10]

Reflecting the community's belief in the environmental underpinnings of crime, Hawthorne's staff, headed by John Klein, the former superintendent of the New York Juvenile Asylum, sought to place the youthful offender in a healthy and carefully designed environment where after an average two-year stay, he would reemerge as a "good and useful citizen." Put differently, Hawthorne attempted to make the Jewish delinquent over into a member of New York's middle class. Every aspect of the facility—from its euphemistic name to its curriculum—was designed to effect that transformation. Indeed, for all its apparent freedom, Hawthorne was a rigorously controlled environment; from six in the morning until eight at night, the inmates followed a strictly prescribed regimen. Awakened at six, inmates quickly showered, dressed, and attended religious services, a "sort of compromise between the reform and orthodox forms of service," related John Klein. After a "nutritious" breakfast, designed to produce "bright-eyed, red-cheeked and healthy" boys, the inmates practiced military drills, a practice which Klein and his coworkers believed improved the inmates' health and taught them "prompt obedience and precision." This, in turn, was succeeded by three hours of classroom study, with a curriculum patterned after that of the public school system. After classes and lunch, inmates were given several hours of vocational training. An integral part of the Progressive ideology of reform, vocational training was one of Hawthorne's chief priorities; together with the three hours of classroom instruction, it was to "assure rehabilitation." Carpentry, plumbing, bricklaying, painting, printing, telegraphy, and woodcutting were taught to each of Hawthorne's "boys"; tailoring, however, and other related skills were studiously avoided. "It would be economy for us to make our own clothing," the superintendent explained, "but as work of this nature would be apprenticeship for sweatshop labor, classes in these trades are not to be recommended." Hawthorne not only believed it necessary to outfit its charges with the skills useful for a future solid economic existence, it was equally determined to retrain the "boys" lest they fall back into traditional Jewish economic practices, practices which Hawthorne's founders apparently perceived to be harmful. Hawthorne's residents, related Julius Mayer, the institution's president, "need to be taught useful trades so that in the years to come they will not be obligated to wear their lives away in sweatshops." "Our boys," Klein insisted, "ought to be fitted for something better."[11]

As part of their training, Hawthorne residents were also taught Hebrew and Judaism. Acting on the belief that a root cause of Jewish juvenile delinquency was the absence of Jewish education, Hawthorne's staff sought to provide the Jewish offender with at least a basic grounding in Judaism, hoping that it would serve as a "restraining influence." "Religion," observed Louis Marshall, "was the safety valve in the unfavorable conditions under which [the Jews] lived in Russia. They've thrown it over here." The poor Jewish education of most of the inmates at the Westchester facility reinforced the authorities' belief that Jewish education was a vital part of the rehabilitation program. Most of the "boy criminals" at Hawthorne were sadly deficient in their knowledge of Jewish life and of Hebrew. Only several could actually read Hebrew; a handful knew of the Jewish holidays, while the majority, lamented the institution's religious instructor, "have no knowledge whatsoever of the Jewish holidays or of any of the Jewish institutions." To remedy that deficiency, Hawthorne set aside several hours each week for religious instruction; in addition, the boys regularly attended synagogue, observed the dietary laws, and said "grace with their caps on."[12]

On the surface, Hawthorne's detailed program of rehabilitation appeared likely to succeed. What with the environmental determinants of crime, the outlook for the youthful Jewish offender was "hopeful": placed in a "healthy environment" and trained in useful and productive skills, Hawthorne inmates, insisted the school's supporters, would ultimately be able to enter the outside world as "Americans of the Jewish faith able to do their fair share in the affairs of men." Or as Louis Marshall poetically put it, there was every reason to believe, now that Hawthorne was a reality, that "the skiff would be restored to its anchorage . . . ." The optimism of Hawthorne's benefactors and its staff was infectious. Pleased by what they had seen and excited by the seemingly attainable prospect of eliminating Jewish criminality and restoring the skiff "to its anchorage," the dedication guests made their way home, "everyone commenting," the *Hebrew Standard* observed, "on the excellent character of the new and important addition to the cycle of institutions which the Jews of the city support." Hawthorne, everyone agreed, was truly a "splendid institution."[13]

THE LOWER EAST SIDE

Habitat of the Underworld

Less than a year after the dedication of the Hawthorne School, its founders began to falter in their optimism; their hopes for a swift and decisive end to Jewish criminality now seemed premature as New York Jews figured more and more prominently in judicial and popular accounts of the underworld. For one thing, the number of Jewish youngsters convicted of pickpocketing and other offenses had grown so rapidly in the interim that Hawthorne was unable to accommodate them. In 1908, over 250 Jewish delinquents had to be sent to a non-Jewish reformatory due to Hawthorne's lack of space; not until after World War I did the number of Jewish delinquents dwindle sufficiently to be handled entirely at Hawthorne. More sobering still was an article by Theodore A. Bingham, New York's police commissioner, in the September 1908 issue of the high-toned *North American Review*. Entitled "Foreign Criminals in New York," Bingham's observations with regard to Jewish criminal activity did nothing to dispel whatever doubts New York Jews might have had as to its transiency.[1]

Armed with a battery of seemingly incontestable statistics, the official stated that an estimated fifty percent of all New York criminals were Jews.

> Wherefore it is not astonishing that with a million Hebrews, mostly Russian, in the city . . . perhaps half of the criminals should be of that race, when we consider that ignorance of the language, more particularly among men not physically fit for hard labor, is conducive to crime.

In fact, according to the police official's calculations, at least eighty-five percent of the Empire City's criminals were foreign born, or as he put it, of "exotic origin." Italians, a people composed of "riffraff of desperate scoundrels, ex-convicts and jailbirds . . . ," comprised twenty percent of the city's criminal element while the remaining thirty percent were divided among "representatives of other alien races" and a few native-born Americans. What is more, Bingham asserted that the Jews (as well as the Italians) had a distinctive criminal nature. "The crimes committed by the Russian Hebrews," he wrote, "are generally those against property. They are burglars, firebugs, pickpockets and highway robbers—when they have the courage; but, though all crime is their province, pocket-picking is the one to which they seem to take most naturally."[2]

Ever alert to what was said about them in the English-language press, especially by high-ranking political figures, the city's Jewish newspapers printed long excerpts from Bingham's article. They also challenged the accuracy of his assertions. Some, as we will see in Chapter 4, quarreled with Bingham's definition of a criminal, others with his statistical tabulations. What could not be disputed, however, was Bingham's basic point: the existence of a sizable Jewish criminal class. Few could question that during the years of mass immigration, the Lower East Side had become a real "police problem," as another, perhaps more restrained, police commissioner put it. Explaining that among residents of the city's most densely populated Jewish quarter, "even vice was an industry," William McAdoo related that the Lower East Side had "produced quite an army of pickpockets and altogether too many burglars." Sad to say, he continued, "the quarter furnishes many recruits to the ranks of unfortunate women in all parts of town." Others echoed the police official's observations. "In certain aspects of Yiddish New York," Hutchins Hapgood wrote, "the enormous vitality of the Jews carries them far in the direction of vice," while George Kibbe Turner, an equally well known journalist, observed that the immigrant Jewish enclave was a "nursery in crime" where Jewish youngsters were given "primary instruction in pickpocketing and prostitution." In an area of only one square mile, authorities estimated there were approximately two hundred disorderly houses, three hundred and thirty-six gang "hang-outs," and over two hundred pool hall-*cum*-betting establishments; dance halls, a rendezvous of pimps and procurers, were found every two and one-half blocks, while gambling establishments blanketed the neighborhood. The East Side, noted the

American Hebrew soberly, "is spoken of as one vast habitat of the underworld."[3]

Vice and crime were not only widespread on the Lower East Side, they were also highly visible. With no segregated crime areas, vice, lamented Abe Shoenfeld, a keen student of the underworld, "was everywhere" and respectable citizenry "rubbed shoulders" with the criminal element. In the cramped quarters of the Lower East Side, it was hard not to. The University Saloon, a notorious haunt of pickpockets and thieves, was but a block away from the eminently respectable University Settlement house—from which, Shoenfeld noted, "it was so bold as to take its name." Abe Ratelles's Second Avenue restaurant, a "terrible joint with two rows . . . two and three men deep of pimps, cadets, disorderly house-keepers, pipe fiends, scoundrels, fences and everything imaginable," was contiguous to a public school. Brothels were scattered throughout the area and their existence, one resident later recalled, was "a matter of common knowledge." If a woman called out to you as you walked down Allen Street, reminisced Jonah J. Goldstein, "you knew she wasn't calling you to a *minyan*." Virtually every street had its own, and sometimes several, disorderly houses, saloons, and poolrooms: Rivington, Broome, Essex, Pitt, Allen, Grand Street, Delancey, Forsythe, Second Avenue—each housed a variety of unsavory haunts.[4]

Frequenting its cafés, saloons, and disorderly houses, the pre–World War I Jewish criminal element also made the Lower East Side—and other Jewish neighborhoods like it—their home. Occupationally Jewish criminals may have been deviant but in most other respects they were not "social isolates": residentially, linguistically, culturally, and even religiously, the Jewish underworld was tied to the larger Jewish immigrant community from which it emanated. Comfortable with their own kind, such well-known Jewish criminals of the prewar period as Big Jack Zelig, a master pickpocket-turned-gunman, and Mother Rosie Hertz, a wealthy madam, lived alongside their more law-abiding coreligionists. At the zenith of his career, Zelig lived on Broome Street in the heart of the Lower East Side, while Rosie chose to live among the more affluent Jews of Borough Park (to whom she boasted of the high cost of decorating her home) rather than reside alone in a well-to-do but non-Jewish neighborhood. Similarly, Lefty Louie Rosenzweig, one of Zelig's associates, lived in Jewish Harlem, where he was known as a "neighborhood boy." Like the other Jewish immigrants

of the Empire City, the members of the Jewish underworld often
spoke Yiddish among themselves. Calling the nervy owner of a sleazy
saloon "Kishkes," a powerful underworld boss "Rabbi," and a tender-
hearted prostitute "Chanele," prewar Jewish criminals also gave birth
to a host of slang criminal phrases of Yiddish origin. A pimp, for example, was known as a "simcha," a detective as a "shomis," and a
loafer and ne'er-do-well as a "trombenik." The Jewish criminal element not only spoke Yiddish but like so many other residents of the
Lower East Side, ate at the Grand Street cafeteria, took the "shvitz"
at the Forsyth Street baths, attended weddings and bar mitzvahs at
Arlington Hall, and even attended the synagogue. Despite her profession, Tillie Taub, a Lower East Side prostitute, was proud of and
firmly attached to her religion. "It makes no difference whatever I do,"
she angrily told Shoenfeld. "On Yom Kippur and Rosh Hashanah, I
go to shoole [sic]." By the same token, Stiff Rivka, a local thief, was
reputed to be knowledgeable as well as devout in her observance of
Jewish ritual. "She knows bible," Shoenfeld reported, " 'dovins' splen-
didly and is as well versed in Judaism as a woman can be."[5]

Thanks to the presence of Tillie, Stiff Rivka, and other Jewish
criminals, the area "bristled" with gangs. Some were little more than
temporary if "rough schools of experience" for American Jewish
youngsters entranced by the hi-jinks of life on the street. Others,
though, were far more pernicious. Lacking what one concerned reformer called "healthy outlets," the youthful residents of the Lower
East Side drifted to the streets where, forming small groups, they
played ball, flirted with girls, and occasionally engaged in acts of
petty thievery; virtually every street, recalled one former gang member nostalgically, had its own gang. Shortly after moving to the
Lower East Side, Samuel Chotzinoff writes, "I applied for admission"
to a local street gang for it "behooved one to belong . . . ." Another
veteran gang member put it this way: "It was the exceptional, almost
abnormal boy who did not join the gang. The gang was romance,
adventure, had the zest of banditry, the thrill of camp life, and the lure
of hero-worship." Parents and teachers worried that their young charges
would become "street bums" and later graduate into the ranks of more
hardened criminals, yet most gangs, notes Irving Howe, "were half-
fraternal agencies for a passage into adult life." In contrast, those
associated with Monk Eastman, Big Jack Zelig, and later Dopey
Benny Fein were no harmless diversions; these gangs, reported one

victim of their exactions, "made the East Side tremble." When not brawling with one another, the major Lower East Side street gangs derived their income and power from two sources: their ability to deliver huge blocks of votes to the local political machine and their unceasing demands for protection money. In the first instance, gang leaders like Eastman, one of the city's first Jewish major underworld figures, an American-born Jew with a "monkey face and a ferocious . . . appearance," saw to it that in return for police protection his outfit delivered the vote to the local pols. By employing "repeaters" at the polls and using not-so-subtle forms of persuasion on the legitimate voters, Eastman ensured the election of Tammany Hall. In later years, Herman Rosenthal and Sam Paul, two infamous gamblers, furthered their careers and lined their pockets by serving apprenticeships under the aegis of either Tammany Hall or the local wing of the Republican party. Herman Rosenthal received his start in the underworld by work- ing for Tammany chieftan "Big Tim" Sullivan, while Sam Paul owed his fortune to having helped Samuel Koenig become the Republican district leader of the Lower East Side. In addition to political work, Eastman was also one of the first Lower East Side criminals to see the potential of protection money. A "licensed bandit," he demanded "tribute" from the area's underworld; he "compelled thieves, gam- blers, and operators of disorderly houses to pay him a share of the profits," one journalist observed. And, as we shall see later on, the ever-ambitious Eastman was also one of the first underworld figures to have furnished small bands of strong-arm men to embattled labor unions and employers. After his passing from the scene—he was ar- rested and convicted of assault in 1904—other "children of the streets" like Zelig and Dopey Benny Fein inherited his mantle. Building upon Eastman's enterprise, the two not only demanded protection money from the area's criminal element but also from its shopkeepers. Dopey Benny routinely walked down Grand Street, "plaster[ing] every storekeeper with two tickets for a ball or a dance. If they had a small store, they would have to buy one dollar's worth of tickets; if their business was larger, five dollars," one eye-witness recollected. From the earnings of such balls or "rackets" (hence the origin of the term), Dopey and his colleagues frequently netted between three and four thousand dollars. When not exhorting or intimidating shopkeepers to buy tickets to a racket, the local street gangs demanded "tribute" in other ways. Interested in opening a restaurant on Delancey Street,

Elias Mandel discovered he first had to pay "key money" to one demanding gang, while hundreds of peddlers were forced to ante up a monthly sum of one or two dollars each for the privilege of operating their pushcarts. Lower East Side criminals, concluded the *American Hebrew*, "exacted tribute as regularly as the rent collector."[6]

Criminal court statistics reflected the "general restlessness" of the Lower East Side: Jews were amply represented on all levels of New York's multi-tiered criminal justice system, from the Magistrates Court, the lowest criminal court, to the Court of General Sessions, the felony and highest criminal court. Established in the mid–nineteenth century and known at that time as the police court, the Magistrates Court functioned as the court of first instance. A person arrested for committing any offense would be brought first to the local police station where his name and charge would be recorded. After this initial booking, he would be taken to the Magistrates Court in his neighborhood; in New York County there were at least nine local or district Magistrates Courts. The magistrate would then determine the category into which the alleged offense fell—whether felony, misdemeanor, or a minor offense—and, once that was ascertained, decide upon an appropriate judicial course of action. Misdemeanor cases were tried in the Court of Special Sessions while the Magistrates Court had summary jurisdiction over instances of vagrancy, disorderly conduct, violations of the Sunday Blue Laws and of the sanitary and corporation ordinances. Felony cases were brought to the attention of the District Attorney who in turn prepared them for a grand jury hearing. If the grand jury saw fit to indict the defendant, his case would be tried in the Court of General Sessions.[7]

Many, perhaps most, of those arraigned in what Raymond Moley has called the "tribune of the people"—the Magistrates Court—were foreign born. During the pre–World War I period, those born abroad accounted for at least half and, on occasion, close to sixty percent, of all those arraigned in the nine district Magistrates Courts of Manhattan and the Bronx; the percentage in the Essex Market Court, a noisy and disagreeable court servicing the Jewish quarter, was even higher. Russians, countywide, constituted the single largest foreign-born element, with as much as one-third of the total foreign-born population arraigned in the lower court (Italians and Irish followed, each with approximately twenty percent). To put it another way, between 1900 and 1914, over one hundred and twenty thousand Russians were actually "held for trial" in the Magistrates Court; doubtless many more Russians were arraigned in the lower court only to have their cases dismissed.[8]

The presence of so many Russians in the Magistrates Court created the impression that as a group they were a rowdy and troublesome lot, "furnishing the magistrate with a vast amount of unpleasant business." To ascertain the truth of such claims, the University Settlement, in 1898, investigated conditions in the "poor man's court." It found that the Lower East Side's reputation for "general lawlessness" was well-founded, and due largely to the proportion "it furnishes of arraignments." Yet after closely examining the court dockets, the settlement's researchers concluded that immigrant Jews could be "absolve[d] . . . from anything like a proportionate contribution to [New York City's] lawlessness." The immigrant Jew, they added, has a "low criminal record . . . ." A decade later, the New York State Immigration Commission drew similar conclusions. Established in 1908 to examine the moral, physical, and social welfare of the "alien" in New York State, it too found the immigrant overwhelmingly dominated the population of those arraigned in the Magistrates Court. In 1908, for example, the foreign born comprised close to sixty percent of all persons held to trial in the lower court. Nevertheless, the commission, whose members included Louis Marshall and Lillian Wald, also observed that in the majority of cases, the offenses for which immigrants were charged "do not imply criminality or criminal motives . . . although they swell the criminal statistics." Instead, most immigrants, they wrote, were charged with the commission of what could only be called minor offenses: the violation of corporation ordinances such as playing handball on the sidewalk and of sanitary ordinances such as improper garbage disposal. Offenses which, as the commission put it, "do not involve moral turpitude," headed the roster of crimes for which most immigrants were arraigned during the pre–World War I period. In 1910, for example, close to half of all offenses for which Russians were arraigned related to the violation of corporation and sanitary ordinances.[9]

In an overwhelming number of cases, then, the prevalence of immigrants in the magistrates courts can be charged up to ignorance of the existing law, not to deliberately unlawful behavior or malfeasance. "They do not realize," observed a sympathetic prison official, "that the code of morality and honesty in the new country may, along certain

lines, differ materially, from that of the old . . . often, they may or may
not be consciously guilty . . . ." "Anyone who has spent a morning in a
magistrates court," related one observer who obviously had, "knows
the number of inconsequential cases of pushcart peddlars, sidewalk ob-
structionists, recalcitrant employers . . . which come up for judgement."
The foreigner's knowledge of American institutions was generally
meager and his cultural and social behavior different from that of the
native-born American. Thus, to the latter, the immigrant's failure to
use a garbage can suggested that he was "simply unable to understand
what constitutes sanitation"—the use of soap and water—where, in fact,
it meant that the immigrant was unfamiliar with the American system
of garbage disposal. A native-born American might contend that drinking and boisterous singing were clear-cut examples of disorderly conduct where an immigrant might find such activities perfectly conven-
tional. Nevertheless, the opinion of the native-born American, especially
when held by New York City policemen, counted, while that of the
immigrant was simply discarded.[10]

For another thing, the police tended to be overzealous at times in
arresting the foreign-born citizenry who unwittingly violated the city's
moral code. As early as the 1850s, an Irish-American newspaper editor
bitterly complained that a "drunken American was never molested
but a drunken Irishman was always clapped into jail by the police."
As true then as it was later, at the turn of the century, the men in
blue lacked sympathy and understanding for the city's newest ethnic
groups. "Police officers are guilty of a savageness, a brutality of manner toward the people," complained the Legal Aid Bureau of the University Settlement as it examined conditions in the Essex Market Court
in 1900. The way they treat local residents, the bureau added, "is at
once shocking and uncalled for . . . rude and brutal." Not surprisingly,
there were relatively few Jews on the police force prior to the Great
War. Of ten thousand police officers, only two hundred, according
to the reliable *American Hebrew*, were Jewish—this in a city which
by 1910 numbered over one million Jews. Alluding to the almost inevitable interethnic tensions experienced by the Jews and the largely
Irish police force, Police Commissioner McAdoo cautioned his officers
to study carefully and be aware of the social customs of Lower East
Side residents. "They are going to stay here and they are going to
become citizens," he chided. Despite his advice, instances of police
brutality were not infrequent. Covering the police beat for the *Evening*

Post, Lincoln Steffens witnessed a "daily scene" at the police station as several policemen were "half forcing, half carrying a bandaged Russian Jew into the police station. . . . Anyway," the journalist continued, "he has done something the police don't like. But they haven't only arrested him . . . they've beaten him up." Growing up on the Lower East Side, Marcus Ravage vividly remembered the fear with which the immigrant community held the police. The "representative of uptown," the policeman "made life miserable for the pedlar while accepting his bribe. As soon as his tyrannical day's work was over, he vanished . . . ." Perhaps the most celebrated encounter of the immigrant community with New York's finest followed the funeral of Rabbi Jacob Joseph in July 1902. As the enormous funeral procession passed by the R. Hoe and Company building on Grand Street, factory workers threw missiles of garbage from the upstairs windows onto the mourners. A large number of infuriated Jews poured into the building, while thousands more took matters into their own hands (literally so!) and in an example of what Irving Howe calls their "new combativeness" retaliated by throwing garbage and stones at the factory workers; a riot ensued. Within minutes, the police arrived to quell the disturbance and, according to one bruised eyewitness, "set to work at once swinging their clubs vigorously as they drove the Jews from the factory. Scores of persons were hurt, mostly by the policemen's clubs." Most of the wounded were Jews.[11]

Immigrants were not only victimized on the street but in court as well. Unaccustomed to the intricacies of the criminal justice system and often unable to understand the language of the court, they fell prey to the unscrupulous activities of crooked bail bondsmen, court clerks, and shyster lawyers. The foreign born, reported the New York State Immigration Commission, are "so easily victims of what appears to be an organized system of graft." At the behest of a consoling yet rapacious lawyer, many desperate immigrants pleaded guilty to an offense they did not commit or paid a steep bail charge so that the lawyer could charge a hefty fee for his services. In his fictional but highly realistic novel of political corruption on the Lower East Side entitled *Haunch, Paunch and Jowl*, Samuel Ornitz has a frantic immigrant woman approach a local shyster lawyer for his help in saving her husband from obviously trumped-up charges. Shaking his head upon hearing the bill of indictment and muttering, "Terrible. Terrible. It's going to be hard. It's going to be hard," the lawyer cheats the woman of her life savings and her most prized possession—a piano—before allegedly freeing her husband. The woman was convinced that "money bought her husband's release," Ornitz writes, when in reality he was found to be completely innocent of any wrongdoing. The lawyer, feeling no remorse for his chicanery, boasts of his success in this and other cases: "I keep the political irons hot . . . ," he trills. "I take care of the boys all the way down the line from the judge on the bench to the bootblack in the criminal court's hallway."[12]

Many Jews, no doubt, were either victims of deliberate chicanery of this sort or of their own ignorance; others, however, knowingly violated the law and committed a felony such as burglary, grand larceny, and on occasion murder. Although during the pre–World War I period Jews never dominated the underworld or even began to approximate the levels of wrongdoing charged by nativists, the commission of felonies by Jews was widespread. Of a sample of several thousand New York County (that is, Manhattan and Bronx) residents arraigned on felony charges between 1900 and 1914, Jews accounted for 21 percent. The New York County District Attorney's docket books for those years show that in 1900 Jews comprised 15.9 percent of all persons brought before the D.A.; by 1915, they comprised a sizable 25.4% of that population. Nevertheless, at no time during the prewar era did Jews have more lawbreakers than their proportion of the population warranted. Rather, Jews were consistently underrepresented among those charged with committing felonies with, on occasion, half as many felony arrests as their numbers allowed. From a purely statistical perspective, Jews did not exceed admissible levels of criminal behavior; from any other perspective, however, Jewish criminal activity in the years prior to World War I was quite marked.[13]

Public opinion not only held the Jews responsible for much of the Empire City's crime, but also linked them to specific types of wrongdoing. Contemporaries ranging from the dispassionate William McAdoo to the intemperate Theodore A. Bingham, from the well-known sociologist and ardent nativist E. A. Ross to an anonymous New Yorker writing in the *Independent*, uniformly maintained that Jews tended to violate property laws rather than those against the person; arson, horse-poisoning, receiving stolen goods (fencing), and pickpocketing were seen as examples of a "typical Jew's crime" where assault, murder, and rape were not. "Their crimes in the main are against property," observed former Police Commissioner McAdoo. "Everything is most ingeniously and cleverly arranged; nothing is left to chance; system, order, great shrewdness and marked ability" characterized the Jewish criminal enterprise. But, he continued, "The East Side Jew rarely commits a crime of violence such as assault and murder. Among themselves disputes are mostly confined to wordy arguments . . . ." For his part, Theodore A. Bingham agreed with his predecessor's assessment; he too found the majority of Jewish criminals to be guilty of violating the property law. Furthermore, implying that, with their nimble feet and dexterous fingers, Jews possessed an inborn talent for petty thievery, Bingham insisted that "pocket-picking is the one [crime] to which they seem to take most naturally," snidely adding, "Jews are burglars, firebugs, pickpockets and highway robbers—*when they have the courage.*" Following Bingham's lead, Ross remarked that "Hebrew immigrants usually commit their crimes for gain . . . rather than the more daring crimes," and, writing in the *Independent*, a popular monthly, one unnamed New Yorker stated categorically that "in certain crimes where cunning is especially needed, Jews furnish most of the criminals."[14]

Such popular observations were, in fact, rooted in reality. Close to 80 percent of all felony charges brought against Jews between 1900 and 1915 had to do with the commission of property crimes: burglary, larceny, arson, horse-poisoning, and receiving stolen goods. In contrast, only 12 percent of these arrests related to the commission of a violent crime, such as assault, murder, or rape. (The remaining 8% were for violations of the regulatory code of law, such as gambling, bookmaking, and policy). "The Jews of this city as a class," observed Harry Newberger, "are possessed of all the vices of the people with whom they live." Thus, Jews did commit assault, engage in rape, abandon their wives, and periodically murder. Nevertheless, as a group, they had far fewer felony arrests for these types of crime than any other ethnic groups—Italians, for example. A sample drawn from the District Attorney's docket books indicates that between 1900 and the outbreak of the Great War approximately half of all felony arrests among Italians had to do with the (alleged) commission of a violent crime such as assault.[15]

It is in this sense that one can speak of "Jewish crime," a term that refers not only to a distinctive *pattern* of criminal activity among the Jews but even more pointedly to distinctive *types* of criminal activity. In virtually every example of a "Jewish crime" committed during the pre–World War I era, the Jewish neighborhood defined its content.

Economically, socially, culturally, and spatially the Jewish neighborhood anchored the activities of its more deviant members. If the drive
for monetary success was as potent among New York Jews as historians have suggested, it was not always expressed through legitimate
channels; with imperative needs but limited means (or patience), some
Jews chose crime as their vehicle of upward mobility. Yet even these
illicit forms of upward mobility were rooted in the ethnic economy of
the Jewish Lower East Side: its heavy concentration of garment manufacturers and contractors spawned a sort of counter-industry in the
selling and manufacturing of clothing. In 1890, for example, at least
half of all employed Lower East Side residents were garment workers;
by 1900, New York Jews "controlled New York's giant clothing industry." With thousands of licensed sweatshops and countless unli-
censed ones located in the heart of the city's Jewish neighborhoods,
and with dozens, if not hundreds, of retail stores specializing in the
sale of dry goods or fabrics, much of the crime involved the theft and
subsequent fencing of clothing by Jews from Jewish manufacturers,
contractors, and jobbers. Proximity to the area's sweatshops and retail
outlets proved to be an attractive, a tailor-made, opportunity for the
local criminal element. "The many burglars of the area," reported one
police official, "confine their operations to robberies of silks, furs and
cloth from the neighboring shops and manufactures." Furthermore, the
occupational profile of most garment industry thieves and burglars contributed to their choice of criminal activity. In many instances, the
Jewish thief or burglar had some connection to the garment industry,
whether as a tailor or cutter, a dry goods store clerk, or a wagon driver.
As tailors, Joseph Marks, a thirty-year-old Russian-born resident of
the Lower East Side, and his friend Max Belsky, a twenty-three-year-old
Russian immigrant, knew from whom to purchase top-quality fabric.
Isaac Greenman's Clinton Street shop housed a lovely collection of
linens, silks, and other dry goods. Apparently unable to afford to buy
these items directly from Mr. Greenman, the two broke into the rear
of the store late one night. Cutting through the two iron bars that protected the rear windows of the shop, Marks and Belsky stole approximately two thousand dollars' worth of fabric. In a second instance,
Harry Goldstein, a twenty-one-year-old American-born garment industry clerk, stole seventeen dozen (!) men's shirts from an Eldridge
Street manufacturer which he then sold to a female fence on Hester
Street. Then there was the case of young David Kalisky. Serving as a

helper to the owner of a wagon delivering rolls of cloth from the manufacturer to a contractor, Kalisky was tempted by the profusion of goods and, when left alone, grabbed as many rolls as he could carry and fled. In each episode, the particular configurations of the Lower East Side's economy defined the crime. "The heavy concentration of property crimes among Jews," explained the *American Hebrew*, "is only another way of saying that they are most occupied in mercantile pursuits."[16]

Dealing in stolen goods or fencing was also an integral part of the criminal activities of New York Jews at this time; like burglary and theft, it too was closely tied to the garment industry. Once an item was stolen from a sweatshop, a retail outlet, or a wagon, it was immediately sold to local fences, a network of which spanned the Lower East Side. Annie Kahn, a twenty-two-year-old Russian-born housekeeper, was one such fence. Together with a male associate, she plotted the early morning theft of five hundred yards of fabric—silks, velvets, and satins—from the Lower East Side shop of Louis Lang. After "burglariously entering" Lang's emporium and stealing thousands of dollars' worth of fabric, Annie's colleague made his way back to her apartment. The two then concealed most of the goods in a trunk, leaving out a few of the choicest items to admire before putting them away. Suddenly the police entered Annie's apartment and, their suspicions confirmed, apprehended the female thief and her partner. The police, it seems, had observed Annie's anonymous partner climbing the fire escape to Annie's apartment, and had come to verify their suspicions of foul play. When asked by the men in blue how she had happened to come by such lovely items, Annie innocently replied that she "didn't know how the things got there." When more fortunate than Annie, most fences, upon receiving the stolen goods, quickly removed telltale marks of identification. Frederika "Marm" Mandelbaum, one of the city's leading fences, rumored to be "as adept in her business as the best stockbroker on Wall Street was in his," defined the usual mode of operations. As the owner of an unassuming haberdashery store on Clinton Street, "Marm" was often aware of opportunities to purchase "miscellaneous booty" at a mere fraction of its market price. After being notified of a robbery, she herself or a "trusted agent" examined the goods; if they met with her approval, she or her agent purchased the "stuff"—and always for cash. The "queen of fences" then took great pains to eliminate any form of identification which might reveal the origins of the item in question. "Her first care was to look for trade-marks," one police official related, "and in this branch of her calling she was very expert. Labels and tags, of course, were immediately removed. Private marks were also searched for." The incriminating trademarks removed, "Marm" would arrange for a buyer. Indeed, reported former New York police chief George Walling admiringly, "she made arrangements for its disposal at a profit." "Everything is elaborately arranged," commented another member of the force. "Two days after [the stolen goods] are gone, the chances are that the owner is probably rubbing elbows in a car with the girl whose shirtwaist is made of the stolen material."[17]

Finally, Jewish labor racketeering was also integrally linked to the Jewish garment industry. In their efforts to unionize the labor force in the needle trades, desperate union leaders turned to local *shtarkes* or "sluggers" who, for a handsome fee, lived up to their names by physically molesting the opposition. Manufacturers, equally desperate, also turned to Lower East Side criminals for their assistance. As we shall see in a later chapter, labor racketeering was a "peculiarly Jewish" enterprise.

Arson and horse-poisoning, two offenses associated almost exclusively with New York's Jews, offer further examples of the importance of the Jewish neighborhood in shaping the criminality of its more deviant members. First, both arsonists and horse-poisoners relied on the insularity of the Jewish community for their respective success. Each created a silent network of individuals—some willingly silent, others reluctantly so—from which they derived their illicit income. Pledged to secrecy, the arsonist, his associates, and those hiring the arsonist reaped huge profits from the overinsuring and subsequent "torching" of property. The horse-poisoner and his colleagues benefited from the fear they engendered among their victims. Terrified lest their businesses be ruined or their families hurt, businessmen and stable owners, though threatened by horse-poisoners, were reluctant to inform the police of their trials. They were thus forced to bear up under the blackmail of the "Yiddish Camorra," the Jewish Black Hand. In each case, moreover, the perpetrators and their victims (with the exception of the horses, of course) were Jewish and the crimes themselves limited to the city's Jewish quarters.

Of all the offenses commonly associated with New York Jews, arson or "Jewish lightning," as it was popularly called, received the most attention. Reading the daily press or even the humor magazines of the prewar period, one is struck by the frequency with which Jews were linked to arson. Of 128 arson cases reported by the *New York Times* between 1875 and 1899, Jews figured in more than one-quarter of them; in the 1890s alone, Jews were implicated in a whopping 44 percent of all arson cases described by the newspaper. Furthermore, popular magazines like *Puck's* and *Life* regularly featured stories and cartoons about arson in which the perpetrators bore names like Blazenheimer, Flameski, Burnupski, and—less imaginatively—Isaac, Cohen, and Goldstein. In one sketch, a stereotypically portrayed Jew with a bulging stomach and an equally protruding nose is asked by a fellow Jew: "What is the only thing our race hates more than pork?" The answer: "asbestos." Because of the widespread association of Jews with arson, insurance companies routinely refused to insure persons with names ending in "sky" or "ski." Fastening every tenement house fire on a "Polish Jew, they note a fire and . . . *of course*, a Jew must have been seen pouring oil over the floor and the tables, then locking the door and hurrying to the synagogue. . . ." "My first thought," recalled one woman as she witnessed the fiery destruction of Mr. Goldstein's store, "was that perhaps Mr. Goldstein had made the fire himself . . . I know among the Jews this is a frequently done thing."[18]

One of the earliest cases of arson involving Jews occurred in November 1878. Acting on information provided him by the New York County fire marshal, Assistant District Attorney Rollins brought charges against a group of Jewish Lower East Side residents. Claiming that Joseph Levy and Charles Bernstein, both tailors, Isaac Perlstein, a peddler, and Abraham Freedman, a cigarmaker, had developed a scheme to defraud insurance companies by overinsuring property in the Jewish quarter and then setting fire to it, the District Attorney indicted the four men on charges of first-degree arson. Touted in the metropolitan press as "the great arson case," it lasted for several months and resulted in the conviction of all four defendants. The proceedings attracted a great deal of publicity. In a bid for acclaim, the District Attorney trumpeted his success in bringing these "four heartless rogues" to justice. Angered by what they perceived to be a strong anti-Semitic bias on the part of the prosecuting attorney and the jury, many Jewish residents loudly protested and called for a fairer trial. The presiding judge firmly denied the charges of prejudice and insisted that the defendants would be tried solely on the basis of the evidence against them. The net effect of the Jewish community's protest was to underscore the extent to which arson was construed as a Jewish offense.[19]

Several years later, in the spring of 1895, New York's then–district attorney, Vernon Davis, indicted the "largest gang of incendiaries ever at work in New York" on first-degree arson charges; once again, the members of what the *New York Times* called a "firebug brotherhood" were all Jews. "It would be hard to find a parallel to the story of organized Polish-Jewish incendiarism in New York and Brooklyn," commented *Leslie's Illustrated Weekly*. "The business of burning down tenement houses teeming with human lives and well-stocked commercial buildings and factories for the sake of insurance money assumed such proportions at times and was conducted with such impunity that the miscreants actually lost consciousness of its criminality." Heading the gang of "miscreants" was Isaac Zuker, a well-to-do Jewish merchant. Together with several partners, he "formed an association of one nationality whose business it was to make fires for the purposes of defrauding insurance companies." With "Oriental cunning and strategy," Zuker first hired fire adjusters, the liaison between the insurance company and the insured party, to inflate the value of a tenement house or a factory. He then employed "mechanics" who, for twenty-five dollars apiece, set the fires. To produce a "mere blaze" that would only slightly damage the property in question, the "mechanics" used plain alcohol; for a "larger conflagration," kerosene. A budding chemist, Zuker even devised his own presumably infallible mixture: a combination of naphtha and benzine so potent that, upon igniting, it produced a loud noise—a "concussion," contemporaries called it—followed by a big blaze. As a result of its exploits, the gang reputedly earned between $500,000 and $700,000 in insurance fees. The defendants were ultimately convicted of first-degree arson: Zuker himself was sentenced to a term of thirty-six years at hard labor.[20]

In succeeding years, the incidence of Jewish arson cases never quite matched the record of the late nineteenth century. Of 123 arson cases reported in the *Times* between 1900 and 1910, Jews figured in only 15 percent. Conceivably the public association of Jews with arson would have faded altogether had it not been for the arrest and subsequent conviction in 1913 of several Jewish members of yet another "arson trust." This affair reignited the public's identification of Jews with the firing of buildings. The leader of the prewar "arson trust" was Isidore

"Izzy the Painter" Stein who, in his career as a firebug, reportedly set over three hundred fires, most of them in Jewish Harlem, a "hotbed of incendiary fires." Posing as a painter, Stein bought large amounts of kerosene, a substance then used for mixing paints; the firebug, though, used it to start fires. Working in tandem with several insurance adjusters and "scouts" who solicited business from local residents, Stein reportedly "did a large business among countrymen from Russian Poland."[21]

Like arson, horse-poisoning was associated almost exclusively with Jews. A form of extortion, it dated back to either 1906 or 1907 and reached its peak in 1912 when an average of twelve horses a week were poisoned in the city's Jewish neighborhoods. Organized in the form of a gang, the horse-poisoners modeled themselves after the Italian Black Hand, an organization which terrorized recently arrived Italian immigrants by threatening to harm their families and homes unless they paid the extortionists. Calling themselves the Yiddish Black Hand, the gang would write a letter to a stableman or a businessman whose concern used horses, demanding a certain sum of money; the latter was euphemistically called a "tax" or a "tribute." Accompanying the letter was the threat that should the victim refuse to comply, his horse would be poisoned: "Pay or we'll drop a horse on you" was the general text of such messages. Furthermore, should the recipient inform the authorities, he ran the risk of bodily harm. Numbering no more than a dozen men, the Yiddish Black Hand had its headquarters in the Suffolk Street saloon of Russian-born Max Schnure. The organization's "bankroll man," Schnure kept the books and disbursed the gang's booty. His saloon not only served as business headquarters for the Jewish horse-poisoners and as the place where they relaxed and socialized with one another, it was also the place to which terrorized merchants brought their cash tribute. Though Schnure was clearly an important figure and his saloon indispensable to the gang, the "brains of the bastard firm," as one partisan observer put it, was Joseph Toblinsky, who went by the evocative name of "Yushke Nigger." Russian-born, five feet seven inches in height, dark-skinned and somewhat plump, Yushke planned strategy for the horse-poisoners and in his time was said to have poisoned over two hundred horses. Other gang members included John Levine, also known as "John L" who did the gang's "lowest work": threatening recalcitrant merchants; Harry McGurck[!], a muscular thirty-three-year-old Russian Jew who acted as the group's strongarm man; "Rob the Pollack" who served, according to one account, as the "firm's cutthroat and chief poisoner" and Louis "Boston" Schneider, a former pimp, burglar, and pickpocket "with a police record a yard wide and all wool."[22]

By 1909, horse-poisoning had become so serious a threat to the city's Jewish merchants that several of them established a fund with which to pay protection money to the gangsters. Apparently this tactic did little to ward off the horse-poisoners and so, a year later, a number of ice cream manufacturers, particularly haunted by the horse-poisoners, banded together and created an insurance fund "so as to protect each other and to prevent further submission to blackmail." For one season, each member of the association contributed a set sum of money to reimburse those who had lost a horse. As that was insufficient to offset their monetary losses, another plan was devised. This time each member would pay an additional five cents per bag of salt, a substance used in the manufacturing of ice cream; the additional income collected would go into a general fund to compensate members in financial difficulties. That scheme was also short-lived; under it, members lost between one and five horses apiece. All alternatives having failed, the ice cream manufacturers' association decided to pay the horse-poisoners a lump sum of one thousand dollars per season to refrain from killing any of the association's horses, thus keeping their animals (and themselves) safe for two years.[23]

In 1912, encouraged by the authorities, the ice cream manufacturers and other victims of the Yiddish Camorra "stiffened . . . to stand up and fight the outrageous conditions under which they had suffered so long" by forming the East Side Horse Owners Protective Association. After regularly giving information to the police on the whereabouts and activities of the horse-poisoners, enabling them to put many of the miscreants behind bars, the ice cream manufacturers were rewarded; within the year, the poisoning of horses, boasted Mayor William Gaynor, "ceased altogether."[24]

The culture and social life of the Lower East Side, as well as its economy, further molded the criminality of some of its residents; in plying their trade, Jewish criminals exploited many of the community's social and cultural institutions. One of the most inventive Jewish criminals in this respect was Stiff Rivka. A noted thief and shoplifter, Rivka's most profitable days were the Jewish High Holidays. "Her principal days of work," Shoenfeld observed, "are Yom Kippur and Rosh Hashanah." After obtaining a front-row seat in the synagogue, from which she had a clear and unobstructed view of the congregation, Rivka would "single out a woman bedecked and like the crackerjack thief she is, make a play for her." As women worshippers left the synagogue following the conclusion of the services, Rivka jostled her victim and stole her brooch. The Schorr brothers—Ikie, Sam, and Max—regularly made the rounds of Jewish weddings and funerals, brushing up against the guests during the ceremony and stealing their jewelry and money. Another pair known only as Hudis and Leah were equally as creative in their criminal activities; they took advantage of the community's culinary proclivities. Noting the immigrants' fondness for eating chicken dishes on the Sabbath, the two women stole chickens from the wholesale poultry markets and, on the eve of the Sabbath, sold the prized items at a reduced price to eager and price-conscious consumers. Even the Jews' predilection for pickpocketing, a crime which they allegedly took to naturally, evolved from the social structure of the Lower East Side. For many area youngsters, the lure of the streets—the opportunity to play, to acquire American street smarts, perhaps even a girl friend—were hard to resist; the streets, comments Irving Howe, "spoke of freedom." Keen observers, "pickpocket bosses" or Fagins exploited the youngsters' affinity for life on the street. "A fagin who has grown up in the same atmosphere," wrote Shoenfeld, "perhaps sees the propensities of the boy, selects him and makes a young grafter of him. The boy is glad that it is known that he is under the protecting wing of Sam so and so or Jack so and so." Besides, he added, the fagin "comes around with ten cent pieces or quarters or half dollars from time to time." Pickpocket bosses not only provided the youngsters with quarters but also trained them in the fine art of grafting by running schools or "cheders" on the Lower East Side. Before he became one of the area's leading labor racketeers, Dopey Benny Fein conducted one such training school. An excellent and caring teacher, Dopey helped out his "talmidim" by providing them with a room at night when they needed one and with money when they were down on their luck; "he never disappointed a friend in need," remarked the *Tog* facetiously. Another well-known pickpocket boss possessed such a kindly mien and was so considerate of his young charges that a puzzled social reformer wrote that he didn't look at all like a criminal, "he seemed more like a rabbi."[25]

Under the watchful eye of their tutors, young Jewish pickpockets
developed their trade into a fine art. Veterans of the underworld spoke
admiringly of the talents of the younger generation of thieves, admit-
ting that the "children of the East Side" were far more adroit than
the "adult professionals of older days." Although trained on the
Lower East Side, the young Jewish grafters did not limit themselves
to that one area; they spread across the city. "The streets of New York
today," complained Frank Marshall White, a well-known newspaperman, in 1906, "are swarming with pickpockets . . . springing up by the
hundreds among the crowded tenement houses, particularly of the East
Side." Crowded streetcars, parks, and marketplaces were the staging
areas of the fleet-footed Jewish pickpockets. Preferring surface cars to
the subway—it was easier to escape—the youthful grafter created a disturbance of some sort. While the travelers were temporarily distracted,
he or an associate "lifted" a watch or a purse and expeditiously jumped
off the streetcar before the theft was discovered. Another tactic of
these gangs was to pretend to start a fight among themselves. As a
crowd gathered to watch the pugilistic display, the youngest and
smallest member of the gang would go through the pockets of those
assembled. Still another much-favored technique was to practice riding
a bicycle through some congested thoroughfare like Orchard, Hester,
or Essex Street. Flailing about as he tried to steady his bicycle, the
pickpocket *cum* fledgling cyclist would fall in the midst of a crowd of
women shoppers. While he "clutches awkwardly here and there" and
attempts to right himself and his vehicle, his confederates, related a
bemused McAdoo, "have been busy picking pockets and snatching
pocketbooks, right and left. The young thief is on his wheel in a
jiffy; the plunder is slipped to him and he is off."[26]

In lifting watches or stealing handbags, Jewish pickpockets rarely
resorted to violence; indeed violent crimes of any sort accounted for
a minor portion of the criminal activities of the pre–World War I
Jewish criminal. Though fierce-looking Jewish gangs stalked the
streets of the Lower East Side, muggings and rapes seldom occurred.
Rarely did "Jews indulge in the sort of anomic and senseless violence
that we who live in the inner city are familiar with today," comments
Albert Fried, an historian of the Jewish underworld. "The Lower East
Side "was a horror but its streets were safe even at night." "East Side
Jews are the most peaceful people I have ever come in contact with,"
observed James Reynolds, head worker at the Lower East Side's

premier settlement house, the University Settlement. In ten years of residing on the Lower East Side, the social worker claimed to have witnessed only an occasional street fight among the Jewish residents. The eschewal of violence among the Jews seemed to be a conscious decision, indeed a kind of cultural inheritance, transmitted from one generation to the next. Committing violent crimes, the *Wahrheit* insisted, "is not in the Jewish blood." In fact, on those occasions when Jews were indicted for murder, the Jewish community was simply astounded and found the association between Jews and violence to be "without precedent . . . in the whole course of Jewish history." For centuries, European Jewry had identified any show of violent behavior with non-Jews and studiously refrained from engaging in it. "The shtetl," write Mark Zborowski and Elizabeth Herzog in their classic anthropological study of Eastern European Jewish life, *Life Is with People*, "is at one in regarding physical violence as 'un-Jewish.' " In the Eastern European environment, Jewish children were taught to differentiate between certain forms of behavior deemed appropriate for Jews and thus "Jewish" and other activities deemed ill-suited to Jews and thus "non-Jewish." "Intellect, a sense of moderation, cherishing of spiritual values and the cultivation of rational, goal-directed activities" were perceived as examples of legitimately "Jewish" conduct, while "emphasis on the body, excess, blind instinct, sexual instinct and *ruthless force*" were perceived as "goyish." Shunning violence, then, was a badge of distinction among the Jews, setting them apart from the more volatile and violent non-Jewish world. Perhaps, too, Jews knew from tradition and habit that when it came to shows of violence or bravado, the non-Jewish world clearly surpassed them. "That Jews are less addicted to crimes of violence," explained the *American Hebrew*, "may be put down to their slighter physique and general tendency to suffer ills without retaliation."[27]

For all these reasons, words—not fists—became the Jew's weapon against a hostile environment and, when need be, against one another. "The Jewish population is not apt, unless under great pressure, to resort to force or to commit crimes of violence," observed police official McAdoo. "Among themselves disputes are mostly confined to wordy arguments. They argue with great vigor and earnestness but the argument ends as it begins." Much the same could be said of the Jewish criminal. Like the more respectable citizenry, they too tended to stay clear of violent crimes and to concentrate on those in which their "cunning" and "shrewdness" could be put to good advantage. "The Christians commit crimes with their hands while the Jews," related sociologist Arthur Ruppin, "use their reason. . . ."[28]

However infrequent, there were occasions in which Jewish criminals of the prewar period committed crimes "with their hands." In many cases, the victims were members of some non-Jewish gang that threatened the safety of the Jewish community. Though the Lower East Side had its fair share of criminals, recalled Judge Jonah J. Goldstein, "in one respect, they rendered a public service: they would take care of those who made fun of and attacked immigrant Jews with beards." Jewish criminals "beat the stuffings out" of those who taunted elderly, foreign-born Jews. "It was that conduct, more than any police . . . that stopped the pulling of beards of the Jewish immigrants," the judge explained. Big Jack Zelig, an American-born, handsome, and well-dressed master Jewish pickpocket, was among those Lower East Side criminals who, in Goldstein's words, "rendered a public service." Angered by what he perceived to be the invasion of his Jewish neighborhood by gangs of youthful Italians in search of women to seduce and businesses to rob, Zelig became a gunman. At first not a great marksman—Shoenfeld wrote of Zelig that he was only a "fair shot with a gun . . . but a fighting terrier . . . a wild cat . . . with his fists"—he practiced until he became "the most feared man in New York," so determined was he to rid the Jewish quarter of Italian hoodlums. When a group of armed Italian thugs showed up at a ball sponsored by a local group of prostitutes and procurers, Zelig, together with his henchmen, 'Whitey Louis' Seidenshner and 'Lefty Louis' Rosenzweig, unhesitatingly opened fire, killing the leader of the gang and sending his comrades scurrying into the streets. "That was [Zelig's] first job," Shoenfeld recalled. In later years, Zelig took steps to prevent the incursion of the Lower East Side by rival gunmen by guarding the area's periphery. So appreciative was the Lower East Side community of Zelig's efforts that when he sponsored a ball at Arlington Hall, not only did the regulars—the underworld community—attend but so did a number of legitimate Jewish businessmen. They came, Shoenfeld noted, "to pay willing tribute to Jack Zelig." Moreover, at the time of the gunman's untimely demise from an assassin's bullet in the autumn of 1912, thousands of local residents clogged Rivington and Allen Streets to get a glimpse of his casket and to pay their final respects. In a kind of paean to the criminal, Shoenfeld unrestrainedly wrote that Zelig cleared East Side dance halls and academies of Italian pimps; he cleared the East Side of Italians who were wont to hold up stuss houses and legitimate business places . . . and he has prevented more hold-ups and other things of a similar nature in his career than one thousand policemen.

Zelig, declaimed the Lower East Side's most keen-eyed crime watcher, "was the great emancipator of the East Side."[29]

Though he had seemingly "emancipated" the Lower East Side from roaming Italian would-be seducers and pimps, Zelig could do little to stop the growing association of Jews with prostitution; indeed, for much of the prewar period, it was Jews, not Italians, who were most closely identified with that area of crime: as procurers, pimps, madams, and prostitutes. Distressed by the proliferation of urban vice yet confident of their ability to curb it, a coalition of civic reformers, ministers, crusading journalists, and social workers made common cause against prostitution in the years preceding the Great War. "In no period of American history," writes Egal Feldman, "did the custodians of American morality direct more serious attention to the eradication of prostitution than they did in the few years preceding World War I." As they crusaded against the "social evil" in urban America, social reformers singled out the Jew for ostensibly commercializing vice; Jews, in short, came under "special attack." Writing in the popular *McClure's Magazine* in the spring of 1909, George Kibbe Turner, one of the country's most respected muckrakers, set the tone for the anti-vice campaign. Boldly and unhesitatingly, Turner indicted the Russian Jew for making a business of prostitution. With his "Jewish commercial acumen," the Jewish procurer transformed what had been an haphazardly conducted small-time business into an organized and thriving enterprise, notorious the world over as the Red Light District, Turner wrote. His success, the journalist explained, was due largely to an alliance with Tammany Hall, the local Democratic machine. In return for police protection, Jewish procurers reportedly gave of their financial resources to Tammany and called on the large number of people in their employ to vote for the political machine at the polls, thus insuring Tammany's hegemony in local politics. Consummating the arrangement, many brothel operators also served as Tammany district captains. "The active Tammany managers of the Eighth District [the Lower East Side]," Turner continued, "were large operators in the sale of prostitution . . . out of the Red Light District has come . . . the great voting power of the organized criminals." Jewish pimps, he dramatically concluded, "have vitiated more than any single agency the moral life of the great cities of America."[30]

In his account of the "professional criminals" of New York, Turner estimated that at least two-thirds of the men and women engaged in the business of prostitution were Jews, drawn from the Lower East Side. Other contemporaries reported much the same finding. With undisguised alarm, the University Settlement reported at the turn of the century that on the Lower East Side "the evil of prostitution . . . seems to exist to an appalling extent and to be on the increase." Several years later, while examining the size of the underworld, Harry Newberger wrote grimly to Rabbi Judah Magnes that "the Jew was one of the first to see the possibilities of the commercialization of vice and to profit by it." The attorney added that New York also had "its full quota of Jewish prostitutes." Prostitutes could be found everywhere, "constantly solicit[ing] from the windows and stoops" of the Lower East Side's overcrowded tenements, a former resident recalled. Allen Street, the "street of perpetual shadow," boasted the densest concentration of Jewish prostitutes. "Sunlight seldom found a way into its rickety tenements because of the elevated railroad which spanned its narrow width," the *American Hebrew* noted. "And not only metaphorically were its residents creatures of the dark . . . the street was infamous for its immorality and vice." "There were a hundred women on every Allen Street corner," Benjamin Antin explained. "Tall women, short women. Fair women. Ugly women. Powdered women, looking at an immigrant boy who stood by in amazement, while they jerked their heads in a beckoning welcome. . . ." Some prostitutes, like Jennie Silver, brazenly walked the streets of the Lower East Side looking for customers. With one hand she "beckoned"; with the other, Shoenfeld reported, "she carried a milk can—as insurance against arrest. "If she is picked up by a cop," he explained, "she will make a 'grandstand play' that she has been looking around for a quart of milk high and low . . . but the stores are all closed." Other prostitutes, like thirty-year-old, Russian-born Rosie Solomon, worked indoors: on the second floor of the rear tenement on Rivington Street. "She does business in a three room flat which is furnished very poorly and kept unclean," the tireless Shoenfeld related. Then there were Maimie and Lizzie of 143 Allen Street. Each had been a prostitute for close to twenty-five years during which time they allegedly "had" a minimum of ten men a day. Calculating that they worked three hundred days a year, Shoenfeld deduced that between them, the two prostitutes had given syphillis to over fifty thousand men.[31]

Perhaps the most well known, certainly the most colorful, woman involved in "the trade" was Rosie Hertz, the "cleverest madam of any disorderly house ever known." The American-born daughter of "Gittel," a Hungarian Jew and allegedly one of the first Jewish madams in New York, Rosie entered the family business as a visiting prostitute. "She would go from one coal cellar to another, from one working basement to another," Shoenfeld reported, and "thus make money." With the funds earned from her peregrinations, Rosie opened her own brothel on East First Street. Popular with the local population, her establishment, reported one judge (perhaps himself a devotee), was "as much a fixture of the Lower East Side as the Brooklyn Bridge." Rosie became a millionaire, and diversified: she bought several parcels of real estate on the Lower East Side, including the land on which her brothel stood, and a home in Borough Park, fenced stolen goods, many of which she later sold to her "girls," and served as a bail bondsman for local residents in trouble with the law. Like many other Jewish "retailers of women," she regularly contributed to both the Republican and Democratic parties and was therefore "never molested." Known to area residents as "Mother Hertz," Rosie exhibited a warm and maternal air. "She wears a wig as a pious Jewess would," reported one eyewitness, "and a large white apron. And when she smiles . . . she pinches your cheek in a motherly fashion." Yet neighbors were warned not to be fooled by Rosie's warm and affectionate personality. Though she often smiled, treated the local children to pennies, and "talk[ed] to God and of God most of the time," she was, Shoenfeld duly observed, "one of the most notorious breeders and incubators of prostitutes this city has ever had." Thanks to her amorous pursuits,

> firesides have crumbled—hearts have been broken—virginity has been polluted—virtue has been contaminated—and the very east side leprously disgraced. . . . Rosie Hertz had been the teacher and mother of more prostitutes, whores, madams etc. than any other individual woman in the world.[32]

Estimates of the number of Rosie's "students" varied. In 1908–1909, "Hebrews" convicted of soliciting and of maintaining disorderly houses accounted for 11 percent of all such cases, while other contemporary sources place the percentage of pre–World War I Jewish prostitutes at close to 20 percent. A 1912 study of 647 prostitutes committed to the Bedford Hills Reformatory found that 123 (19.0%) had listed themselves upon admission to the reformatory as Jewish; 266 (41.1%) as Catholic, and 252 (38.9%) as Protestant; 6 (0.9%) had no affiliation. A later study, conducted by the members of the Spanish-Portuguese Synagogue sisterhood, indicated that on the eve of World War I, Jewish women accounted for approximately 17 percent of all women arraigned in New York County's Women's Night Court on charges of prostitution. Though probably underrepresented as far as their proportion of the population is concerned—Jews *in general* comprised one-quarter of all New York City residents prior to World War I—Jewish prostitution was fairly widespread.[33]

Contemporaries not only believed that the Lower East Side furnished its share of Gotham's prostitutes and procurers; they also held the area's residents responsible for introducing a new form of commercialized vice: white slavery. "An international trade in the procuring, either with or without their consent, of girls and women for immoral purposes," white slavery appeared to be one of the leading sources of prostitutes in urban America; authorities estimated that three thousand women annually were "decoyed" into prostitution by white slave traders prior to World War I. Furthermore, the authorities believed that the majority of white slave traders were Jews. "It is an absolute fact," insisted Ernest Bell, one of the nation's leading anti–white slave crusaders, "that Jews are the backbone of this loathsome traffic in women." Though the French "maquereaux" or procurers had been among the earliest promoters of white slavery and continued to be among its more active participants during the pre–World War I era, Jews, most observers argued, "are the chief sinners." Accordingly, Americans were warned to be on their guard against the "Polish pollution . . . which is already corrupting the manhood and youth of every large city in the nation." Jewish names riddled the pages of virtually every published anti–white slavery tract; the exploits of such infamous Jewish panderers as Motche Goldberg, "King of the Vice Trust," and Abe "the Rabbi" Ratelles, a pioneer white slave trader, were "household tales." According to students of the "traffic in women," the Jews' involvement had its roots in the Old World. "Out of the racial slum of Europe has come for un-numbered years the Jewish *kaftan* leading the miserable Jewish girl from European civilization . . ." wrote Turner. "He comes out of

Galicia and Russian Poland," the muckraker continued, "with his white face and his long beard—the badge of his ancient faith—and wanders across the face of the earth. . . ." Reviving the time-honored, anti-Semitic canard of a network of international Jewish organizations conspiring to control one form or another of the global economy, social reformers suggested that Jewish "merchants of vice" banded together, in a kind of cartel, to control the white slave trade. "The business of traffickers in white slavery is thoroughly organized," reported *Outlook*, "with affiliated bodies in many of the principal cities"; white slavery, reported another periodical, is "organized and specialized . . . exactly as all other businesses have done . . . ."[34]

With its headquarters in New York, the "center" of the white slave trade, the Independent Benevolent Association was the most successful trade organization of its kind. It numbered two hundred panderers or "ladies managers," each of whom had to pass a rigorous screening test before being admitted to membership. Not everyone who applied was admitted: Sam Jaffee, also known as "African Jake," was denied entry to the organization because "his record was too bad." At monthly meetings the members monitored the trade, from Odessa to Buenos Aires, from Paris to New York. "Matters of mutual trade interest" were discussed at these gatherings, and "when the more enterprising men in it found larger opportunities in the other cities of the country, its members would naturally inform one another of conditions . . . in the different sections," wrote one observer. It was also widely believed that, thanks to their political leverage, members were able "to exert a continual influence . . . to prevent the punishment of individual members."[35]

The white slave trade took many forms. At first procurers—Jewish kaftans—inveigled unsuspecting young Eastern European Jewish women into coming with them to America. Often promises of marriage were made and, having "heard wonderful stories of America as a land of liberty and justice," young women accepted them gladly. In Mendele Mocher Seforim's "The Magic Ring," for example, the protagonist Bayla is seduced into prostitution in just this way. Upon arriving in America, the young and handsome women were taken immediately to houses of ill-repute where, robbed of self esteem, unable to speak English, and with no one to turn to, they became "prisoners"—and, in due time, prostitutes. Using the same strategy, procurers also traveled throughout the interior of the United States, recruiting innocent Midwestern women. *House of Bondage*, a graphic account of white slavery, and a bestseller of its time, describes the fate of one young woman unknowingly trapped "in the life." One day Mary meets a nattily dressed and urbane New Yorker named Max. Promising her a life of excitement and prosperity if only she will marry him, Max succeeds in persuading the Midwestern woman to come away with him. After several days during which Mary is drugged and physically abused, she awakes from her stupor to find herself in a brothel. Gradually, Mary comes to terms with her new status. Yet one thing continues to gnaw at her: what happened to her friend Max? Summoning up her courage, Mary asks a patron about the urbane New Yorker. He responds: "Don't you know that the Yid who got you into this makes a business of such things . . . there is a whole army of them that do."[36]

As thousands of single women like Mary or Bayla traveled, unescorted, to New York and other major urban areas, the expense and trouble of importing prostitutes became unnecessary. Hiring suave, well-groomed, and handsome young men—the public called them "cadets"—to entice the new arrivals into a life of vice, enterprising procurers broadened their base of potential recruits. Railroad stations and Ellis Island, the gateway to America, were main recruiting areas. Cadets would "scan the immigrants as they come down the gangplank of a vessel," investigators reported, "and 'spot' the girls who are unaccompanied by fathers, mothers, brothers, or relatives to protect them. The girl who has been spotted as desirable . . . is properly approached by a man who speaks her language and is immediately offered employment at good wages. The only thing," the investigators delicately added, "is to accomplish her ruin by the shortest route." Employment or intelligence offices, as they were then known, were another "hunting-ground" of cadets; dance-halls a third. Employment offices hired "runners" who, fluent in several European languages, made friendly overtures to immigrant women in search of work. "Assuring them in the most flattering terms of opportunity for work and 'easy money,'" explained Frances Kellor, a leading Progressive reformer, runners would then place the unsuspecting immigrant in a brothel. On the Lower East Side alone, Kellor estimated there were eighty-five employment offices supplying women to brothels. Like the intelligence offices, dance halls exploited the need of the immigrant women for friendship and employment. A cheap form of amusement, dance halls with exotic names like Palais de Danse and the Non-pareil dotted the Lower East Side, often providing the only relief from its gray tenements. "The town is dance mad," observed reformer Belle Israels. "If you walk along Grand Street . . . the glare of lights and the blare of music strike you on every side . . . Columbia Street, Delancey, Stanton, Allen, Houston, all have their quota of places." In the gay atmosphere of the dance hall, smooth-talking and affable young men sought out immigrant women. "Ignorant and dazed by the strange conditions of an unknown country," reported an eye-witness, immigrant women are "very easily secured by promise of marriage or even partnership." Another habitue of the dance hall added, perhaps tongue-in-cheek, that "mass defloration . . . is a nightly event."[37]

Whatever the locale, the strategy of the cadet—that "missionary of the devil"—remained the same. He dazzled the immigrant woman with his charm, winning her affections. "He dresses better than the ordinary neighborhood boy, wears an abundance of cheap jewelry and has usually cultivated a limited amount of gentlemanly demeanor," wrote the Committee of Fourteen, New York City's most energetic anti-vice organization. "By giving the young girl glimpses of a standard of living which she had never dared hope to attain," the Committee explained, "friendship rapidly ripens into infatuation." After several dates, the young woman "find[s] herself at the mercy of her supposed friend," the reformers noted. Disgraced, the woman clutches at her "supposed friend's" offer of marriage, only to end up as a prostitute.[38]

As images of the Jewish bearded kaftan and of urbane cadets took hold of the American imagination, the nation's moral custodians seemed deliberately to blur the boundary between fact and fiction. No allegation was too far-fetched, no description too fevered to be used in the service of the anti-vice crusade. What is more, much of the literature had a pronounced nativist and anti-Semitic bias. It was a "prevalent notion," writes Feldman, that "behind the scenes of urban vice were found the nation's newcomers. Surely it was the foreigner, a good many upright Americans were convinced, who was organizing, supporting, and thriving upon the lucrative traffic of prostitution. Serious discussions of procuring and pimping inevitably led to an anti-Semitic rhetoric." Similarly, Arthur Goren notes that among the New York reformers eager to topple Tammany Hall, the politics of prostitution frequently took on an ugly anti-Jewish cast. "The muckraker sacrificed accuracy and balance for the sake of sensationalism . . . and referred mainly to immigrant Jews," he writes in his classic account of prewar New York Jewry. Nowhere is the anti-Semitic animus of the social

evil reformers more transparent than with respect to their claim that
Jewish white slavers monopolized the entire traffic in women. What
Turner and others believed to be a vast conspiratorial network was
actually a set of voluntary organizations. Joined together by common
business interests and a common ostracism, pimps and procurers formed
their own social clubs where they could fraternize freely and exchange
business information. Like the *landsmanshaft*, a staple in the social landscape of the Lower East Side, groups like the Independent Benevolent
Association provided pension benefits, funeral arrangements—including
a plot in Flatbush—and a congenial social environment for their
constituents. In fact, the Independent Benevolent Association was
duplicated on a far larger scale in other centers of Jewish underworld
activity. Buenos Aires, a leading entrepôt of the white slave trade,
contained many synagogues, *landsmanshaften*, and cemeteries catering
exclusively to the members of the Argentinian Jewish underworld.
"There has been much talk in the newspapers," explained the Dillingham Commission in its study of the white slave traffic, "of a great
monopolistic corporation whose business it is to import and to exploit
these unfortunate women. The Commission has been unable to learn
of any such corporation and does not believe in its existence." The
anti-Semitic and nativist sentiments of the social reformers also colored
their descriptions of the dimensions of Jewish involvement in the
white slave trade. Admittedly, reliable statistics are hard to come by;
the nature of the business, reported the Dillingham Commission's researchers, "precludes of course exact statistics." The limited available
information suggests that social reformers like Turner inflated the
extent of Jewish participation. In fiscal 1908–1909, for example, "Hebrews" accounted for a relatively small ten percent of all persons
deported from the United States for procuring; the French, in contrast,
accounted for close to one-third of this population.[39]

In the final analysis, no matter how tainted or suspect contemporary
pre–World War I reports of widespread Jewish involvement with
prostitution and white slavery may have been, they cannot be entirely
discounted. "It may very well be," observed Isaac Hourwich, a statis-
tician with the United States Census Bureau and a close student of the
underworld, that recent articles on white slavery "were inspired by
anti-Semitic animus; the charge of prejudice does not disprove, however, the facts . . . . While there may be some inaccuracies and exag-

gerations, prostitution and the business of the procurer," he concluded, "are no longer unknown to the Jews."[40]

In all its manifestations—whether procuring or horse-poisoning, theft or pickpocketing—Jewish crime was both widespread and unique. Enmeshed in and tied to the Jewish environment of the New World, the types of crimes indulged in by Jews were significantly different than those, say, of the Italians. As the years went by these differences became less pronounced; indeed, instances of Jewish criminality became fewer. But during the prewar period, Jewish criminals, as one law official put it, displayed a "definite selectiveness" in their criminality. As such, Jewish criminality became a major source of worry and of consternation for New York Jewry's very own social and moral custodians.[41]

TWO "PARTICULAR OCCASIONS"

The Bingham and Rosenthal Affairs

Although Jewish criminals were everywhere on the Lower East Side "befouling" the neighborhood, crime, writes Irving Howe, "was never at the center of immigrant Jewish life. . . . In the life of the immigrant community as a whole, crime was a marginal phenomenon, a pathology discoloring the process of collective assertion and adjustment." Despite great poverty and the psychic and cultural disruptions caused by their movement from the Old World to the New, the overwhelming majority of first-generation Jews lived out their lives without becoming caught in the coils of the criminal law. Those who appeared on the dockets were but a small fraction of the Jewish population and the behaviors for which they were apprehended a most unrepresentative sample of the activities of most immigrant Jews at the time. Most immigrants went about their business, trying to eke out an honest livelihood, pay the rent, clothe and school their children. Admittedly, it was hard at times to avoid coming into contact with the community's Jewish criminal element, yet most law-abiding Jews tried to keep their distance. They knew that to avoid being solicited by Jewish prostitutes they must not walk on certain streets; to avoid meeting pimps and thieves they should stay clear of certain restaurants. "It is better to stay away from Allen, Chrystie and Forsyth Streets, if you go walking with your wife, daughter or fiancee," cautioned the *Jewish Daily Forward*, "for there's an official flesh trade there." "Ask any girl—bar none—who has ever passed Second Avenue and gone by 76 Second Avenue [a gang hangout] if she knows of the place . . . without hesitation she will answer in the affirmative. Hundreds of them have been molested by this gang," reported Shoenfeld.[1]

Most Jews, it seems, not only attempted consciously to steer clear of the Jewish criminal element and its haunts, they also kept the problem of Jewish criminality at arm's length in a social and psychological sense as well: by keeping silent about it. At times the Yiddish press, disturbed by the growing incidence of Jewish crime on the Lower East Side, fulminated against the community's apathy, seeking to rouse the local residents from their customary indifference; their appeals fell on deaf ears. Whatever their reasons—and there were many—most Jews kept quiet. "Ostrich-like, they buried their . . . heads . . . they refused to see the glaring fact or to hear the urgent call," reported one dismayed contemporary. Some, perhaps many, were so taken up with earning a living that they remained ignorant of the "rotten problem" of Jewish crime or, as Harry Newberger put it, "have the remotest notion of the extent to which this thing has taken hold." Unaware that their children learned the Torah of fighting rather than the Torah of Moses, that they returned home bearing scars instead of textbooks, many parents were caught off guard by the criminality of their children. "While the father goes to the synagogue," one contemporary perceptively observed, "the son goes to jail." Hard-working, religious, and even learned, Mr. Rosenzweig had no idea that his son Lefty Louie spent all his time loafing on street corners, rolling drunks, and stealing. The same was true of Mr. Horowitz. An active member of a local synagogue, he believed that his son "Gyp the Blood" was an excellent student. True enough—but "Gyp" was an excellent student of fisticuffs, not of academics! Often upon becoming aware of the wrongdoing of their children, parents like Mr. Rosenzweig and Mr. Horowitz were so troubled, so taken aback that, noted Shoenfeld sympathetically, "for shame, they keep it to themselves." Community leaders did much the same thing, preferring to keep discussions on Jewish criminality "to themselves." "East Side leaders and institutions," writes Howe, "were steadily worried, more than they allowed themselves to say in public or admit to the gentiles. . . . And over the years," he continues, "the Jews had developed a cultural style encouraging prudishness and self censorship; there were things everyone knew, had no choice but to know, yet only rarely was it deemed proper to speak or write about them. Life was hard enough without indulging in luxuries of revelation." Then, too, some Lower East Siders—how many we do not know— were not at all troubled by Jewish criminality; they simply "did not care." Though not criminals themselves, they probably consisted of those who profited from their financial and political association with the Jewish underworld: persons like the tenement house owner who reaped huge profits by permitting prostitution on his property; the garment manufacturer who sanctioned the use of violence to undermine the labor movement, and the labor leader who in turn sanctioned the use of violence to undermine management; the politician who protected members of the underworld against arrest.[2]

The Lower East Side community, then, had many reasons for "burying its head." In fact, only when the outside world pointed an accusatory finger did New York Jews of the prewar community address the problem. "The trouble is," one disgruntled New Yorker complained, referring especially to the downtown community, "Jews are inclined to let this matter sleep and do nothing unless some particular occasion calls forth action." The Bingham affair of 1908 and the Rosenthal affair four years later were two such "particular occasions," two events that focused a reluctant community's attention on the emerging Jewish underworld. Commissioner of Police Theodore A. Bingham's article in the September 1908 issue of the *North American Review*, which charged that New York Jews comprised at least half of Gotham's underworld element, undid the positive image most Jews had held of themselves and that others had held of the Jews. Catching the community off guard, the Bingham article, with its seemingly irrefutable statistics, pointed up the discrepancy between New York Jewry's collective self-image as "a nation of priests" and the reality behind that image. Unwilling at first to accept Bingham's charges at face value, New York Jews mounted an elaborate campaign to discredit both the police official and his allegations. Ultimately, though, a growing number of them had to concede that the police commissioner's characterization was not entirely wrong.[3]

Barely had the community sufficient opportunity to regain its equilibrium before its reputation was assailed once again; this time, in the summer of 1912, by the Rosenthal affair. The murder of Herman Rosenthal, a well-known Jewish gambler, by several Lower East Side youths rocked New York Jewry to its very core, sparking an internal review of the New York Jewish experience and forcing the community to marshall all its resources toward solving the problem of Jewish crime. As an excited metropolitan press treated the public to continuous discussions of the haunts and the personalities of the Lower East Side underworld, New York Jews found they could no longer freely boast of their deep-seated morality; the Rosenthal case made a mockery of such claims. Interpreting the Rosenthal case as a cruel indictment of

New York Jewish life and ultimately as cause for its restructuring, an anxious and uneasy community launched a campaign to eliminate Jewish criminality once and for all from its precincts.

Within days of the publication of Bingham's inflammatory article, the editors of New York's Yiddish newspapers printed long excerpts from the essay. They also strongly denounced it, calling Bingham's remarks "anti-semitic poison" and a "modern form of the ancient blood libel," and even going so far as to call for a public apology from him. When none was immediately forthcoming, the Lower East Side "rose in wrath" and demanded Bingham's resignation. The Anglo-Jewish press as well as several metropolitan newspapers joined in denouncing Bingham. The usually restrained *American Hebrew*, for example, labeled Bingham's allegations "overcolored," "venomous," and inappropriate for a civic official. The *New York American* found Bingham's remarks "as idiotic as they were atrocious" and roundly criticized the official for its intemperateness. "With the recklessness of a man in a bar-room altercation," the paper editorialized, "Mr. Bingham takes these figures, incorporates them in an article meant for wide circulation and solemnly sets them forth as truth. . . . But Mr. Bingham," the paper continued, "himself stands indicted of an irresponsibility that is as dangerous in his office as the malevolence he disclaims. . . ."[4]

Determined to prove that the police commissioner's accusations were mistaken and reckless, the Jewish press tried feverishly to account for his figures. Some papers suggested that the official had erroneously labeled as criminals all persons arrested for committing such trivial offenses as peddling without a license, while others contended that the police, in an effort to appear industrious, had fabricated a number of the arrest reports, many of which contained Jewish names. Still other contemporaries believed that the damning statistics were simply false. Bingham's comments, one daily claimed, were "little more than a hodgepodge [lit.: *kasha*] of unsubstantiated quotes, clippings and interviews."[5]

On the evening of September 5, while the furor was at its most fevered, one hundred New York Jews, representing a broad spectrum of the community's ethnic and political divisions, met to discuss the implications of Bingham's allegations. Troubled both by the substance of the *North American Review* piece and by their inability to respond in a united and organized fashion to it, they deliberated until two in the morning. Some of those in attendance hesitated to take action against the police official; others urged an immediate and bold response. Ultimately, the group decided on several courses of action: to establish a community-wide organization which would be able to speak in the name of and for the polyglot New York Jewish community; to examine available court and police records as soon as possible to "combat" the commissioner's assertions; and, finally, to engage in a long-term study of Jewish criminality. Ironically enough, not only was the Kehillah—the name given to the overarching Jewish communal organization—spawned as a result of New York Jewry's involvement with crime, it was also to spend a sizable portion of its budget and much of its energies in later years combating Jewish criminality. In the meantime, fashioning an effective rebuttal to the police commissioner was the group's most pressing task.[6]

This stress on the importance of presenting a statistically oriented reply to Bingham was in part a response to the terms of the debate set forth by the police official in his article. To mount a convincing rebuttal, defenders of the Jews would have to meet the commissioner on his own terms: with numbers. In this respect, too, Jewish communal leaders were responding to the tenor of the times. As part of the "factual generation" of the prewar period, they, like their gentile counterparts, tried to address difficult social problems—housing, poverty, and crime—objectively and empirically. During those years, writes Robert Bremner, "the solution to every problem seemed to lie in submitting it to a group of good citizens and disinterested experts . . . the path to reform lay through research." As a first step toward eliminating Jewish criminality, community leaders planned to submit the issue to a panel of statisticians who would initially determine the extent of the phenomenon and then—and only then—suggest remedial measures. Constructing elaborate pyramids of numbers to repudiate Bingham, Jewish leaders sought to show that when population, age, and location were controlled, the Jews had significantly fewer criminals than did native-born Americans. And yet, despite the community's professed trust in numbers, one cannot help but suspect that by casting such an inherently emotional issue in the neutral language of statistics, by assuming a pose of objectivity, the community was actually trying valiantly to mask its true feelings of dismay and consternation.[7]

In what must have seemed like a stroke of good fortune to those in search of objectivity, the community had available a highly professional

A sad-looking Jewish gang of the 1920s.

A recent photograph of one of the original Hawthorne School cottages. (*The Jewish Board of Family and Children's Services*)

The Essex Market Police Court, "Tribunal of the Poor." (*New-York Historical Society, New York City*)

"Drilling a Youthful Street Gang." (*Photo Library Department, Museum of the City of New York*)

Allen Street, "Street of Perpetual Shadow." (*New-York Historical Society, New York City*)

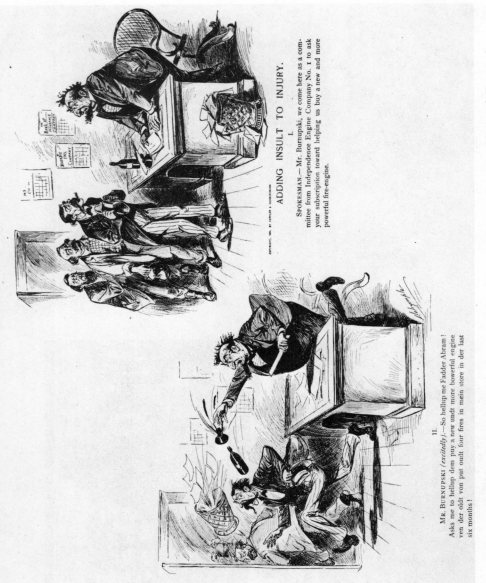

ADDING INSULT TO INJURY.

I.

SPOKESMAN.—Mr. Burnupski, we come here as a committee from Independence Engine Company No. I to ask your subscription toward helping us buy a new and more powerful fire-engine.

II.

MR. BURNUPSKI (*excitedly*).—So hellup me Fadder Abram! Asks me to hellup dem pay a new undt more bowerful engine ven der oldt von put oudt four fires in mein store in der last six months!

A *Puck* cartoon satirizing the connection between Jews and arson. (*General Research Division, The New York Public Library, Astor, Lenox and Tilden Foundations*)

Marm Mandelbaum's dinner party, conducted with "as much attention to the proprieties as though Mrs. Mandelbaum's establishment was in Fifth Avenue instead of in a suspicious corner of the East Side." (*General Research Division, The New York Public Library, Astor, Lenox and Tilden Foundations*)

Gyp the Blood and Lefty Louie, two "echt" Americans. (*UPI*)

An ethnically mixed gang of the interwar era.

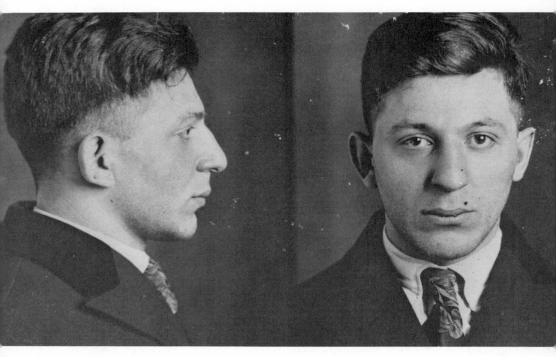

"Lepke" Buchalter.

"Gurrah" Shapiro.

The garment center. (*Collections of the Municipal Archives of the City of New York*)

Female garment workers. (*Photo Library Department, Museum of the City of New York*)

Factory interior, Moe Levy and Company Clothiers. (*Photo Library Department, Museum of the City of New York*)

Chicken pullers—"rough birds themselves"—at the Washington Poultry Market. (*Collections of the Municipal Archives of the City of New York*)

Arnold Rothstein's Orthodox Jewish funeral.

The candy-store headquarters of Murder Inc. (*Collections of the Municipal Archives of the City of New York*)

A victim of Murder Inc. (*Collections of the Municipal Archives of the City of New York*)

study of Jewish criminality that had been commissioned only months before by the Federation of Jewish Organizations, a group which (theoretically at least) represented five hundred Jewish societies throughout New York State. The Federation's decision to sponsor such a project was fueled by several factors, among them the unavailability of detailed statistics on ethnic criminality. As early as 1907, Edward Lauterbach, the organization's president, had asked the New York police department to furnish him with a breakdown of arrests by nationality. A comment by journalist Frank Marshall White that two-thirds of recent additions to the infamous Rogues Gallery were Russian Jews had caught the community leader's attention and he wanted the police department to verify it for him. A year passed and Lauterbach's request went unanswered. In the interim, members of the Federation's Executive Committee became alarmed by what they saw as the growing incidence of Jewish criminality and suggested the Federation "shed light upon this important problem." Accordingly, in February 1908, Lauterbach assigned his private secretary, Mark J. Katz, the task of combing through the most current records of the Court of General Sessions—those for 1907—to determine the number of Jews charged with committing felonies. Five months later, Katz published his findings in the June issue of the *Federation Review*, the house organ of the Federation of Jewish Organizations. His figures showed that in relation to population, Jews were half as likely as non-Jews to be convicted of a felony. Katz also found that Jewish convicts accounted for 16.4 percent of the total convicted population in 1907, hardly the 50 percent of Bingham's tally. Katz's study, observed one contemporary, shows that "Jews are to be congratulated on the low percentage of criminality among them. . . ."[8]

The release of the study was timely indeed; within days after Bingham had sent shock waves through the Jewish community, the Jewish press widely and proudly disseminated Katz's study. Armed with his statistics, the leaders of the community hoped to deliver a "crushing and convincing reply" to Bingham. In fact, the community's campaign to win some measure of redress was apparently successful. On September 17, just two weeks after having published his article, Bingham issued a public apology. In his statement, carried by all the major newspapers, the police official contended that he had no animus against the foreign population of New York. The purpose of the *North American Review* article, he explained, "was not to enter upon a scientific inquiry into the race or religion of those charged with criminality but solely to make a plea for a secret service fund in order that criminality might be more effectively dealt with than is now possible. The idea which I sought to impress," he continued,

> was that the number of foreigners with whom the police come in contact is very large and that a special knowledge of racial customs and manners is essential to the attainment of the best results by the police in the investigation of crimes committed by and against those of foreign origin.

The police official then concluded by "repudiat[ing]" the figures upon which much of his article rested: I do so, he stated, "frankly and without reserve."[9]

What is one to make of this episode and of New York Jewry's response to it? After all, Bingham was clearly not the first to have alluded to the existence of a Jewish underworld, and yet his statement seemed to carry more weight and to cause far more alarm than those of his predecessors. For one thing, Bingham's statement was buttressed by seemingly unassailable statistics and was therefore not easily dismissed out of hand as the ravings of an ill-informed and anti-Semitic mind. In fact, his sophisticated and ostensibly objective description lent credence to the claims of nativists that Russians (and Italians) were decidedly inferior: Ross and other immigration restrictionists often cited Bingham directly as a source for their anti-immigrant position. For another thing, Bingham's statement was made publicly, thus reaching a wider audience than those who followed court proceedings or political trials. Unlike an earlier official, police chief Thomas Devery, who was reportedly kind enough to have *whispered* his views on Jews and criminality to Jacob Schiff and Felix Adler lest he publicly embarrass the Jewish community at large, Bingham *broadcast* his opinion through the published word, publicly shaming New York Jews and robbing them of their cherished self-image as a community of law-abiding and hard-working men and women. Accustomed to seeing themselves as morally "unblemished," Jews were now branded as members in full of the city's "dangerous class," an image they could not easily shake. In the final analysis, observed the *Jewish Daily Forward*, Bingham "may retract his silly figures a thousand times. Still, the enemies of the Jews will make use of them"; the *Judisches Tageblatt* added that it was "very naive" to think that Bingham's retraction settled the issue: "The world," it explained, "will believe the Commissioner more than us. . . ."[10]

But what of Bingham himself? Was he so immature a politician that he felt his remarks would go unnoticed by the city's immigrant groups, or such a statistical innocent that he was simply unaware of the implications of his remarks? Or was the police official an unabashed xenophobe sharing his thoughts (fears?) with kindred spirits through the *North American Review?* Bingham was probably a little bit of all three. By all accounts a man of little tact and less discretion, Bingham had become a thorn in the side of Mayor George B. McClellan who had first appointed him as police commissioner in January 1906. "He was always getting himself and incidentally me into hot water," the mayor later recalled. His article might well have been just another one of the many blunders committed by this "bluff [former] soldier" of a city official. Yet it would also seem that Bingham shared no fondness for the city's numerous ethnic groups. In charge of an armed police force in daily contact with the city's millions, surely he calmed no fears when he used words that suggested that he was three-quarters prejudiced, one-quarter fair. Bingham referred to a city that teemed with immigrants; in expressing his ethnic biases, he arrayed himself not against the law-breakers but against the citizenry. Nor was the September 1908 article the first time that Bingham had expressed such anti-immigrant sentiments. Writing in the annual report of the New York police department two years earlier, in 1906, he had casually noted that a "large number of these emigrants are criminals." In this respect, Bingham reflected the views of a considerable segment of the American public at this time. Even after he had issued his retraction, magazines carried statements by readers agreeing with the police commissioner's description of the Jews. "The dishonest among them [the Jews]," wrote one correspondent in the *Independent,* "are all out of proportion to their numbers"; another New Yorker wrote that "Police Commissioner Bingham was right in his idea about the large proportion of Jewish criminals."[11]

Ultimately, winning a retraction from Commissioner Bingham was only a limited victory for New York Jewry. Its success at challenging the high-ranking official, compelling him to qualify his earlier statement, no doubt gratified many New York Jews, even vindicating their belief in the notion that the Jews, after all, were "the people who gave the world its moral standard." Buoyed by their recent political success, most Jews refused to concede that Jewish criminality was indeed a serious and growing Jewish social problem; instead they dismissed Bingham's allegations out of hand, preferring to think of them as suspect, the product of sloppy research. True, there was much to quarrel with in Bingham's description of the city criminal element. There could, however, be no quarrel with its basic premise: regardless of the actual number of Jewish criminals, a Jewish underworld existed. Some Jews, horrified by the implications of the *North American Review* article, either redoubled their efforts in support of the Hawthorne School or became involved for perhaps the first time; Hawthorne's list of contributors grew slightly in the year following the Bingham affair. Most, though, persisted in clinging to the notion that Jews and crime was an impossible combination and refused to concede its seriousness. Now that the community had proved that Jews do not constitute fifty percent of all New York's criminals, admonished Louis Marshall, it would doubtless "relapse into that state of self-satisfaction which has characterized [it] in years past. . . . Let us not deceive ourselves with the belief that we are entirely kosher."[12]

On the evening of July 16, 1912, Herman "Beansey" Rosenthal, a small-time gambler and hustler with large pretensions and former protégé of Tammany Hall chieftain "Big Tim" Sullivan, was shot to death only hours before he was to have testified before a grand jury on police-underworld ties. Harrassed by the police and consequently unable to pursue his calling as a gambler, Rosenthal had walked into the New York County District Attorney's office on July 15 and volunteered a great deal of information on Gotham's underworld. Among his more startling allegations was that Police Lieutenant Charles Becker, the head of an anti-vice squad, was his silent partner in a West 45th Street gambling parlor.[13]

Within days of Rosenthal's untimely demise, the case was being touted as one of the more extraordinary crimes of the decade; Charles Whitman, New York's ambitious district attorney, accused Becker point-blank of having plotted the murder of his erstwhile business associate lest he reveal to the grand jury the extent of the comfortable and financially rewarding police-underworld nexus. After a number of trials and retrials, Becker was convicted of having conspired to murder Rosenthal and was executed by the state in July 1915. Becker, though, was not the only one on trial; the mounting evidence of po-

litical corruption which Whitman gleefully unearthed implicated
Mayor William Gaynor and his administration as well. The Rosenthal
case, noted the *New York World*, reveals that "the system [of organized graft] does not stop with Becker and his kind but extends right
into police headquarters." The murder of the gambler, another contemporary wrote, "revealed a condition of official debauchery often hinted
at but never before revealed." For his part, District Attorney Whitman,
whose efforts in prosecuting Becker later earned him the governorship
of New York State, felt the murder was a "challenge to our civilization."[14]

While New York Jewry shared the general public's outrage at
Becker's crime, it was far more upset by the involvement of approximately twelve Jews in the murder. Not only had the victim been
Jewish but the gunmen later accused of killing him, with one exception,
were also Jews; so were those allegedly hired by Becker to arrange
the details of the shooting—to rent and drive the getaway automobile,
dispose of the gun, and hide the gunmen. For months, the metropolitan
press prominently displayed such demonstrably Jewish names as Harry
Horowitz, Jack Rose, Louis Rosenzweig, Sam Schepps, Jacob Seidenshner, and Harry Vallinsky on its front pages. Most New York
dailies did not dwell openly on the ethnicity of the participants but
concentrated instead on such themes as municipal corruption, police
inefficiency, and Gaynor's political ineptitude. Still, the press did not
need to highlight the Jewish involvement in the Rosenthal murder; the
facts spoke clearly for themselves. The *New York American* probably
succeeded best in publicizing the murder as the handiwork of Jewish
Lower East Siders when it published profile photographs of gunmen
"Lefty Louie" Rosenzweig, "Gyp the Blood" Horowitz, and Jacob
"Whitey Louis" Seidenshner, all of whom had stereotypically Jewish
noses. That this display, perhaps more than any editorial or news story,
touched raw nerves was demonstrated by the response of one Yiddish
journalist who, upon seeing the photographs, exclaimed: "And for this,
the Jewish people have been chosen?"[15]

Guilt-ridden over the involvement of its "sons" in the Rosenthal affair,
New York Jewry regarded the episode as "its greatest moral crisis"
and with "courageous recognition" observed grimly that "the entire
affair from start to finish . . . is Jewish through and through." "The
Jewish heart bleeds from shame and horror that the Jewish people have
'merited' such a place in the annals of American criminal history,"

lamented the *Judisches Tageblatt*. Another contemporary remarked that in the wake of Rosenthal's demise, "sorrow descended upon us. We are all in trouble today." New York Jewry found everything about the case profoundly unsettling, from the large number of Jewish youth involved in the crime to the type of crime itself; to its mind, the case suggested that the American Jewish experience was a failure. After all, of the twelve Jewish participants in the Rosenthal murder, six had been born in America; the other half, though born abroad, had migrated to America at a young age and were reared in New York. As "echt Americans," with no criminal ancestry, the murderers and their accomplices had had all the advantages of a public school education, had grown up "under the free skies of the republic and with all the privileges of other native Americans." William Shapiro, the owner of the getaway car, "comes of respectable parents," wrote one confused journalist, while Lefty Louie, one of the gunmen, was raised by his family as a "well-educated [individual who] knows how to conduct himself—and is very refined in his manners. . . ." If the Jewish criminal element had such respectable antecedents, what did the future of American Jewry hold? the community asked itself. Furthermore, that Jewish boys had actually committed murder was "astounding" to most New York Jews, for murder was something foreign to the Jewish historical experience or so Jews liked to think. For centuries, Jews had not only prided themselves on their "comparatively clean bill of moral health" but also on the absence of crimes of violence; the latter, explained the *American Hebrew*, "were the rarest thing." "While it had never been thought that there were no evildoers among the Jews," Cyrus Sulzberger, a leading Jewish community leader, related, "the belief was general and well-founded that their malefactors were of a different kind. Here are crimes," he added, referring to the Rosenthal murder, "which heretofore in all countries have been alien to the Jewish nature and to which the history of the Jews in all lands and times offers no parallel." What, then, had gone awry? How was one to reconcile the promise of America with the reality of a Lefty Louie?[16]

Determined to find the causes, each of the community's newspapers, from the fiercely religious *Judisches Tageblatt* to the staunchly Socialist *Jewish Daily Forward*, proffered its own theory sparking, in the process, an internal review of the New York Jewish experience. Years before, the Jewish proponents of Emancipation had intently and publicly scrutinized every aspect of the European Jewish experience in an effort to encourage the authorities to grant political and civic rights to Jewish residents. Eager to prove to the state that the Jews were capable of assimilating to the larger body politic, these Jewish leaders investigated sharply every phase of Jewish life, from the religious practices of its members to their occupational makeup—all with an eye toward the community's eventual reconstruction. In a functional sense, the furor that resulted from the Rosenthal case provided New York Jewish leaders, a century and a continent away, with a similar opportunity. To be sure, the granting of civic or political rights to Jewish New Yorkers was not an issue in the summer of 1912, but the future and the shape of the New York Jewish experience was. Taken aback, even stunned, by the involvement of its "sons" in one of the decade's most dastardly crimes, New York Jewry sought desperately to find the etiology of Jewish criminality; as Jewish newspaper after Jewish newspaper searched for the origins of a Lefty Louie or a Gyp the Blood, no feature of Jewish life in the Empire City was left untouched. For its part, the religious community attributed the Rosenthal murder to a pervasive moral decay in American life. "In America," the *Judisches Tageblatt* complained, "Jewish children are reared without the benefit of God, without religious training and worst of all, without a firm moral upbringing." "Emancipated from all connection with Judaism," added the *American Hebrew*, "the majority of youngsters take their education into their own hands": the result—a Rosenthal, a Gyp the Blood, a Lefty Louie. Those of a more sociological bent found New York Jewish life as a whole to be wanting. The Rosenthal case, *Wahrheit* explained,

> is but the logical outgrowth of conditions on the Lower East Side . . . where anomie [lit.: *hefker*] prevails. Go into the cafes, the dancing schools, the race-track, the gambling houses . . . the social "clubs," the sport associations . . . and listen to what the inhabitants talk about and how they talk . . . ask them what they aspire to, what their calling [lit.: *beruf*] is, what sort of ideals they cherish and you will understand how it was possible for such types [as the Rosenthal murderers and their accomplices] to emerge.

Equally troubled by this seeming explosion in Jewish criminality, the *Jewish Daily Forward* pronounced the case a clear-cut example of the dangers of capitalism, which, the paper maintained, was responsible for delinquency by breeding conditions in which honest laborers remained poor while criminals grew wealthy. "Such a society," it explained, "is neither Jewish nor Christian; neither American nor European. It is capitalist."[17]

Even as they traded recriminations, the Jewish press developed a consensus on the origins of Jewish criminal behavior: whatever the specific analysis, no one doubted any longer that crime was a social consequence of the community's earlier reluctance to admit to its existence, a consequence of its own inattentiveness to the conditions fostering delinquency and vice. "It is we, the members of the New York Jewish community, with our apathy and our blindness," *Wahrheit* insisted, "who are responsible for this great moral crisis." The *American Hebrew* fully agreed: the problem of Jewish criminality, the weekly explained, "has undoubtedly been due to a certain reluctance to recognize it openly. The desire to keep the fair name of Israel unspotted from scandal has in the last resort led to worse scandals. We have wanted a prophet to rebuke us, as of old, and we still need his chastening influence." Though by 1912 New York Jews had formed the Hawthorne School and were beginning to build a similar facility for Jewish girls as well, these institutions, the Rosenthal case demonstrated, were not adequate to the task of eliminating Jewish criminality. If nothing else. the Rosenthal case indicated that Jewish crime was far more deep-seated than anyone had suspected, existing "to an extent far beyond what we ourselves had dreamed."[18]

Given the newly discovered dimension of Jewish underworld activity, "cleaning up the Jewish house" by fighting crime became a necessity, the only way by which Jews could hope to restore their name "to its rightful place." Lending an additional note of urgency to the community's decision was nativism which, by 1912, was at its height. "The times," one alarmed observer wrote in the aftermath of the Rosenthal affair, "are exceptionally critical." Jewish criminality, the underside of the immigrant experience, not only reflected the inadequacy of existing Jewish institutions to cope with the masses of new immigrants but, more to the point, it threatened the well-being of the community at large. Disclosures of large-scale Jewish criminal activity subjected New York Jewry to what was perhaps the most sustained and intense public scrutiny in its entire history, a scrutiny which laid bare the community's weaknesses for all to see. Moreover, the Rosenthal revelations provided nativists with the ammunition necessary to compel repatriation or, worse still, to press for the imposition of immigration quotas. "After the exposures which have now been made," wrote

Cyrus Sulzberger to Rabbi Judah Magnes, president of the Kehillah, "it needs no preliminary investigation to convince us that such conditions as exist not only imperil the good name of the Jews but place in jeopardy the whole immigration problem. . . . It is a time for getting busy and doing something to root out the disgrace." Other Jews apparently agreed, for, in the months following the Rosenthal affair, dozens of schemes were proposed. Some members of the Jewish community suggested forming Jewish civic groups; others advocated establishing more Americanized synagogues capable of appealing to the disaffected younger generations, while *Wahrheit* put forth what was surely the boldest of all possible anti-crime ideas: the formation of a "vigilance committee." A "Jewish secret service" to monitor the activities of the Jewish criminals and, with the help of the police, to suppress them, it explained, would eliminate Jewish criminality where the other schemes would not. "If one were to go into the Hall of Records, one would find that Jews have more organizations than any other nationality," the paper noted. "One would find Jewish organizations whose purpose is to observe the Sabbath; Jewish organizations promoting the observance of Jewish dietary laws. Would it not then be an easy thing to establish an organization which protects the interests of *all* Jews?" The Kehillah promptly provided the answer: on August 1, 1912, scarcely three weeks after Rosenthal's death, it called a meeting of German Jewish leaders and representatives of local Lower East Side organizations to consider the "advisability of forming a Vigilance Committee and Bureau of Information and Investigation." New York Jewry, argued Magnes, had a "double duty" to support such a bureau. "As good citizens and Americans, we Jews ought to cooperate with all movements intended to strike at the root of this colossal evil." It was the civic responsibility of the Jewish community to help sponsor a municipal cleanup campaign. But, as Jews, he continued, "We have a holy obligation, a duty to ourselves and to our community, to uproot the tendencies towards moral and political corruption in our community." The vigilance committee, the rabbi added, was simply a "family gathering of Jews to devise means for saving our fair name."[19]

The Kehillah's plan was not without its critics. Some felt the establishment of a Jewish detective agency was unprecedented; while Eastern European Jewry had a long tradition of forming kehillot, there had never been a Jewish communal agency designed to eradicate corruption within the Jewish quarter. Lacking historical roots, a Jewish detective agency could not be easily countenanced. Others, especially those of a religious cast of mind, felt the formation of a Bureau of Information and Investigation was only a stopgap measure; it was not enough, argued one newspaper, to weed out Jewish criminals; what was needed was a positive program of Jewish education. "Networking the city with opportunities for education in Jewish religion and tradition," urged the *American Hebrew*, "is the chief instrument for the remedy of the evils from which we suffer." The strongest opposition to the Kehillah's suggestion, however, came from the *Morgen Journal*. Piqued by its very existence, the paper's editor urged New York Jews to stay clear of the Kehillah and its brand of "Californian vigilance," a sarcastic reference perhaps to Magnes's Californian origins. The Kehillah could not even reduce congestion in a tenement house, the paper sputtered; how could it hope to combat criminality? Going a step further, the *Morgen Journal* argued that crime fighting should be left to the municipal authorities. In a strongly worded editorial entitled "The Stupidity of Regarding Crime as a Jewish Social Problem," the paper exhorted its readers to participate in city-wide cleanup efforts but to shy away from exclusively Jewish ones; crime, it added, is not a Jewish question but an American one.[20]

Nevertheless, sufficient consensus on the legitimacy of and the necessity for a Jewish vigilance committee existed within the Jewish community to enable the Kehillah to establish what it euphemistically called the Bureau of Social Morals. "While the Beckers are only a civic problem," *Wahrheit* explained, summing up the community's support for such an agency, "the 'Gyp the Bloods' and the Roses [are] OUR WORK, JEWISH WORK." Under the Kehillah's direction, bureaus of information were formed throughout the city enlisting the cooperation of residents in alerting the Kehillah to the whereabouts of known local criminals. In late August, Magnes, playing a "Jewish Parkhurst," hired his first salaried investigator, Abe Shoenfeld. The son of a Jewish labor leader, Shoenfeld had had considerable experience investigating crime as a member of the Rockefeller-funded Bureau of Social Hygiene, an outfit looking into prostitution. Posing as a writer, Shoenfeld was able to collect information from many of the city's Jewish criminals; he later transcribed these confidences into 750 stories and 2,516 index cards which he then forwarded to the police. Eventually, Shoenfeld broadened the base of his operations by hiring eight additional investigators. To shore up the legal end of the Bureau,

Magnes also enlisted the help of Harry Newberger, the scion of a distinguished German Jewish family, as the Bureau's counsel. Under his direction, the Kehillah's anti-vice agency worked in tandem with Mayor Gaynor and his police department, supplying them with the information that ultimately "led to gambling raids, revocation of licenses and the arraignment of individual criminals." With admirable thoroughness, the Bureau compiled hundreds of dossiers on the Jewish underworld. Much as the police would routinely write up the particulars of a case on a "yellow sheet," Shoenfeld and his associates transcribed all sorts of personal bits of information about Jewish criminal figures onto index cards. Each card not only provided the name, age, birthplace, nationality and type of "graft" of the criminal under surveillance, but also the address of his business and his "hangout," details of his physical appearance, police record, material and marital status, the number and name of children—whether legitimate or illegitimate—and the criminal's history "before entering the graft." With this information, the detective explained, ". . . We creep right into their home affairs—into their lawyers' offices, and we know what goes on. There is not a time we cannot lay our hands on them, and there is not a man on our lists who is not known to one or more of our investigators. Nothing," Shoenfeld added, "is ever used on hearsay only— nothing entertained unless it is solidly backed up by argument and in most instances corroborated in some way or other." When the police, acting on information provided them by the Bureau, visited a brothel or a gambling den, they were invariably "armed with a complete history of the place and every man therein," Shoenfeld related. Then, too, Mr. Newberger or one of his assistants would also be at the scene of a raid, "ready with legal books and the strength of the Committee [the Kehillah] behind them."21

After a year and a half of energetic crime-fighting, the Bureau claimed proudly that it had successfully closed all stuss houses below 14th Street and that streetwalkers on the Lower East Side were "merely a memory." In the First Inspection District embracing the city's most densely populated Jewish neighborhood over "sixty crap houses, horse racing poolrooms . . . saloons, gambling hangouts and restaurant hangouts" were shut down thanks to Shoenfeld and his sleuths as were over one hundred brothels, sixty-five pool parlors, and sixteen opium dens. Frightened lest the Bureau of Social Morals report their activities to the authorities, the local criminal element either moved away from the neighborhood, from the long arm of the Bureau, or kept a low profile. "Whenever we walked into an underworld dive," Shoenfeld proudly recalled, "they'd say 'Zechs,' which meant 'Stop talking, the Kehillah's here.'" Writing at the height of the Bureau's anti-crime efforts, its supporters boasted that "as a consequence of the Kehillah initiative, the Jewish parts of the Lower East Side of New York were never freer from vice and crime than they are today." The Bureau, Shoenfeld added, "made a lasting impression, a powerful impression. . . ."[22]

By 1915, though, the Bureau seems to have become only minimally effective in reducing crime. In January of that year, Shoenfeld complained to Magnes that although much had been done to eliminate crime in the Jewish areas of the city, there was yet much more to do. "The field," he observer, "still needs harrowing and weeding . . . we want the East Side clean . . . beyond reproach." Poor relations between the Kehillah and Mayor John Purroy Mitchel, who had assumed office in January 1914, frustrated the Bureau's continuing efforts at "harrowing and weeding." Although the Bureau continued its practice of sending monthly vice reports to both the mayor and his police commissioner, Arthur Woods, they "received only perfunctory notice or none at all." Far from welcoming the activities of this volunteer anti-crime unit, as Gaynor and Police Commissioner Waldo had done, the new administration regarded it as an "irritation" and resented the work of these "self-appointed critics." The poor working relationship thus hampered the efficacy of the Bureau's efforts. Compounding this situation was the fact that by World War I, the climate of reform, of which the Kehillah's Bureau was so clearly a part, had waned; consequently, the Kehillah lost much of its financial support from formerly anxious German Jewish leaders like Cyrus Sulzberger and Jacob H. Schiff. Nevertheless, the persistent Shoenfeld continued with his anti-crime work, leaving a unique legacy, until 1917 when the Kehillah as a whole disbanded.[23]

"We expect to stand higher than others, to be a nation of priests, a holy people," wrote *Wahrheit*, articulating what was for many Jews a staple of their Jewish identity. Yet in the aftermath of the Bingham and Rosenthal affairs that notion seemed to be honored exclusively in the breach. Together, the 1908 and 1912 episodes punctured the Jewish community's vaunted self-image. By publicly demonstrating that Jews figured prominently as gamblers, pickpockets, prostitutes, and even murderers and that, moreover, they constituted a sizable portion of Gotham's underworld, the two events shattered the idea that Jews were immune to the corrosive effects of poverty and dislocation; that they were, in a word, a singular, a Chosen People. As a result of these two "particular occasions," New York Jews no longer had the luxury of regarding their criminal element as a "rare deviation from the norm." "A criminal CLASS has developed among the Jews," admitted the *American Hebrew*, "where no such class ever existed before. Of course, sporadic cases of crime always occurred. But they were clearly sporadic. There were no classes of Jewish gunmen, of Jewish pickpockets, Jewish horse-poisoners, Jewish gamblers, Jewish prostitutes or Jewish white slavers. All of these now exist. . . ."[24]

Forced by the cumulative impact of the Bingham and Rosenthal affairs to temper and recast their own self-image, New York Jews, on the eve of World War I, began to move their concern with Jewish criminality from the wings to the center stage of New York Jewish life; by 1912, Jews had come openly to recognize Jewish crime for the serious problem it truly was and to make its elimination a central part of the communal agenda. That is not to say that New York Jews were completely obsessed with the Jewish underworld during the prewar period; that they dared not open the pages of the daily press lest they find themselves discussed on its front page. Nor did New York Jewry at this time do nothing else but combat and discuss Jewish criminality. Nevertheless, the unmistakable evidence of wholesale Jewish criminality forced the community to take stock of itself, to reevaluate its social, cultural, even its religious, institutions. Their self-esteem sorely "wounded," New York Jews surveyed the landscape of Jewish New York in search of answers to the unprecedented burst of Jewish criminal activity in the Empire City; what they found suggested that New York Jewish life was wanting. The inadequacy of Jewish education; the failure of the synagogues to touch the lives of the younger generation of New York Jews; the overly congested living quarters—each factor highlighted the difficulties of adjustment to life in the New World even as it propelled large numbers of Jews into becoming criminals. Reflecting the limits of community in America, the emergence of crime as a distinctly Jewish social problem ultimately called into question nothing less than the community's traditional self-image as a "holy people, a nation of priests," and its future in the New World.

FROM SANCTUARY TO MARKETPLACE

Jews and Prohibition

As the Great War drew to a close, New York Jews began to make great strides both economically and socially and to move out of the Lower East Side of their early years to middle-class neighborhoods. In doing so, they were leaving behind them not only the gray cramped tenements of the city's densest Jewish quarter but its social dislocation, poverty, and criminality as well—or so they hoped. Thanks in large measure to their social advancement and in part, too, to the efforts of the Bureau of Social Morals, Jewish criminality, most Jews believed, was the "outcome of conditions of nearly a generation ago, which are not likely to recur. . . ." In all probability, this hope would have been fully realized had it not been for the passage of the Eighteenth Amendment to the Constitution: Prohibition. This national attempt to legislate morality by outlawing alcoholic beverages, writes Albert Fried, was a "deus ex machina" which drastically disrupted what many observers held to be the gradual disappearance of Jewish criminality in the Empire City. By offering unprecedented economic and social opportunities both to veterans of the underworld and to newcomers as well, Prohibition served as a catalyst for a new chapter in the history of New York Jewish crime, a chapter which radically altered the existing underworld. With the passage of the Eighteenth Amendment and its companion, the Volstead Act, criminals, observed police officer Cornelius Willemse, "went joyfully to work."[1]

At midnight on January 16, 1920, constitutional Prohibition went into effect throughout the United States. In New York City, law enforcement authorities had braced themselves for what they thought would be an evening of "spontaneous orgies of drink." Much to their surprise, all went quietly; the anticipated outbursts of merriment did

85

not materialize. "Instead of passing from us in violent paroxysms," noted the *New York Times*, "the rum demon lay down to a painless, peaceful . . . death." The very smoothness with which the Eighteenth Amendment overnight became the law of the land contrasted with the intense drama preceding its passage: few issues in American history had been so hotly debated. Advocates of Prohibition argued that it would cure a variety of ills commonly associated with modern civilization. Abstinence, believed the members of the Women's Christian Temperance Union and the Anti-Saloon League, would reduce crime, benefit the economy, instill habits of thrift and providence, and Americanize the immigrant. Prohibition's detractors, like New York's Governor Al Smith and Columbia University President Nicholas Murray Butler, argued that far from being a boon, outlawing alcohol would increase the crime rate, irreparably damage the economy, instill habits of extravagance, and impede the integration of the immigrant into American society.[2]

For the most part, Jews did not actively participate in this debate; New York Jews *qua* Jews had little to say on the general social value of Prohibition even though individual Jews advocated both sides of the issue. Stephen S. Wise, a national Jewish leader and prominent Reform rabbi, favored the national experiment, as it was called, arguing that Jews had a civic obligation as Americans to support the Eighteenth Amendment and to comply with the provisions of the Volstead Act. Louis Marshall, on the other hand, did not. "Had it been left to me to decide," the American Jewish Committee president wrote in 1924 to Emanuel Celler, "I would have been strongly opposed . . . police power should not be vested in the Federal government." Yet neither Wise nor Marshall actively promoted their respective beliefs in the public arena; their views remained their own. "Prohibition," noted Louis Wolsey, a leading Reform rabbi, "is an Anglo-Saxon–Protestant issue that we Jews ought to keep out of." As both a reflection of reality and a recommendation, Wolsey's statement went to the heart of the Jewish response to Prohibition: organized Jewry was to be found neither in the vanguard of the movement in support of Prohibition nor in the vanguard of the movement for its repeal.[3]

Not that America's Jews necessarily approved of the national experiment. For one thing, drinking was an accepted and integral part of their religious and cultural life. Jews were accustomed to sanctifying the Sabbath, the Jewish holidays, or any other joyous event with a

glass of wine or a shot of whiskey. "It is almost a desecration of the joy
of the Sabbath, not to have a little brandy before the fish course, once
with the course and once after," reported Charles Bernheimer with
just a pinch of exaggeration. Whether in commemoration of a holiday
or in celebration of a family event, Jews liked to drink a "l'chayim," a
toast. As one observer put it: "The wine and brandy bottle have their
place in every [Jewish] home." For another thing, instances of alcoholism, one of the major reasons for Prohibition's enactment, were rare
among the Jews at the time. "The Devil Rum," the *American Hebrew*
observed, "never did succeed in making any inroads on the life or
morals of the Jew." "The Russian Jew," added Maurice Fishberg,
chief medical examiner of the United Hebrew Charities and an authority
on Jewish diseases, "is not a teetotaler but he has no need for the
solicitous guardianship of a temperance organization." The ritualized
use of wine among the Jews, coupled with their fear of being censured
by the outside world for unruly and excessive behavior, controlled the
amount of liquor they imbibed. "The Jew knows," one contemporary
related, "that it does not pay to be drunk." Jews tended to drink under
very specific and controlled circumstances; random and arbitrary
drinking "for the fun of it" was all but unknown among Jews of the
pre–World War II period. Among them, noted one social worker,
"there must always be some reason . . . for drinking." Furthermore,
whatever drinking was done took place largely within the home; unlike
the Irish or the Germans, whose affection for the saloon was legendary,
the Jews did not frequent bars. "The Russian Jew," wrote Bernheimer,
"does not lean on the bar nor does he sit around in the saloon; drinking
. . . is done in the house." Indeed, pundits suggested that one could tell
a Jewish neighborhood by the paucity of gin mills; whereas Irish and
German neighborhoods were dotted with them, Jewish communities
were characterized more by their cafés. "Where other nations use
alcohol," reported Fishberg categorically, "Jews use tea." Statistics on
alcoholism and related health matters reflected this temperate use of
alcohol. Fishberg found that, among the unclaimed Jewish dead at the
city's morgue, a strikingly low proportion had died from diseases
directly or indirectly caused by alcoholism; in contrast, an estimated
seventy-five percent of the unclaimed non-Jewish dead had died from
alcohol-induced or related diseases. "Alcoholism," the doctor concluded,
"is a negligible quantity in the etiology of poverty and dependency
among Jews." Similarly, data collected by the U.S. Army during

World War I indicated that Jews accounted for a slight 0.5 percent of those soldiers diagnosed at the time as inebriates, whereas the Irish accounted for 10.1 percent of that population. A still later study, conducted between 1929 and 1939, indicated that the tendency for restrained drinking among the Jews continued during the interwar period. Of those admitted to the New York State hospital system for treatment relating to alcoholism during those years, Jews accounted for 0.5 percent; the Irish, in turn, comprised 25.6 percent of those treated for extreme inebriation.[4]

Perhaps because of their long-standing reputation for moderation, Jews made light of the national experiment. Jewish newspapers throughout the 1920s poked fun at the difficulties faced, on the one hand, by a public unwilling to do without liquor and, on the other, by law enforcement authorities forced to compel adherence to an unpopular law. In biting articles entitled, "How Is One to Manage without a Little Drink" or "75,000 Policemen Cry 'Catch a Drunk,'" the *Jewish Daily Forward* satirized the ineffectualness of the police and the overzealousness of Temperance advocates. The *American Hebrew*, despite its usual sobriety, also lampooned Prohibition. "Having banished the beer glass and the whiskey bottle, Puritan Alexanders are now longing for more worlds to conquer. Is the ice cream parlor next?" inquired the weekly. A third, perhaps more Jewish, example of the lighthearted attitude of New York Jewry toward Prohibition was the publication in the midtwenties of a volume entitled "Tractate Prohibition." Using the talmudic text of "Tractate Shehitah" as its source and written in Aramaic, the book poked fun at the vagaries of Prohibition by employing the rhetoric of the Talmud and the perspective of a modern-day, obviously disgruntled, American. Thus, in explaining the phrase "everyone drinks," one commentary noted that the expression refers not only to the general public but more specifically to the fact that even the lawmakers disregard the provisions of the Volstead Act by routinely having a daily drink.[5]

The satire notwithstanding, Jewish community leaders favored obeying the Eighteenth Amendment and the Volstead Act. Some, drawing on the old Jewish adage that "the law of the land is the Jewish law," argued that it was one of the tenets of Jewish life to abide by all the dicta of the host society. Most, however, understood obedience to the Volstead Act as a civic responsibility befalling America's Jews not so much as Jews but as Americans. "The prohibition question is no

Jewish question," explained Rabbi Stephen S. Wise. "It's an American problem. Do not let us think about ourselves but let us think of the welfare of the whole country." Following the rabbi's logic, other Jewish figures urged compliance with the letter and the spirit of the law "even if it hurts." The drinking of sacramental wine—wine used for ritual purposes—however, was an entirely different matter. Unlike abstinence, which affected America's Jews as Americans, the use of sacramental wine affected them directly as Jews; sacramental wine, as one Jewish leader put it, "was a Jewish question."[6]

According to Article 7 of the National Prohibition Act of 1920, every American family was permitted to use up to ten gallons of wine annually for religious purposes; this was known officially as "sacramental wine." Christians would drink the wine while taking the sacrament in church; Jews would use it not only in the synagogue but at home as well, for, in celebrating the Sabbath and Jewish festivals, wine was an essential part of the ritual. The sacramental wine provision had been one of the original features of the National Wartime Prohibition Act of November 21, 1918, the basis for the Eighteenth Amendment. In all likelihood, the privilege had been incorporated into the amendment as a matter of course; granting religious groups the right to use sacramental wine would be guaranteed under the First Amendment to the Constitution. There is nothing in the public record to suggest that its inclusion was the result of lobbying efforts by concerned clergymen, although one suspects that, in determining the annual allotment of sacramental wine, Prohibition officials did confer with priests, ministers, and rabbis. According to the provisions of Article 7, members of the clergy could obtain the wine for their congregants by requesting a specific allotment from the local Prohibition administrator; the more congregants one had, the greater one's need for sacramental wine. The Prohibition official would then forward the clergyman's request to a winemaker, or in some instances to a wine dealer, who would deliver the shipment directly to the rabbi, priest, or minister. The latter would then personally oversee the distribution of the commodity. Sometimes this took place within the precincts of the church or synagogue, at other times, in a legally recognized adjunct known as a "wine store," which served as a depot where church or synagogue members could purchase their bottles of wine without disturbing the quiet of the sanctuary.[7]

Immediately after the machinery for regulating the distribution of sacramental wine was put into effect, several Jewish organizations made known their opposition to the sacramental wine privilege. Early in 1920, Rabbi Leo Franklin, president of the Central Conference of American Rabbis (CCAR), the rabbinical arm of the American Reform movement, informed his colleagues that although legally they were entitled to ask the government for sacramental wine, they should not do so. Since Dr. Kaufmann Kohler, "Nestor of American Judaism" and president of Hebrew Union College, the movement's rabbinical seminary, had sanctioned the use of unfermented wine or grape juice for all religious purposes, Franklin strongly suggested that his fellow rabbis persuade their congregants of the "desirability of using unfermented instead of fermented wine." Like its more liberal counterpart, Conservative Jewry was also troubled by the sacramental wine provision. Early in 1921, several of its leaders had asked a leading rabbinic authority, Dr. Louis Ginzberg, to ascertain whether "fermented wine is indeed essential to the performance of any religious ceremony." After months of research, Ginzberg presented his findings in the form of a rabbinic responsum; they were later published in the *American Jewish Year Book* to ensure the widest possible circulation. The rabbinic scholar concluded that unfermented wine "possess[es] the same status as fermented wine in regard to its use for religious purposes. . . ." With Ginzberg's imprimatur, the Conservative movement vowed to grant "official sanction" to the use of grape juice.[8]

Of all New York Jewry's religious movements, only the Orthodox steadfastly refused to join in the virtual boycott of the sacramental wine privilege. Hoping to convince Orthodox Jewry to change its mind, Louis Marshall wrote to Rabbi Moses Z. Margolies, dean of the Orthodox community, which at the time was represented by two major organizations, the Union of Orthodox Jewish Congregations of America (UOJCA) and the Union of Orthodox Rabbis, or Agudath Harabonim. Founded in 1902, the latter was uncompromisingly anti-modern and spoke for first-generation American Jews, unwilling to accommodate to the American environment, at least religiously. The UOJCA, in contrast, represented a younger, generally native-born constituency, one more inclined to take into account the conditions of modern American life. In his dual capacity as rabbi of Kehilath Jeshurun, one of New York's most influential "modern" Orthodox synagogues, and as a high-ranking official of the Agudath Harabonim, Margolies (also known as the Ramaz) spanned both groups and was thus ideally suited to speak on behalf of Orthodox Jewry *in toto*. Marshall therefore appealed to the Orthodox community leader for his assistance. Worried that use of the privilege would lend itself to multiple violations and thus place the American rabbinate and by extension American Jewry in a "false light," the civic leader gently suggested to the religious leader that he reconsider the use of grape juice in religious ceremonies and possibly write a responsum to that effect. "If unfermented wine is indeed permissible," Marshall wrote, "Jews should act on such a ruling and abstain from placing themselves in the position of asking for *exceptional treatment*." Rabbi Margolies was not swayed by Marshall's arguments and refused to support the anti-wine campaign. Nor was Marshall successful in prevailing upon the Orthodox community in New York (or elsewhere for that matter) to desist from using wine. In a rare show of consensus, both the UOJCA and the Agudath Harabonim, more often than not at loggerheads with one another, joined forces and publicly insisted on the use of wine on all religious occasions. The UOJCA, for example, went on record as "favoring the provisions in the federal law which enable Jews to continue their religious observances," while the Agudath Harabonim contended unequivocally that "wine is required for . . . gracing the Sabbath and holidays." Still other Orthodox Jews went a step further and attacked the Reform movement for its seeming insensitivity to religious tradition. "No consideration was shown the sentiments of the Jews who for two thousand years attached a sanctity to the use of wine in connection with festive celebrations," commented the editors of the *Jewish Forum*, a popular Orthodox publication. "The innocent must suffer for the malpractice of those who act dishonestly in the name of religion."[9]

What lay behind the efforts of Marshall and other concerned Jewish leaders to substitute grape juice for wine and in effect to neutralize the provisions of the sacramental wine clause? Why all the fuss over grape juice? Marshall and his associates, it seems, were motivated by two considerations. First, they strongly feared that the sacramental wine privilege was in essence a special dispensation: the American correlate to the European pre-Emancipation edicts which had segregated the Jews from the rest of the body politic by treating them legally and otherwise as a group apart. To their mind, granting the Jews special treatment would simply not do. The champions of grape juice were also quite concerned lest Jews exploit the sacramental wine privilege by diverting wine from the sanctuary to the marketplace and thus blacken (once again) the Jewish reputation. The sacramental wine privilege, cautioned the American Jewish Committee president, "can create much public discussion and lead to unpleasant insinuations. . . ." To Marshall's way of thinking, the federal government's granting of special privileges to its Jewish citizens was anathema. Jews, he insisted repeatedly, "have no right to ask for any indulgences. . . ." Choosing to ignore the fact that in framing the original legislation the government had had all religious groups, not just Jews, in mind, and dismissing the possibility that not every violator of the sacramental wine privilege was Jewish, Marshall and his colleagues viewed the provision as nothing less than a specially designed attempt to grant the Jews special treatment. America, writes historian Ben Halpern, is "different. . . . What is characteristic of American Jewry and what makes it different . . . is that it began its real history as a post-Emancipation Jewry. Emancipation," he continues, "was never an issue among American Jews: they never argued the problems it presented in America. . . ." Fearful lest America reverse its course and turn back the clock by treating the Jews as a group apart, Marshall campaigned ardently for the use of grape juice. Rejecting the sacramental wine privilege was his way of demonstrating that America was indeed different. Then, too, compounding Marshall's discomfort with the sacramental wine provision was fear that its use would engender ill will between the Jews and other Americans. Because the requirements of Judaism were such that Jewish users consumed wine in far greater quantities than non-Jews, the Jewish civic leader worried lest *others* interpret Article 7 of the National Prohibition Act as a legally mandated effort to distinguish the Jews from the rest of the American citizenry. Attuned to the nuances of American ethnic politics, he wished American Jewry to avoid potential problems with its fellow citizens. The average American, explained the *Tog*, elaborating on Marshall's apprehensions, does not pay much attention either to politics or to the Jews. But tell him that the Jew has more liquor than he does and he automatically becomes a Jew-hater. To avoid such a situation, suggested the paper, Jews should follow Marshall's lead and desist from using wine. It is only in this context that efforts to enforce a community-wide boycott of the sacramental wine privilege can be understood. In order to demonstrate that every American Jew wholeheartedly accepted the quid pro quo inherent in the process of integration, that every Jew wholeheartedly accepted the notion that America was different from Europe, a communal consensus was imperative. "It would be unfortunate to make this a movement of a particular section of the Synagogue," wrote Marshall urging all Jews to refrain from taking advantage of Article 7 of the National Prohibition Act; "We want . . . to present a united front," added grape juice devotee Rabbi Leo Franklin.[10]

Proving American Jewry's willingness to accommodate to the larger American environment was only part of Marshall's agenda; equally important was his determination to prove that Jews stood steadfastly behind the government's attempt at regulating social behavior, that they were, in Marshall's own words, "practically unanimous in frowning down any attempt that may be made to evade the law." Alarmed by the growing association of Jews with bootlegging, Jewish leaders like the AJC president tried to put an end to that association by removing what they believed to be one of its sources: sacramental wine. By having the entire Jewish community collectively foreswear wine, he hoped to prove dramatically that Jewish bootleggers were not in the least representative of the larger Jewish community. In this respect, using grape juice was itself a kind of crime-fighting: to prove its moral probity, American Jewry was to refrain from availing itself of the sacramental wine privilege.[11]

Marshall's fears were not entirely unjustified, as evidence linking Jews to bootlegging mounted rapidly during the 1920s. Contemporaries widely believed that Jews were among the nation's leading purveyors of illicit alcohol; many also believed, almost as a matter of course, that within moments after the Volstead Act took effect, illegal distilleries by the hundreds sprang up in virtually every immigrant neighborhood, including that of the Jews. Writing in the popular *World's Work*, Burton Hendricks asserted that, with their history as tavernkeepers and liquor distillers in Europe, "Jews had more than their fair share of bootleggers," a charge strongly seconded by Imogen Oakley, chairman of the Federation of Women's Clubs and a passionate "dry." "Russian Jews," she insisted, "predominate among the bootlegging population." What is more, a 1926 study of the effects of the national experiment upon the nation's immigrants claimed to have found evidence that on the Lower East Side "there is *undoubtedly* a very heavy traffic in illicit liquor." "Many," the study went on to say, "are enjoying economic satisfaction from the manufacture and sale of 'concoctions.' " Indeed, Jewish bootleggers like Waxy Gordon, Longy Zwillman, and beer

baron Arthur "Dutch Schultz" Flegenheimer regularly made the headlines of the metropolitan papers with their dazzling feats of law evasion.
In New York, according to one recent study of bootlegging, an estimated nine out of seventeen leading rumrunners were Jews. Jews
were also amply represented among the more amateur bootleggers of
the 1920s. Between 1924 and 1932, for example, close to twelve percent
of all persons arraigned on charges of violating the Volstead Act were
Jewish; relative to their proportion of the population, though, Jews
were slightly underrepresented. Some of those caught making and distributing "hooch" were doubtless guilty of violating the law. Others,
however, were probably making wine for home consumption; among
immigrants this was particularly widespread. "Wine is to the Italians,"
explained a sympathetic Italian official, "as coffee is to Americans." To
the foreign born, drinking liquor was not a defiant act but a part of their
normal round of activities. "The foreign born population," this official
added, "do not quite grasp or assimilate the thought that drinking carries
the moral meaning which so many Americans place on it."[12]

To be sure, some Americans may not have grasped the social and
political implications of the new legislation. Others, however, like Waxy
Gordon or Dutch Schultz, grasped its potential immediately. To Waxy
and his fellow second-generation Jews, the manufacture and distribution
of illegal alcohol represented an almost unparalleled opportunity for
making large and continuous sums of money. Like the movie industry,
a business which attracted the talents of a similar group of immigrant
Jewish young men, bootlegging was a "big growth industry." "A
bright young Jew could get in at the start without having to trip
over established gentiles along the way," writes Howe of the movie
industry. And, so it was, too, with bootlegging: for much of its early
history, the illegal manufacture and sale of liquor was unorganized and
uncrowded. The owners of established liquor companies and breweries
of the pre-Prohibition era had all but walked away from their businesses, leaving the field wide open. Similarly, the established underworld figures of the period also chose (at least initially) to ignore
bootlegging as a profitable field of endeavor. "Precisely because legitimate liquor dealers abandoned the business and established underworld
leaders often remained on the sidelines, bootlegging," writes Mark
Haller, "was an area of illegal enterprise that was seized by newcomers."
Graduating from membership in street gangs to distributing and eventually manufacturing their own liquor, "ambitious yet relatively un-

known men" like Gordon, Schultz, and Longy Zwillman (and their Italian counterparts, Lucky Luciano and Bill Moretti) found Prohibition a fulcrum for their ambitions and talents. Bootlegging, explained John Landesco, one of the earliest professional students of the underworld, "was a new criminal occupation with less risk of punishment, with more certainty of gain and with less social stigma than the usual forms of crime like robbery, burglary and larceny."[13]

Far from stigmatizing the bootlegger and rendering him socially unacceptable, this new profession enhanced the credentials of the upwardly mobile second-generation American Jew and opened doors hitherto closed to him. Socializing with the members of café society, many of them customers, frequenting the same speakeasies and attending the same parties, bootleggers blurred the once-tight boundaries between the legitimate and the illegitimate, between the underworld and the "upper-world." Moreover, by investing or laundering illegally obtained profits in such legitimate businesses as the theater and real estate, they blurred the boundaries in a financial sense as well. Their newly acquired economic and social capital enabled them to move "uptown," leaving their traditional base—the immigrant neighborhood—behind. With the exception of Waxy Gordon, who lived among the "alrightniks" of West End Avenue, most neither lived in the Jewish quarter nor derived their incomes from it. So little drinking took place there that Jewish bootleggers found it more profitable to look elsewhere for customers; they were selling wine "largely to the well-to-do Americans outside their neighborhoods," as one student of the national experiment remarked. Indeed, nothing distinguished the Jewish bootlegger from his non-Jewish colleague other than, of course, his Jewish origin. The two shared the same or a similar class of customers, resorted to the same techniques in manufacturing and distributing illegal liquor, and most importantly, employed ethnically heterogeneous gangs. If Prohibition served, as has been claimed, as a swift vehicle of upward mobility for America's criminals, it was also a crucible for eliminating the various social and cultural distinctions which had previously distinguished the various ethnic groups of the underworld from one another; ethnically diverse gangs were on their way to becoming the norm of the underworld.[14]

The career of Waxy Gordon, one of New York's most eminent and successful bootleggers, illustrates these trends. Born on the Lower East Side at the turn of the century, "the son of poor tenement folk,"

Waxy took to the streets while a youngster and became a member of Dopey Benny's band of skillful pickpockets. When Dopey moved into strong-arm work, Waxy went with him, soon becoming one of his chief lieutenants. After Dopey was arrested in 1915, the gang disbanded and Waxy engaged in a variety of criminal activities, among them bookmaking. With the promulgation of the Eighteenth Amendment, Waxy quickly realized the potential of Prohibition and after raising the necessary capital from fellow criminals, among them Arnold Rothstein (see chapter 7), he began to smuggle liquor in from Canada, England, and the West Indies. Posing as a real estate entrepreneur with a suite of offices in a respectable West 42nd Street office building, Waxy hired freighters ostensibly to transport much-needed building materials from abroad to New York. On board, however, were hundreds of boxes of liquor. By 1925, Waxy's "real estate" business was flourishing; he was depositing over $200,000 a month in his bank account. With his newly found wealth, writes one historian, the bootlegger "cultivated a persona . . . a gentleman about town conspicuous by his fancy dress and limousine and companions." Circulating between a lavishly appointed ten-room apartment on Manhattan's Upper West Side and an equally splendid home on the Jersey shore, Gordon "cut his own swath of respectability."[15]

To feed his expensive tastes and at the same time to avoid continued conflicts with the law, Waxy ceased to import liquor from abroad and began instead to invest in and operate breweries. An extremely astute businessman, Waxy allegedly "controlled the brewery syndicate" in New York and New Jersey by the end of the 1920s; together with his associates Max Greenberg and Max Hassell, the bootlegger-turned-beer baron owned over twenty of the metropolitan area's major breweries. Though the Volstead Act prohibited the manufacture of beer containing more than one-half of one percent of alcohol, it permitted the manufacturing of beer with a lower alcoholic content, known as "near beer." But, as one historian explains, "it was impossible . . . to manufacture legal beer of a lower alcoholic content without manufacturing an illegal product first." Thus, genuine beer was produced and then "de-alcoholized until it reached the legal limit." Waxy took advantage of this loophole in the Volstead Act to produce thousands upon thousands of gallons of beer at great profit. Operating breweries in Paterson, Newark, Union City, and Elizabeth and presumably manufacturing only legal beer, Waxy devised a system whereby hundreds of thousands of gallons of real beer were pumped through hoses in underground sewers to bottling plants in "garages" miles away. To avoid any suspicion of wrongdoing, trucks carrying shipments of near beer left the breweries daily. And to avoid hijacking, Waxy hired a gang of "triggermen" to ensure the safety of his trucks as they transported both near and real beer to roadhouses and speakeasies throughout the east coast. Headed by Abner "Longy" Zwillman, a native of Newark's Third Ward, the gang was an ethnically heterogeneous mix of Jews and Italians which, prior to working together with Waxy, had spent most of its time hijacking trucks carrying large shipments of liquor. Placed on Waxy's payroll, given both a percentage of the profits and their own brewery as a "token bonus," Zwillman and his associates ensured the safety of Waxy's operations, growing prosperous in the process.[16]

Though Waxy and his fellow bootleggers had little to do with the manufacture and distribution of sacramental wine, within months of the Volstead Act's passage sacramental wine had become one of the nation's largest sources of illegal liquor and consequently the object of much governmental concern. As early as 1920, the New York State Prohibition administrator, perplexed by what seemed to be excessively large shipments of sacramental wine to New York City, hired a Lower East Side resident and former postal worker named Izzy Einstein to find out why "there was such a remarkable increase in the thirst for religion." Donning various disguises, Einstein and his partner Moe Smith effected the arrest of close to two hundred persons for allegedly bootlegging sacramental wine on the open market. Many of those arrested by Einstein were in fact rabbis who knowingly violated the Volstead Act. In need of money, some rabbis let themselves be talked into "certifying" bogus rabbis, for which service they received a handsome sum; rabbis were also known to have sold their legitimately acquired wine permits to bootleggers. In one famous episode, a clergyman named S. Margolies traded on the similarity between his own name and that of the leading Orthodox rabbi, Moses Z. Margolies, by fabricating a religious organization which he named the Association of Hebrew Orthodox Rabbis of America, a title easily confused with the Union of Orthodox Rabbis (Agudath Harabonim). Margolies' association received wine for some seventy congregations simply on the strength of its letterhead until Einstein unmasked it as a fraud. In other instances, the two rum sleuths found rabbis claiming their synagogues had over a thousand members when in reality they had no more than a hundred; rabbis presiding over congregations whose members bore

names like Sullivan, Moriarty, and Wilson; and rabbis forming synagogues whose sole purpose was the acquisition and distribution of wine;
these were popularly called "wine synagogues." "Gentiles staging
celebrations at their home," reported one contemporary, "pridefully
offered their guests wine from bottles marked with a Hebraic inscrip-
tion." In California, where abuses of the sacramental wine privilege
were also widespread, the growth in the number of synagogues would
have startled even the most ardent believer in the strength of Judaism.
A small Oakland congregation, barely able to assemble the necessary
prayer quorum, suddenly found itself overwhelmed with members;
that many of those seeking admission to the synagogue lived several
hundred miles away and that some were even black seemed to matter
hardly at all. Other synagogues went still further in their religious
zeal and enlisted persons long since dead as new members. Of course,
not all congregations were "wine synagogues," nor were all rabbis
involved in shady bootlegging deals; often innocent rabbis became the
unwitting accomplices to bootlegging schemes. In one well-publicized
instance, a Lower East Side, foreign-born rabbi, unfamiliar with the
"tricks of the trade," authorized two wine dealers to serve as his representatives to buy wine for his small congregation. Without the rabbi's
permission or knowledge, the two sold his written authorization to
a bootlegger for one thousand dollars.[17]

Not all those arrested for distributing sacramental wine illegally
were Jews. Often individuals simply posed as rabbis or sextons, receiving thousands of gallons of wine which they subsequently sold
on the open market. Shirt ironers, delicatessen proprietors, prize-
fighters, and even students masqueraded as rabbis in order to get hold
of large quantities of sacramental wine. Testifying before a congressional committee on the enforcement of the Volstead Act, an astonished
Roy Haynes, the United States Prohibition Commissioner, told an
equally astonished audience that among those bootlegging sacramental
wine were "Irish rabbis." "Yes," he reported, "they have Irish rabbis
and rabbis of every description."[18]

Despite the publicity surrounding the use and abuse of the sacramental wine clause, American Jewish leaders made little headway in
their efforts to convince the entire American Jewish community to
use only grape juice. For all their cajoling, the centrifugal and overwhelmingly voluntaristic nature of Jewish life in America defeated
them. In Europe, Jewish leaders backed in part by the state had the

authority to enforce compliance with a communal decision, no matter how unpopular; payment of the hated *karobka*, the Russian tax on kosher meat, is a case in point. American Jewry's representatives, however, lacked such power; at best, they could only attempt to persuade their fellow Jews and congregants to adopt a communal recommendation. In the absence, then, of any communal consensus, compelling adherence to a policy like the nonuse of wine was virtually impossible. Statistics on the consumption of sacramental wine reflected the powerlessness of American Jewish leaders. Between 1922 and 1925, at the height of the anti-sacramental wine campaign, requests for wine on the part of New York residents actually increased. During those three years, the amount of wine shipped to New York for sacramental use grew from 597,645.90 gallons to 1,776,136.30 gallons, an all-time high.[19]

As the demand for sacramental wine continued to spiral, federal Prohibition officials labeled sacramental wine one of the chief sources of illegal liquor in the nation. Furthermore, calling the record level of usage a "national scandal," they saw the problem as largely a Jewish one. Testifying in 1925 before a congressional committee on the enforcement of Prohibition, Roy Haynes declared that the illegal use of sacramental wine "did not happen in connection with any other religious sect [*sic*] than the Jews." When pressed by the members of the committee to account for this anomalous state of affairs, Prohibition's highest-ranking officer explained that the structure of the Jewish religion was such that inspecting possible abuses in the use of sacramental wine was extremely difficult. "In the case of the Catholic church," Haynes observed, "the priest takes communion but in the case of the Jewish congregations, the individual members take the communion." And that means, he added, "covering miles of territory in checking up each one of those persons. . . . When you get to interfering with the religious rites of a religious congregation, you are getting on delicate ground . . . ."[20]

The obvious difficulty Haynes and his staff had in understanding the structure of Jewish worship and religious behavior in America was of a piece with the federal government's inability to regulate the distribution of sacramental wine on the one hand and to enforce compliance with the Eighteenth Amendment and the Volstead Act on the other. In the hope that reorganization of the Treasury Department would improve its poor record of arrests and convictions for the violation of the Prohibition laws, the Treasury appointed Lincoln C. Andrews in the spring of 1925 as Assistant Secretary of the Treasury in charge of the Coast Guard, Customs, and Prohibition enforcement. A former army man, Andrews approached his new post with zeal. Determined to improve the quality of Prohibition enforcement agents, boost morale, and eliminate, once and for all, the sacramental wine problem, Andrews promptly convened a conference of representatives of the UOJCA, the CCAR, and the RA.[21]

Working together with religious authorities was not new to the department. Since the sacramental wine provision was so tightly bound up with the issue of religious freedom, Prohibition officials from the very outset had been wary lest they step on anyone's religious sensibilities. As early as 1921, members of the New York State Prohibition office had conferred with ten "Jewish rabbis" about releasing a shipment of wine for the upcoming Passover holiday. Similarly, E. C. Yellowley, New York State's Prohibition director, had held several meetings during his tenure in office in the mid-twenties to discuss ways of curtailing the growing number of sacramental wine violations. What distinguished Andrews's meeting from earlier efforts was that it was the first time that the federal government had called for such a conclave, thus attesting to the seriousness of the problem. Moreover, breaking with the precedent of allowing Jews (and other religious groups) complete autonomy in regulating their own communal affairs, Andrews's meeting represented perhaps the first time in American history that the federal government had actively intervened in the internal workings of one of its religious groups. Finally, the absence of any non-Jewish clergy at this gathering underscored the Prohibition office's understanding of the problem as a Jewish one.[22]

After meeting with the representatives of American Jewry's three major denominations, Andrews late in November 1925 devised a plan certain, he felt, to end all future abuses. It had several significant features; the most far-reaching aspect called for Prohibition agents to guard against fake or "wine" rabbis by "hav[ing] the assurance of some known recognized Jewish authority that [the] applicant is a bona fide rabbi." To that end, the CCAR, the RA, and the UOJCA promised to supply a list of names of approved and legitimately "certified" rabbis. American Jewry's religious organizations agreed to this procedure because they realized that the process of ordination in the New World lent itself to abuse; that the sacramental wine problem, at bottom, reflected the drawbacks of the Jewish ordination process. In America, candidates for the rabbinate could either enroll in one of the country's three major rabbinical schools or study privately under the direction of a learned sage. If the latter course was decided upon, the student could qualify for ordination after demonstrating his proficiency in Jewish law to the satisfaction of his *one and only* teacher. With no organized hierarchy of authorities to oversee private ordination, it was entirely possible for unscrupulous persons to pass themselves off as rabbis. To check this abuse, the CCAR, the RA, and the UOJCA each agreed to Andrews's suggestion. In the future, should a rabbi apply for permission to buy sacramental wine, his credentials would be checked by a Prohibition official supplied with an "authorized list" of legitimately certified rabbis. Only if his name was found on the list would he be permitted to buy the ritual wine for his congregants. In addition, only individual rabbis per se could apply for and distribute the sacramental wine allotment; no longer were they legally allowed to delegate the job to an associate—either a fellow clergyman or a lay wine dealer; the use of permits or "zettels" was now outlawed. Finally, Andrews limited the amount of wine to be granted to each family. Earlier, each adult family member had been permitted two gallons of wine annually, not to exceed ten gallons of wine per family; now each adult family member would receive one gallon of wine annually, not to exceed five gallons of wine per family.[23]

Eager to put an end to the "disgraceful transactions" of sacramental wine bootlegging, New York Jews, for the most part, approved of Andrews's new regulations. Some grumbled about the decrease in their allotment of wine, arguing that it would interfere with the proper observance of Jewish ritual. "This law (*gezarah*)," complained the religious *Morgen Journal*, "affects the Jewish home most severely." The majority, though, were willing to try any scheme that would "help religious congregations regain their prestige." "It is not for us to decide whether or not fermented wine is required for all Jewish rituals; that we leave for others more qualified to decide," commented the *Tog* in what was probably the fullest communal response to Andrews's new proposals. "But we are able to offer an informed opinion with respect to the latest Prohibition regulations," the paper continued, "for those affect all Jews equally—secular Jews, religious Jews, *kiddush*-Jews and non-observant Jews. Uniting all Jews, regardless of religious affiliation, is the fear of desecrating God's name (*chillul hashem*) and if nothing else, the sacramental wine privilege has thus far provided altogether too many opportunities for the desecration of God's name." Accordingly, concluded the daily, "we welcome any attempt to avoid future cases of this sort."[24]

Ultimately, whatever hopes New York Jewry and Assistant Secretary Andrews had for eliminating sacramental wine abuses soon evaporated in the face of mounting evidence that the 1925 plans were not effective. Within the first few months of 1926, more than one-half of the yearly allotment of sacramental wine had already been withdrawn. After releasing this statistic to the press, Chester Mills, then New York State Prohibition director, contended that the current shipments of wine to New York alone were "without doubt far in excess of the actual religious needs of the Jewish race." Angered by the apparent failure of his new and much-touted regulations to curb the flow of wine withdrawals, and without explaining what had gone awry, Andrews issued a series of new and "drastic" orders in August 1926. First, all existing permits were to be voided. At the end of the month, each rabbi who needed wine had to appear in person before a local Prohibition administrator and "present his needs." Second, Andrews ordered the closing of all "wine stores"; from this point on, the distribution of sacramental wine was to take place only within the synagogue (or church). Finally, the Assistant Secretary indicated he would step up raids against those rabbis who persisted in trading in sacramental wine.[25]

This time, New York Jews did not accept the new rulings with equanimity. Tired of being made the scapegoats for the failure of the Volstead Act and angered by Andrews's seeming hostility, they spoke out against the latest batch of regulations. In a campaign spearheaded by the eight-hundred-member Association of Orthodox Rabbis and the Union of Orthodox Rabbis, an extremely orthodox group, the community forcefully decried the new regulations as unduly harsh and punitive. Coming on the eve of the holiest days on the Jewish calendar, argued New York Jewish attorney Samuel Joseph on behalf of the Association of Orthodox Rabbis and the Union of Orthodox Rabbis, the timing of the new guidelines was inexpedient. Busy with preparations for the Jewish New Year, the rabbis were simply unable to apply in person for their wine. And even if they had ample time to do so, he continued, many would refuse to visit the local Prohibition administrator: insecure in their knowledge of English and anxious lest they receive the "third degree," many would prefer to obtain their wine from bootleggers than deal directly with potentially unfeeling and hostile government officials.[26]

Whether or not Joseph's predictions were actually fulfilled cannot, of course, be ascertained. What is known, however, is that withdrawals of sacramental wine decreased sharply within a few months of Andrews's 1926 edict. This drop was due not only to the closing of several hundred "wine stores," and to the increased vigor with which Prohibition officials clamped down on potential offenders, but more importantly still, to a federal grand jury investigation into illegal sacramental wine usage. Early in the summer of 1926, even before Andrews had issued his latest orders, Emory Buckner, United States Attorney for the Southern District, had begun quietly to investigate bootlegging in sacramental wine. Two months later, reported the press, the U.S. Attorney's office indicted four rabbis for illegally obtaining and trafficking in sacramental wine—but not before having looked into the affairs of over six hundred metropolitan rabbis.[27]

Coming on the heels of Andrews's stringent regulations, these indictments further shocked and dismayed an already troubled Jewish community. Some Jewish newspapers manifested their dismay by printing angry headlines such as "Grand Jury Picks On Rabbis"; others displayed cartoons showing a man with a bottle of sacramental wine in his hand being taken away by Prohibition agents; the captions read "Never Mind, *Boreh P'ree Hagafen*" (the Hebrew prayer for wine). Yet beneath the defiant tone of these cartoons and editorials was a genuine concern that the rabbinate was being dishonored and ridiculed by its continued association with the sacramental wine privilege. "We expect our rabbis," noted the *Tog*, "to be both a source of pride and honor for us as well as models of behavior. Suspected of wrongdoing, they now stand as a reproach to the entire profession and as a *Chillul Hashem* to the community at large." Even the subsequent acquittal of the four rabbinical defendants failed to still the community's disquiet over the sacramental wine problem. Though, happily, "all the commotion [*tumelt*] resulted in nothing," the *Tog* observed, the Jewish community's reputation had been sullied.[28]

Indeed, the paper's assessment of the situation proved to be correct. Shortly after Buckner's indictment of the four Jewish clergymen was announced, Andrews appeared before the House Appropriations Committee to press his agency's case for additional funding. Using the sacramental wine problem to illustrate the difficulties his agents had in enforcing the law, the Prohibition official testified that "the distribution of sacramental wine has resulted in diversion to beverage use of wine in the big cities. That is almost exclusively on account of the Govern-

ment's efforts to satisfy the Jewish faith. . . . The Jewish faith is not
organized as *our* hierarchical churches are. There is no discipline and
no control. Anybody can become a rabbi. . . ." Nevertheless, Andrews
was optimistic that his administration would succeed where others had
failed in eliminating the diversion of sacramental wine into illegal channels; he concluded his testimony by saying that he anticipated no future
abuses.[29]

What the Assistant Secretary did not anticipate, though, was the
volley of criticism leveled against him in the wake of his congressional
appearance by Harlem Congressman Fiorello La Guardia. An outspoken
foe of Prohibition as well as the representative of a large Jewish district,
La Guardia was eager to lock horns with Andrews. In a letter to the
Prohibition official, which later appeared in the press, La Guardia took
issue with his assertion that Jews were largely responsible for the illegal
use of sacramental wine and subtly implied that Andrews and many of
his fellow Prohibition officials were anti-Semitic. "You surely must have
been misinformed," he wrote Andrews on December 8, 1926, "for there
has been no greater percentage of diversion of sacramental wine allowed to the Jewish faith than any other faith." The feisty congressman went on to say that the problem lay not with the Jews but with
the corruption rampant among members of the Prohibition staff: "May
I be permitted to state that you had better reorganize your own Department before you try to reorganize the ancient Jewish religion."[30]

Andrews hurriedly had his subordinate, Chester Mills (the New York
State Prohibition director), refute La Guardia's charges. "In curtailing
the withdrawals," stated Mills emphatically, "we have been extremely
careful not to start a religious persecution." But La Guardia was not
convinced. For several months thereafter, he continued to take Andrews
to task for "harassing and annoying rabbis" and "formulating impossible
and ridiculous rules." Andrews, in turn, countered that he had tried
his utmost to resolve what was inherently a difficult and sticky problem.
"There is perhaps no other phase of my duty of administering the
Volstead Act," he wrote the congressman in May 1927, "which has
given me as serious concern as this." In pointing to the lack of hierarchy
in Judaism, Andrews explained, he was not "criticizing the Jewish
Faith but simply stating the fundamental fact which had made regulation so difficult." La Guardia appears to have accepted Andrews's ex-
planation, for the exchange went no further. Nor, for that matter, had
it resolved anything. Both the Reform and Conservative movements

steadfastly continued to insist on noncompliance with the sacramental wine privilege while the Orthodox community, equally firmly, insisted on compliance. The Prohibition office, for its part, continued until the cessation of Prohibition to issue new regulations in attempts to tighten the number of sacramental wine shipments. In 1927, for example, it required all rabbis requesting wine to submit an alphabetized list (in English, stressed the Prohibition office) of the names and addresses of those who would consume the wine. This time, it seems to have met with more success: between 1926 and 1932, shipments of sacramental wine to New York dropped from 1,765,566.95 gallons to 394,648.24 gallons.[31]

Although the La Guardia-Andrews exchange may not have settled the differences between the federal government and American Jewry, it summarized, in its own way, the central issues of the problem: difficulties in regulating withdrawals of sacramental wine were embarrassing to both sides. Failure to solve the problem reflected poorly on the administration; time and again, a Prohibition official would publicly announce that illegal use of sacramental wine was being checked, only to find it as slippery and resistant to control as before. This proved disquieting to the Jews as well, blackening their reputations and subjecting the internal workings of the community to public scrutiny. Thus, the lack of internal consensus was now made a matter of public record; as Louis Marshall observed, the sacramental wine problem created "an unpleasant spectacle for the general public. . . ." Tension and ill will were inevitable. After all, neither the federal government nor the American Jewish community had much previous experience working with one another—especially when it came to resolving internal religious matters. Thanks to the enactment of the Eighteenth Amendment, both sides were thrown together, forced quickly to get acquainted and to resolve, under tense and difficult circumstances, relatively tough issues. Compelled to work together at a time when their respective reputations were on the line, it was no wonder that misunderstandings and friction arose. Ultimately, though, the two parties ironed out their differences and went on to become adept at the politics of accommodation. Seen from this perspective, the national experiment was an experiment in more ways than one.[32]

UNSAVORY CONNECTIONS

Jews and Racketeering

Racketeering, "the art of levying and collecting tribute by violence and intimidation," was to the 1930s what Prohibition was to the 1920s. Like the national experiment, it was the subject of hundreds of magazine articles and countless government inquiries. It was also very much a by-product of that era: as Prohibition drew to a close, many bootleggers, alarmed by the imminent drying up of their income, moved from rumrunning to extortion. It was, reported one law official, "a simple step." With the skills and contacts acquired over a decade of illegal activity, many second-generation Jews (and Italians) intimidated business and labor into "working together" with them. The disorganized structure of the small marketplace, characteristic of so much of the ethnic economy, facilitated their entry. Jews took advantage of the decentralized conditions in the kosher poultry and garment industries while the Italians followed suit by exploiting their countrymen in the fish, fruit, and vegetable markets. With competition keen and labor problems a fixture, the small merchant was an easy mark for the racketeer who promised increased profits and a minimum of labor disturbances in return for a slice of the proceeds. Labor racketeering was also quite prevalent. From popular accounts of the Mafia, like Donald Cresey's *Theft of a Nation*, one sees the racketeer invading a union, taking it over against its will, dislodging and even killing its leaders. That is only part of the story; the reality of labor racketeering was (and continues to be) far more complex. In some instances, the presumably noncriminal leadership of a union sought the services of gangsters for defensive purposes: as protection against the anti-union practices of employers. In other instances, union leadership used gangsters to help organize workers and even to terrorize union members suspected of disloyalty. Finally, there were instances in which union leaders resorted to the use of gangsters to further their own careers or to line their pockets: sweetheart agreements and kickbacks are two examples of this brand of trade union corruption.[1]

Periodically during the interwar years the federal, state, and municipal governments announced a "war on racketeers," but such efforts rarely succeeded. After several years of halfhearted and ineffectual antiracketeering activity, New York Governor Herbert Lehman served notice on the underworld by creating in 1935 the office of Special Prosecutor. He hired Thomas E. Dewey, a thirty-three-year-old former Chief Assistant United States Attorney, to lead the crusade against racketeering and vice in New York County.[2]

To the casual observer, the flurry of interest in racketeering which culminated in Dewey's appointment suggested that the phenomenon was a recent one. Actually, racketeering—especially labor racketeering—had a long history, stretching back to the early years of the century. "Racketeering is a new word," observed Frederick Kernochan, Chief Justice of the Court of Special Sessions, before a Senate committee investigating rackets, "but what they do is old." The forerunners of the 1930s racketeers were the Paul Kelly, Eastern, Hudson Duster, and Dopey Benny gangs that dotted the Lower East Side and the Hell's Kitchen area of the West Side during the early 1900s. Known as *shtarkes*, guerillas (or gorillas), or strongarm men, they were closely aligned with local politicians and worked on primary and election days to ensure their election. These gangs also preyed on local merchants, compelling them, often at gunpoint, to pay protection money; occasionally, too, the city's early gang members served either as strikebreakers for management or as strike enforcers for the nascent labor unions.[3]

Unlike most of his contemporaries, however, Dopey Benny broke new ground by taking up labor racketeering as his primary calling card and relegating electioneering and the protection racket to a sideline. In fact, Dopey was the first Jewish underworld figure to make labor racketeering a full-time and highly profitable business for himself and his fellow gang members. He placed the "gangster business," reported the *Times*, "on an economical basis." Born on the Lower East Side in 1889 as Benjamin Fein, the son of poor immigrant parents, Dopey took to the streets at an early age, stealing packages from delivery trucks, rolling drunks, and picking pockets, a skill in which he excelled. Despite an adenoidal condition which made the gangster look sleepy—and which earned him his nickname as well—Dopey was so adroit at "grifting" that he opened a school to train other would-be pickpockets. By 1910, he left pickpocketing for labor racketeering, cleverly taking advantage of the then-unsettled conditions of the Jewish marketplace. In the aftermath of the great cloakmakers' strike of 1910, one of the most brutal and debilitating labor struggles of its time, Jewish civic and labor leaders drew up the Protocols of Peace, a document which established the fifty-hour work week and the preferential open shop and abolished inside subcontracting. If winning the Protocols was in many respects a decided victory for labor, the rights of Jewish workers were still not nearly as recognized nor as respected as Jewish labor leaders might have wished. In their continuing efforts to broaden the base of the unionized needle trades, implement the provisions of the Protocols, and win support for the labor movement in general, overzealous union leaders at times relied on force. "Violence," writes Louis Adamic, "was often all that could save unions in the face of the brutality of many employers, with their gunmen, police, militia and anti-labor unions." Accordingly, in the aftermath of the 1910 strike, Dopey Benny became an integral aspect of the Jewish labor movement: for four years he and his henchmen were placed on the payroll of the United Hebrew Trades (UHT), the linchpin of the Jewish labor movement.[4]

Initially, at the turn of the century if not earlier, unions relied on their own membership, particularly those well endowed with brawn, to do the "dirty work" of physical intimidation. Eventually, though, professional gangsters replaced the volunteers, for their methods were both less dangerous and far more effective than those employed by "husky and devoted union men." Monk Eastman was one of the very first Jewish underworld personalities to have used his fists on behalf of the nascent Jewish labor movement of the 1880s and 1890s. Adding to the considerable revenue he generated from his protection rackets, Monk also "furnished for hire small gangs of 'strong-arm' men to employers for assaulting strikers, to unions for assaulting 'scabs'. . . ." Dopey Benny, however, institutionalized the practice. During his four-year association with the Jewish labor movement, the butchers', bakers', garment workers', hat frame and neckwear makers', ragpickers', sign-painters', and umbrella makers' locals reportedly turned to the racketeer for assistance. Indeed, Abe Shoenfeld claimed that Dopey was present any time the UHT or one of its affiliates conducted a strike. "Since the Dope has become so popular," the detective reported, "every strike that took place on the eastside, under the auspices of the UHT—the Dope was contracted to do the guerilla work." Placed on the payroll either on an annual basis or for the limited duration of a strike, Dopey and his men were given union cards as pickets and union delegates. "Every time we went out on a strike," Dopey explained, the union "would give us a pink sheet of paper, four by six inches, stating General Strike Committee and signed by the ILGWU, 32 Union Square . . . . The meaning of the paper was we were general picket men and we were allowed to walk the street. . . ." Using bats, clubs, and blackjacks—but, boasted the gang leader, rarely guns—Dopey's gang protected striking workers from physical attack by management's hired help by masquerading, thanks to their pink sheets, as fellow pickets. At other times, their job was "to chase everyone out of the shop and beat up some of the people . . . break up partitions, machines and everything." And at still other moments, Dopey hired a band of female thugs who, wielding sharp hairpins and umbrellas weighted with lead slugs, attacked nonunion female workers, persuading them to join the union. Dopey's gang also helped to ensure control of one or another local by its leaders in the face of dissent from the rank and file. In 1913, for example, a painters' strike had been settled after weeks of tortuous negotiations. Though the leadership of the union appeared satisfied with the terms of the proposed contract, the general membership was not. Gathered at a Second Avenue theater to ratify the document, several union members were prevented from airing their dissatisfaction by the presence of Dopey and his gang. "The minute a painter attempted to object," one eyewitness related, "he was immediately threatened and pounced upon by a guerilla and told that if he did not keep still, he would get himself in trouble." The contract was ratified forthwith.[5]

For such services, Dopey charged between $25 and $50 a week and an additional $10 a day (of which he pocketed $2) for each of his men. He also had a schedule of prices for different tasks: shooting a scab or "guard" in the leg cost the union approximately $60; breaking an arm $200; the wrecking of a nonunion shop anywhere between $150 and $500 depending on its size; murder commanded a steep $500 per victim. "Dopey Benny's practices," commented the *Times*, "were medieval but he conducted them under modern conditions." Reportedly

an "expert organizer," Dopey Benny also insisted on a contract with
the unions according to which the latter, in addition to paying the
racketeer a regular salary, agreed to pay him $5 a day should he land
in jail, and also to arrange for legal counsel. In April 1914, for instance,
all UHT affiliates were ordered to buy tickets to a show at Kessler's
Second Avenue theater. The proceeds were used to enable Dopey, then
broke and convicted of assaulting a police officer, to appeal his sentence.
In an extra show of largesse, the union sent Dopey's father a weekly
check for $25 while his son was temporarily indisposed. "During the
time you were in State's Prison," the District Attorney once asked
Dopey Benny, "did you or anyone for you receive any money from
the Waist and Dressmakers Union, Local 25?"

> Yes sir; they got my payroll.
> That is, your regular weekly wage?
> Yes, and I guess they got some money besides toward collection
> for my defense fund.
> They contributed to your defense at the time you were on that
> charge.
> Yes sir. . . .[6]

Like union leaders, manufacturers or "bosses" also made frequent use
of gangsters; an estimated thirteen firms specialized in providing
shtarkes or strongarm men to management. One firm, located at 125
Broadway, numbered 125 persons in its employ, many of them retired
policemen and assorted hoodlums. Posing as detective agencies or
guard services and often licensed as well, these firms rented out their
services on a *per diem* basis. As "guards, detectives or doormen," the
shtarkes terrorized strikers into returning to work and protected nonunion or "scab" labor from the ire of striking workers. Located at 35
Spring Street, the Browne & Myers Detective Agency routinely canvassed the offices of clothing manufacturers boasting of its ability to
"supply strike breakers, guards, protectors and fellows 'who can do
everything necessary.'" Manufacturers also sought to enlist Dopey
Benny and his agile band, offering him large sums of money to work
on their behalf. Yet, despite these attractive financial offers, Dopey
steadfastly refused to work for management. "My heart," the racketeer
explained, "lay with the workers." In the latter part of 1912, a successful
white goods manufacturer offered Dopey $15,000 "just to move over

on his side" but Dopey firmly refused. "He put fifteen $1,000 bills in front of me . . . and I said to him, 'No sir, I won't take it,' I said, I am on the level now; I won't double cross my friends." Closely monitoring Dopey's activities, Assistant District Attorney Lucien Breckenridge commented that "the man really had a conviction that he was helping along in his own way a cause in which he believed. He would talk with glowing eyes of the way he turned down offers to guard the shops of employers . . . he had standards of a sort."[7]

Dopey Benny not only had "standards," he was also an astute businessman who sought to control competition from rival gangs by forming alliances with them. In the wake of the 1912 Rosenthal affair, the police became increasingly more vigilant in following the activities of the underworld. Keeping a close watch on the city's casinos and brothels, the men in blue made it both unprofitable and dangerous for the city's criminals to continue their traditional endeavors. By the same token, the prospect of working in tandem with the politicians, histori-cally a highly rewarding and stable source of income for the under-world, was foreclosed as well. Their reputations damaged as a result of the Rosenthal imbroglio, politicians stayed clear of the underworld and "dared not employ" its members. Deprived of a livelihood, the city's gangs searched for new alternatives. Dopey found his, coinci-dentally enough, in the labor field and for several years enjoyed a virtual monopoly of labor racketeering. But soon other gangsters like Joe "the Greaser" Rosenzweig, a twenty-six-year-old, dark, and well-spoken criminal who "doesn't look as his name implies" and the Sirocco gang, a band of gun-toting Italians, followed Dopey's lead as their sources of income diminished considerably. Foreshadowing the strategy later made famous by Chicago gangster Johnny Torrio in the 1920s, Dopey divided the city into districts patterned after police precincts. He then parceled out strikes on the basis of geography. If a labor union called a strike on the Upper West Side, the "turf" of the Hudson Dusters, they and only they had exclusive "rights" to it; if a strike was called on the Lower East Side, Dopey's gang laid claim to it. By transcending the limits of his neighborhood through these alliances, Dopey not only rationalized the business of labor racketeering, in the sociological sense of the word, but broadened his base as well. Although firmly rooted in the Jewish ethnic economy, Dopey enlisted the coop-eration and friendship of gangs throughout the entire city. By doing

so, he adumbrated the behavior of the post–World War I Jewish criminal who was to break with existing norms of Jewish criminality in a
search for new and illicit forms of income.[8]

In the fall of 1914, the police caught Dopey Benny threatening to
kill B. Zalmanowitz, the disgruntled business agent of a butchers' union.
A year earlier Zalmanowitz had contracted with the Dope to protect
striking butchers. Apparently the job had not been performed to the
agent's satisfaction and he refused to pay Dopey's $600 fee. Dopey
repeatedly threatened Zalmanowitz; frightened, the business agent
called in the police and they watched in the wings one September day
as the gang leader repeated his threats, then promptly arrested him on
first-degree extortion charges. The gangster expected that once bail
was set he would be released immediately as he had been in previous
years. But none of his associates came forward with the bail money.
Liable at the time for approximately $8,000 in bail money stemming
from previous arrests, Dopey may well have become too much of a
fiscal liability to the union. Languishing in jail, angered by what he
perceived to be the "double-cross" by his friends and employers, Dopey
agreed to tell District Attorney Charles Perkins what he knew of the
underworld's ties with labor. In return, the "Lower East Side's greatest
gang captain" was released from jail and his case "deferred indefi-
nitely."[9]

Dopey, reported the *New York World*, "spun an amazing tale."
Several hundred pages long, his testimony was a veritable history
of gang life in New York. Naming names, among them Sam Liebowitz,
president of the United Hebrew Trades, and several ILGWU higher-
ups, Dopey indicated that these men were "the people that got me all
that work; hav[ing] something to do for me." Having been provided
with the material he needed to launch an all-out "crusade" against
Gotham's underworld, the District Attorney established what he called
a "shtarke's bureau" to monitor their activities. Following a month-
long investigation, Perkins empaneled a grand jury to hear and reflect
on his findings. After listening to his presentation for over three months,
the grand jury in May 1915 charged twenty-three labor leaders and
eleven gangsters with murder and the lesser charges of extortion, assault, and riot. The bill of indictment contended that the defendants
had conspired to murder one Herman Liebowitz, a cloakmaker and
member of the Cloak and Suitmakers' Union, who had taken a job at
a nonunion shop in upstate New York at the time of the 1910 cloak-

makers' strike. Upon returning to union headquarters, charged the
D.A., the cloakmaker was severely reprimanded by union officials and
ordered not to return to his "scab" job, after which, on orders of the
union leaders, the offending worker was beaten to death. The defendants, the state explained, "pushed out" Liebowitz, "struck him in
the head" and then "threw him in the street whereupon all stepped on
him with their feet." Believed responsible for the brutal murder were
Solomon Metz, UHT president; Morris Sigman, secretary-treasurer
of the ILGWU, and five other prominent members of the Cloak and
Suitmakers' Union. Upstanding members of the Lower East Side community and dedicated unionists, they were unlikely murderers.[10]

Immediately upon learning of the grand jury's charges, representatives of the Jewish labor movement vociferously and passionately denounced them. Calling the indictment a blood libel and a bald attack
on labor, the *Jewish Daily Forward* accused the District Attorney of
using the indictment as a pretext for "breaking the back" of the Jewish
labor movement. "This is a scandalous conspiracy," the Socialist daily
cried. "It is one of the most brazen (*chutzpadik*) attacks capital has
ever dared to make. . . ." Also much unnerved by the grand jury's action, the UHT quickly convened a conference at which it issued a
series of carefully worded resolutions protesting the indictment. First,
it unequivocally endorsed the innocence of the seven major Jewish
unionists. Second, it argued that since the indictment was built on the
testimony of two "jewels"—the "zaddik" [saint] Dopey Benny and the
well-known 'fixer' and ne'er-do-well Max Sulkes—the D.A. had no case.
Then, in an abrupt switch, the UHT took the offensive, blaming the
manufacturers for the presence of gangsters in the needle trades. "All
delegates know full well," read one of the UHT resolutions, "that the
bosses have taken strong measures in their efforts to eliminate the
workers. It is a well known fact that strong arm men are used at every
strike to beat up the workers." Through these resolutions, the UHT
hoped to move its constituents into unequivocally supporting the defendants—and they succeeded in doing so. All those at the meeting
eagerly embraced the notion that the Jewish labor leaders were the
victims of a conspiracy. Shouting their support for the seven cloakmakers, the unionists vowed to wage a vigorous and unrelenting fight
to free the "sacrifices upon the altar of anti-labor sentiment." To that
end, they also established a defense fund "to fight our cause clean and
to vindicate our comrades." Thus, the ILGWU levied a tariff of one

dollar on each garment trades worker, even distributing ardently worded circulars to its supporters nationwide calling upon them to come to the "defense of our Brothers." In the excitement of the moment, no one stopped to realize that neither the ILGWU nor the UHT had denied the validity of the charges leveled against Metz and Sigman; instead they had excused them.[11]

The outrage of the UHT and the *Jewish Daily Forward* was not simply precipitated by the announcement of the charges; it had been slowly building for months as the labor movement in general was at a "critical juncture" in its history. Finding the provisions of the Protocol to be "irksome," many manufacturers had not only begun openly to flout them but, by May, had also abrogated them. Whatever substantive gains the movement had won since 1910 were gradually being eroded. "The clothing trade," reported Shoenfeld at the time, "seems to be at a standstill." Writing to AFL president Samuel Gompers, Benjamin Schlesinger, the ILGWU's beleagured president, observed, "Since the arrests of some of our officers, I felt as though the manufacturers are ready to take advantage of the 'gangsterism in the unions' cry put up by the New York District Attorney, to crush our Organization." Coming at a particularly demoralizing moment in labor union history, the indictment of the seven prominent labor leaders added insult to injury; union supporters could not help but feel that public opinion had turned against them. "The Bosses," wrote the *Forward* angrily, "are as tied to the gangsters as Cossacks were to the Czarist government," and it expressed outrage at the lack of indignation over that connection. Even temperate Morris Hillquit, Socialist leader of the Lower East Side, saw the forthcoming trial as an effort to discredit the Jewish labor movement; it was for that reason that he undertook the defense of the seven accused cloakmakers. Years later he was to write that the "existence of the union depended" on the trial. "No case I've ever handled caused me greater anxiety and concern."[12]

Not all New York Jews were as exercised and disturbed by the indictment as the Jewish labor community. In fact, the nonlabor elements of the Lower East Side reacted rather calmly at first to news of the murder charge. Perhaps unsure as to the innocence of the dedendants and holding no brief for labor, they neither rushed to the defense of the seven cloakmakers nor proclaimed the forthcoming trial a conspiracy to destroy the Jewish labor movement. Instead, each of the non-labor Yiddish newspapers urged restraint and a cool, measured examination of the available facts. "This is surely no time for hysterics," cautioned *Wahrheit* (at the time no longer a Socialist paper), while the *Morgen Journal* (still a religious daily) recommended that the guilt or innocence of the defendants be resolved solely in a court of law and not through heated and public denunciations of the District Attorney or the American criminal justice system. The uptown community, for its part, stayed clear of the entire episode.[13]

Before long, however, the non-labor elements of New York Jewry abandoned their dispassionate and "above-the-fray" attitude. By September 1915, as the defendants came to trial, it had become as indignant and concerned over the trial as labor had been several months earlier. "Not only workers but all Jews, even business people," the *Morgen Journal* commented, "are touched by the case." "It will be a black day for all Jews," said *Wahrheit*, "if the defendants should be found guilty." With mounting alarm, each Jewish newspaper urged its readers to support the accused union officials and to donate funds toward their defense. "The fate of the seven cloakmakers," exclaimed one non-labor paper, "will be on our conscience if they are judged wrongly because of a weak defense." What accounts for the shift in attitude is not clear. Perhaps the non-labor community had received new information on the particulars of the case which led it to affirm the defendants' innocence. Even more likely, the general Jewish population came (belatedly) to understand that in the event of a conviction, the reputation of all Jews was likely to be tarnished. With the case coming on the heels of the 1912 Rosenthal affair, New York Jews could not afford to be dragged into the limelight and their good names muddied once again.[14]

The trial of the seven union officials in the criminal branch of the New York State Supreme Court began on September 24 and lasted for two tense weeks. Daily hundreds of angry unionists jammed the courtroom, sometimes overflowing into the streets, while the Jewish press followed the proceedings avidly, devoting page after page of coverage to the trial and, occasionally, a special edition as well. Covering the trial for his paper, Abraham Cahan, the editor of the *Jewish Daily Forward*, described it as a "battlefield on which the entire working class and the entire capitalist class of America will collide." Though meant rhetorically, his description captured the tensions of the pro-labor audience as it watched its leaders on trial for murder. Led by Assistant District Attorney Lucien Breckenridge, the prosecution claimed, as it had earlier in May 1915, that the defendants had conspired to kill Herman Liebowitz for his failure to strike at the time of the 1910 cloakmakers' strike, planning to use his death as a warning against future incidences of "scabbing." To prove its case, the state brought forth as its key witness Isaac Levine, an often unemployed cloakmaker with a faulty command of English, who claimed to have heard the defendants order the death of the offending worker and then to have actually witnessed it, and Max Sulkes, the founder of a rival cloakmakers' union called the ILGWU of the World, who corroborated Levine's account. Branding the state's case as "outrageously tainted," Hillquit and his fellow defense lawyers sought to show that both Sulkes and Levine had much to gain by seeing Metz and Sigman behind bars. Sulkes was a "fixer and a steerer," related Hillquit, and "one of the most notorious crooks on the East Side . . . never been known for years to have earned an honest dollar." Organizing a private detective agency "making strike breaking a special business and operating under the guise of the labor union in order to . . . befool the public . . . and to induce cloakmakers to go to him for scabs," Sulkes had formed the ILGWU of the World. A man of whom the impartial Shoenfeld wrote that "he has been raising a lot of dust around here . . . shaking down the shops, the bosses and so on," Sulkes apparently decided to "dig up that case of 1910, of Liebowitz" to destroy the legitimate union. The defense charged that Sulkes, together with Levine, who coincidentally was president of Sulkes's ILGWU of the World, deliberately sought to make political capital out of what had been a tragic and unintended consequence of the 1910 strike: Liebowitz's untimely death. Reconstructing the events of that fateful day, Hillquit described how some "ill advised strikers . . . in no way acting in a responsible position, acting in defiance of the union and its officers and these defendants, . . . might have dealt the unfortunate blow. I say they might," he added. "We don't know." What was known, he concluded, was that there was never any "conspiracy to assault . . . to do anything in the slightest degree with the murder."[15]

On October 8, the jury found the seven defendants not guilty. The entire courtroom broke into applause and a "frenzy of joy, emotion, tears and hysterical laughter burst forth"; the court, wrote one eyewitness, resembled a "kissing-bee." Well-wishers waiting outside also burst into tears and applause upon hearing the verdict and "threw their caps in the air, clapped their hands and shouted hurrah." After triumphantly leaving the Supreme Court building, the seven defendants and their families were taken to the *Forward* building on East Broadway where yet another crowd of supporters had gathered to express its congratulations and delight. "Today is a *yomtov*, a holiday," exclaimed the pleased *Jewish Daily Forward* following the acquittal. "It is a day of festivity, a day of victory for workers everywhere." Equally relieved, the non-labor community joined in the celebration. "The acquittal is happy news for all American Jews," proclaimed the *Morgen Journal*, "for once again the Jewish name has been cleared."[16]

And yet, despite the Jewish community's relief at the outcome of the trial, the acquittal of the seven cloakmakers was only a limited victory. In its eagerness to clear its name of wrongdoing, New York Jewry had concentrated most, if not all, of its efforts on proving the innocence of the labor leaders and correspondingly, in publicizing the anti-labor sentiments of the prosecutors. By so doing, the community had overlooked what was central to the trial: the underworld's involvement with the Jewish garment industry. From May through October 1915, the Jewish newspapers as a group devoted hundreds of pages of text to the trial; yet they barely touched on the fact that, willy nilly, Dopey Benny and his ilk had become an integral aspect of the Jewish economy, influencing conditions in the marketplace and threatening the integrity of the labor movement. What is more, neither before nor during the trial did any of the Jewish papers express surprise at—or even take exception to—Dopey's disclosures; to many Jews, they were obviously not the revelations they were touted to be. To be sure, Dopey was not the first Jewish criminal to have made money from the Lower East Side's economy; long before him, Jewish underworld personalities had derived much of their illicit income from the area's sweatshops and retail stores. What distinguished Dopey from his predecessors was the *degree* of his association with the ethnic economy. By providing what Jewish labor leaders believed to be an indispensable and necessary service, Dopey and his fellow racketeers moved from the periphery of the Jewish economy to its very center. New York Jews, though, were slow to realize just how deeply entrenched Jewish racketeering had become.

Between 1915 and 1930, racketeers went from being employees of the garment manufacturers and needle trade unions to being their employers, from "mere hirelings" to "robber barons"; during the 1920s,

the Jewish labor racketeers came into their own. Like Dopey Benny
and the other pre–World War I racketeers, this generation also exploited the unsettled political and economic conditions of New York's
largely Jewish "rag trade" and gradually seized control of the entire
industry. In the early 1920s, the ILGWU was split by two rival
factions, the Communist or left wing and the established, more centrist
leadership. In 1925, Max Sigman, now the union's president, responded
to the threat of a takeover by suspending all Communist-dominated
locals and by physically removing Local 22, the leading Communist
local, from its headquarters. Angrily, Sigman charged Locals 2, 9, and
22 and their officials with "permitt[ing] the affairs of their locals, their
policies and acts to be directed and managed for them by outside Communist groups, wholly alien to our organization. . . ." With the aid of
"Moscow money," the union president charged, these locals sought
to "publicly slander and defame" the ILGWU and its officers and,
worse still, to take over the union. In retaliation, the ousted Communist
locals set up the Joint Action Committee—in effect a rival union—to
coordinate all left-wing activity in the ILGWU. Within a year, the
Joint Action Committee had succeeded in winning the support of most
ILGWU workers, many of whom were dissatisfied with the existing
leadership of the union and who therefore sought to dramatize their
collective discontent by aligning themselves with the "opposition." By
1925, the "vast majority of the workers were with the left wing and not
the ILGWU" related Benjamin Stolberg.[17]

In the summer of 1926, events within the factionalized ILGWU came
to a head. The by now Communist-dominated New York cloakmakers'
locals rejected a labor program jointly sponsored by Governor Al
Smith and the ILGWU leadership and called a general strike. It lasted
for an unprecedented twenty-six weeks, affected close to fifty thousand
workers, and threatened the existence of the union. In the course of
the strike, both labor and management made heavy use of gangsters to
strengthen their respective positions: the Communist-led ILGWU reportedly hired Jacob "Little Augie" Orgen, a well-known Jewish
gangster and the current "king of the East Side gunmen" to protect its
workers; the manufacturers allegedly turned to Jack "Legs" Diamond,
a former bootlegger turned slugger, to protect its shops and nonunion
work force. Management, reported Max Sigman, in an open letter to
the ILGWU rank and file in September 1926, has "not hesitated to
hire notorious gangsters with well known criminal records to beat up

and shoot up the strikers on the picket line"; the ILGWU, for its part, also shared in the blame, having "fostered gangsterism . . . " within the union. Furthermore, both sides apparently turned to Arnold Rothstein, the financier of the underworld, for his support. In a recent interview, Charles "Sasha" Zimmerman, one of the leaders of the Communist takeover of the ILGWU, told of how he first came to know Rothstein. Zimmerman had complained in 1925 or thereabouts to a fellow union official that the Legs Diamond gang was beating up his pickets. The friend arranged for Zimmerman to meet with Arnold Rothstein who, by most accounts, controlled the activities of the Legs Diamond gang, among others. "To me," Zimmerman recollected, "Rothstein didn't mean a darn thing. I didn't know of such an underworld character." Telling Rothstein of his current labor difficulties, Zimmerman was surprised to hear the financier of the underworld tell him not to worry. "And like magic," the ILGWU official continues, "they [the strike-breakers] were taken away. The firm came down to settle. . . . Natu-rally," he adds, "I was friendly with him [Rothstein]." Though a fuller rendering of Rothstein's dealings with the Jewish labor movement will be drawn in Chapter 7, Zimmerman's account of his involvement with Rothstein in this particular context suggests the extent to which labor (and, of course, management) drew on Rothstein. As Zimmerman himself put it, "Everything was all right. He was doing me favors."[18]

After inflicting a heavy toll on the industry, the strike ended in De-cember 1926—but not before it had drained the finances of the "rag trade" and sapped its moral strength as well. Workers estimated their losses at over thirty million dollars; manufacturers placed theirs at "scores" of millions; the union, one observer related, "was a wreck." Ap-pealing to the industry's desperate need for stability, racketeers cleverly took advantage of its weakened state and entrenched themselves still fur-ther. Called in as an "ally," reported the *Times*, the racketeers became the industry's "master." With promises of both financial assistance and the elimination of industrial strife, racketeers were able to move into the ladies' garment trades with ease; once "invited," they refused to leave. Racketeering, commented newspaperman Mike Berger, is akin to the fable of the camel: "He first put his foot into the Arab's tent and gradually worked in all his bulk."[19]

The men's clothing industry was equally affected by the "cancer" of racketeering. Determined to resist the unionization of their businesses by the increasingly successful Amalgamated Clothing Workers Union, the umbrella organization of men's clothing workers, many men's clothing manufacturers turned to gangsters for harassment of Amalgamated labor organizers in order to prevent the establishment of union shops. In other instances, manufacturers who in principle had agreed to the formation of a union shop violated the terms of the labor agreement with the active connivance of racketeers. Union delegates visiting presumably union shops to discuss compliance with union regulations were often assaulted. To "fight fire with fire" and to compel manufacturers to abide by union procedure, labor officials also resorted to gangsters to assault noncompliant manufacturers. Because of the growing need for their services on the part of both management and labor, racketeers here too became progressively more powerful. In fact, within a very short time they were in a position to install their own representatives in key union positions. Thus, Phil Orlovsky, manager of Local 4, the cutters' union of the Amalgamated and a vitally important part of the men's clothing business, was reputedly the henchman of racketeer *par excellence* Louis "Lepke" Buchalter. "The strategic New York cutters' local," observed J. B. S. Hardman, a close student of Jewish labor activities, "fell under underworld dominance in the early 1920s. . . . the entire membership . . . suffered from the abuses the racketeers inflicted on the trades via the cutters' corrupt leaders. The masses of them were badly scared."[20]

After tolerating and in some instances actually welcoming the participation of racketeers in the garment trades, businessmen and labor officials finally took steps to dispossess them in the summer of 1930. In July of that year, David Dubinsky, secretary-treasurer of the ILGWU, Isidore Nagler, manager of the New York Cloak Joint Board, and several other union officials visited New York County District Attorney Thomas Crain, taking with them a list of names of over twenty manufacturers who had allegedly paid $100,000 in tribute to garment center racketeers within the last year or two, and asked his assistance in stamping out racketeering. Crain promised he would look into the matter. Calling racketeering a "grave menace," he invited fifty prominent civic leaders, among them John D. Rockefeller, Charles Schwab, ILG president Benjamin Schlesinger, and Rabbis Nathan Kraus and David de Sola Pool to help him find a "cure" for racketeering. Despite Crain's good intentions, little was done; the civic leaders failed to come up with any concrete suggestions on how to fight organized racketeering.[21]

Undaunted, labor leaders persisted in their campaign to "shake off the unsavory connections" between racketeering and the garment industry. Less than a year after Dubinsky's visit to Crain, in June 1931, Sidney Hillman, president of the Amalgamated, startled a gathering of his top labor officials by squarely addressing the issue: "We might as well be frank here, and say out in the open what we have been saying to each other in private. What the New York market is suffering from more than anything else is the racketeering evil." To dramatize the importance of eliminating racketeering once and for all, Hillman ordered his men to strike a firm reputedly associated with racketeers. After a brief encounter between the Amalgamated's strikers and the firm's *shtarkes* that resulted in many bloody noses and fractured limbs for both sides, Hillman publicly called on New York Mayor Jimmy Walker and Edward Mulrooney, the city's police commissioner, to destroy the "organized blackmail system" in the garment trades. Explaining that the racketeers operated undeterred in the "rag trade" by creating a climate of fear and physically terrorizing both workers and manufacturers, the labor leader vowed that he and his associates were "definitely determined, come what may, that we are not going to recognize [the racketeers] as the government in this city." Hillman then appealed to the mayor to let the racketeers "know who is the government of New York City," and secured promises from Walker and his administration that the city would use "every ounce of . . . power" to that end. The labor leader then staged a massive protest against the "curse of underworldism" as, for two months in July and August 1931, 30,000 men's clothing workers stayed off the job.[22]

What prompted Hillman to take up the cudgels in defense of his union against racketeering when he did can only be guessed at. Some observers suggest that the labor leader was slow to realize the profound and morally enervating influence of the racketeers not only over several of the Amalgamated's locals but over the garment industry as a whole, but that when he did, he took immediate and dramatic steps to combat it. Others, less charitably perhaps, suggest that Hillman, by all accounts a master politician, believed the strength of his office was great enough to control the racketeers—and to use them as he saw fit. When, by the end of the 1920s, Hillman saw his power eroding and that of the racketeers increasing, he sought to eliminate this challenge to his authority. Whatever his motives, the Amalgamated's president fought vigorously against racketeering.

As the strike continued and violence between the union's pickets, the manufacturers' nonunion workers, and the racketeers' *shtarkes* grew in intensity, Hillman engineered his boldest move: he ousted Phil Orlovsky, Cutter Local 4's manager and boss, from his position. This was tantamount to throwing down the gauntlet to the garment center's racketeers, for Orlovsky was rumored not only to be an associate of theirs but also, and more importantly, their liaison with the Amalgamated. In August, Hillman filed charges against Orlovsky before the union's Executive Board accusing the cutters' manager of "racketeering, misappropriation of funds and scabbing." After refusing to come before the board to answer these charges, Orlovsky was dismissed, in absentia, from his position. To concretize the Amalgamated's dismissal of Orlovsky, Hillman and his followers seized control of the headquarters of Local 4 and "effected a coup d'état": all of Orlovsky's associates were forcibly removed from the local. Thanks to his energetic and large-scale attack on Orlovsky and racketeering in general, Hillman succeeded, it seems, in eradicating (if only temporarily) the "organized blackmail" system of racketeering from the garment industry.[23]

The architect of labor racketeering in the garment industry and elsewhere and the object of both Dubinsky's and Hillman's antiracketeering efforts was Louis "Lepke" Buchalter. In 1935, at the zenith of his career, he allegedly controlled the baking, flour-trucking, dressmaking, fur, and garment industries and employed an army of 250 men, supervised by his longtime friend Jake "Gurrah" Shapiro, to ensure that control. Born on the Lower East Side in 1897, one of eleven children, Lepke had been a quiet and rather ordinary child who, according to one contemporary who knew him well, "should have turned out better." With the death in 1910 of his father, an unsuccessful hardware store owner, Lepke left school and worked at a variety of odd jobs. It was at this time that he became friendly with Gurrah; together the two robbed pushcarts and extorted minor sums of money from Lower East Side merchants. In 1915, at the age of eighteen, Lepke was arrested for the first time on burglary charges. Though ultimately cleared, he subsequently embarked on a rather active criminal career: between 1916 and 1922, he was arrested at least three more times, generally for burglary. When released from Sing Sing in 1922, he teamed up with his old friend Gurrah and another aspiring gangster, Hymie "Curly" Holtz. Like many other criminals of the period, they became sluggers (*shtarkes*), sometimes working for Little Augie Orgen, at other times independently.[24]

On the evening of October 16, 1927, Little Augie was killed on a Lower East Side street corner. Police investigating the murder discovered that, shortly before his death, the gunman had quarreled with Gurrah over the "rights" to a labor strike then in progress in Brooklyn. The police brought Gurrah and his partner, "Louis Buckhouse" (another of Lepke's aliases), in for questioning but ultimately dropped the charges for want of evidence. Following Augie's death, Lepke merged what remained of the deceased gangster's followers with his own growing gang and consolidated his hold over industrial disputes. For the next eight years Lepke and Gurrah, as one police officer noted, "worked efficiently and unobtrusively," extending joint control over many New York industries including trucking, the bakery business, and the fur trade; it was in the garment industry, however, that the duo—known either as "L and G" or, more to the point, as the "boys"—made their mark.[25]

Like Dopey Benny and other pre–World War I racketeers, L and G operated almost exclusively within the Jewish economy. Themselves products of the immigrant experience, they were familiar with the cultural idiom of the largely Jewish "rag trade" and used that familiarity to their own, criminal, advantage. Insiders in an insiders' business, L and G knew the industry's soft spots—labor's continuous battles against nonunion or runaway shops; the manufacturers' overriding need to keep costs down—and effectively exploited them. Furthermore, by relying on the insularity of the garment trade, on its homogeneity and its mistrust of strangers, the two racketeers ensured their hegemony. Frightened of exposure yet in need of the racketeers' assistance, labor and management agreed to the demands of Lepke and Gurrah. Then, too, the growing division between the marketplace and the home enhanced the racketeers' effective domination of the industry. In the wake of the Great War, more and more city dwellers began to live in one area and to work in another; earlier, the home and the work place were often the same, or, as one contemporary put it, "the homes of the Hebrew quarters are its workshop also. . . ." Yet by the 1920s, increased social mobility on the one hand and the rapid technical development of the marketplace on the other redefined the once traditional arrangement. Formerly located on the Lower East Side, the garment center gradually moved uptown, first to the area north of 14th Street and later to its present location in the West Thirties. Led by the "Save New York Committee" of 1919, the needle trades were "removed" from their lower Manhattan headquarters to the "Seventh Avenue district." The move, one proponent predicted, "will guarantee that New York will remain for all time the manufacturing center of the needle trades for the United States." This change not only augured well for the financial success of the clothing manufacturers but also affected the Jewish criminal enterprise: the exactions of the racketeers now took place in the market and not on the "Jewish street" of the prewar period. The Jewish community could no longer rely on informal neighborhood channels, as it had earlier, to curb crime; the underworld had removed itself from the center of the average person's daily life. In the long run, the breakdown between the work place and the home would have serious repercussions for New York Jewry's efforts at combating Jewish criminality. In the meantime, Lepke and his comrades effectively took advantage both of this development—of their decreased visibility, in other words—and of the insularity of the garment industry to blackmail labor and management into cooperating fully with them.[26]

The key to Lepke's mastery of the garment industry was his stranglehold on trucking: the transportation of goods held together the various aspects of the business, from the contracting, cutting, and finishing of the garments to their distribution. It also linked the nonunion shops to the garment center. By seizing control of the trucking business, either through operating his own trucks outright or by placing lieutenants in key positions within the truckers' unions, Lepke had management and labor at his mercy. To avoid a potential paralysis by a truckers' strike, one which would force workers out of work and bankrupt the manufacturers, both sides paid handsomely, sometimes in cash (estimates of the amount earned by L and G ran as high as one million dollars annually—a staggering figure during the Depression), sometimes in what Victor Herwitz, one of Dewey's assistants, called "perks." ILGWU and Amalgamated officials and garment manufacturers, he related, "knew not to interfere" with any Lepke-operated or protected trucks, lest they be saddled with a strike or have their goods damaged.[27]

Lepke broadened his hold over the industry still further by buying

into several ostensibly legitimate manufacturing concerns, either pur-
chasing the firm directly or having "legitimate" businessmen front
for him. In 1934, for example, S. W., a partner in the Perfection Coat
Front Company, manufacturers of coat fronts, a vital ingredient of
suits, approached I. R., a men's clothing manufacturer, and suggested
they go into business together. "I am in partnership with L and G"
said S. W., promising the reluctant manufacturer there would be no
future labor problems to worry about. "The union is in their hands . . .
the union takes orders from them." I. R., in turn, was sufficiently per-
suaded of the merits of his associate's proposal to become his partner.
Their relationship continued for several years until I. R., for no recorded reason, became frightened and spoke to Dewey about his
venture with L and G. Lepke's business arrangements were not always
so amicable, though. In the fall of 1933 I. F., the owner of a cloth
sponging business, which applied chemicals to fabrics to prevent them
from shrinking, was approached by J. M., a fellow businessman, and
asked "to pay some money . . . to the boys." I. F. refused but subsequently received so many threats from L and G's gang of hoodlums that
he paid them one hundred dollars a month for over four years.[28]

In other instances, clothing manufacturers who ran into difficulties
with the garment unions contacted various Lepke intermediaries either
to avert or to settle a labor problem. In the late 1920s, for example,
M. B., a clothing manufacturer, used nonregistered contractors—that is,
contractors not approved by the Amalgamated—to make men's suits.
Upon discovering this irregularity, the Amalgamated's Joint Board informed M. B. that unless he contracted with registered cutters, the
union would pull its men from his factory. The manufacturer refused,
and his cutters immediately went out on strike. Consequently, M. B.
went to see L and G's representative with the Amalgamated to discuss
his predicament. After M. B. had paid L and G a "fee" of between
two and three thousand dollars, the cutters returned to work and, as
M. B. himself later put it, he "heard no more from the Joint Board"
about using nonregistered contractors. Women's garment manufacturers
also had their L and G representative bargaining on their behalf before
the ILGWU. Benjamin Levine, a middle-aged, Russian-born clothing
manufacturer, was reportedly Lepke's "contact man" with the women's
clothing union. Prior to becoming a manufacturer of women's coats,
shortly after World War I, Levine had met and become friendly with
Pasquale Muccigraso, director of the ILGWU's organization commit-

tee, the person in charge of recruiting new members to the union. Lepke and Gurrah, who at the time had a major interest in a contracting firm that did business with Levine, knew that "in order to gain control of the industry it would be necessary to make contact with some union official." "They likewise knew," reported Frank Hogan, one of Dewey's right-hand men, "that Levine was a close friend of Muccigraso." L and G contacted Levine who, in turn, introduced them to Muccigraso. Years later, Hogan explained to Dewey,

> word got around the garment trade that Benjamin Levine could settle matters with Lepke and Gurrah and the union and thus avoid the stench bombs and threats of personal violence which were prevalent at the time. As a result many manufacturers in the garment industry contracted Benny Levine to intercede in their behalf. Benny Levine acted as intermediary and go between on many such transactions.

Thus, in one recorded instance, a dress manufacturer was fined several thousand dollars in back wages for his failure to comply with ILGWU regulations. He promptly turned to Levine for help in getting the penalty rescinded. Levine, reported the dress manufacturer, "clear[ed] it with the union" and the fine was substantially reduced. Levine was well compensated.[29]

Virtually the same situation obtained in the men's clothing industry. In fact, despite the observation made by Matthew Josephson, Hillman's authorized and admiring biographer, that following Orlovsky's dismissal the "Lepke gang, weary and discouraged, began to look for other fields to plow," L and G continued to maintain ties with the Amalgamated. Danny Fields, a former amateur boxer who became one of Gurrah's sluggers, told Dewey that shortly after the 1932 "coup d'état" two Amalgamated officials, Sam Katz, a business agent, and Bruno Belea, a union organizer, had asked him to be their "go-between for the union with Lepke." Eager for the money, Fields accepted the offer and for fifty dollars a week served as the Amalgamated's liaison with L and G. In one case, he arranged a meeting with Katz and Lepke in the basement of the Kolmer Marcus manufacturing plant. At this meeting Katz reportedly said to Lepke that "the union wanted [him] to work for them as he had worked for Orlovsky . . . whatever could be done for the union they [L and G] should do." Lepke agreed. Between 1932 and 1936, Danny Fields personally delivered $280 a week in cash from the Amalgamated to the racketeer.[30]

Through these various arrangements, some *sub rosa*, others more aboveboard, L and G. maintained what Herwitz called "relative peace" in the garment industry. Manufacturers were able to proceed with the production and distribution of garments, while unions were able to provide their members with employment. Seeing to it that the garment industry operated smoothly gave L and G great satisfaction, one which they translated into dollars and power. Not for them the altruism of Dopey Benny. For L and G, profit and power were the sole objectives And yet, the "relative peace" cultivated so assiduously by L and G was not without its price. For one thing, law enforcement authorities estimated that manufacturers and labor leaders paid several millions of dollars in tribute to Lepke during the early and mid-1930s. For another, the clothing trade was so frightened of L and G that many manufacturers and union workers preferred to go to jail rather than testify against the two gangsters and risk losing their lives.[31]

This was not an exaggerated fear. In September 1936 Jacob Rosen, a former garment trucker, was killed by Gurrah's thugs for talking to Dewey about the racketeers. Rosen had operated a trucking business known as the New York and New Jersey Trucking Company, which transported unfinished garments from the manufacturers to contractors in New York and New Jersey. The Amalgamated apparently told Lepke in 1932 that it wanted a "stoppage" of clothing trucks to protest nonunion contracting in New Jersey and elsewhere. Lepke obliged, ordering all truckers belonging to Local 240, the Clothing Drivers and Helpers Union of the Amalgamated, not to deliver to nonunion firms in New Jersey. Rosen, however, refused to go along. He then indicated an interest in expanding his business into Pennsylvania. Warned by Lepke that he was "entitled to so much and no more," Rosen again ignored the racketeer. This time he found that many of the goods he transported were being systematically damaged and, worse still, that manufacturers and contractors were refusing to give him any business, presumably acting on Lepke's orders. "They made some excuse," related one of Rosen's children, "not to give them [Rosen's business] the trucking which they had had for years." The pressures grew so great that Rosen quit the business. In an effort to buy his silence, Lepke "threw him a bone—two or three days work a week"— but that was not enough for Rosen and his family to live on. The trucker therefore opened a candy store on Brooklyn's Sutter Avenue. Shortly thereafter, at the urging of his family, Rosen wrote to Dewey, exposing the "dirty methods" used by L and G and Max Rubin, the business agent of Local 240 and Lepke's representative in the trucking union. Somehow Lepke found out about Rosen's letter and sent Rubin to bribe him; Rubin also suggested that it would be wise for Rosen to leave town. When Rosen refused to accept either the advice or the money, he was murdered.[32]

By 1935, Lepke's empire was beginning to give way under the pressure of mounting indictments against him. In October of that year, as one of his first acts as Special Prosecutor, Dewey announced that his office was seeking an indictment against the "leaders of the most dangerous outfit in New York City—Lepke and Gurrah" and welcomed the testimony of anyone who had been a victim of their exactions. A year later, in November 1936, the federal government tried and convicted the two of violating the Sherman antitrust laws in the rabbit dressing industry. The two gangsters, the government claimed, had forced all furriers to join the Protective Fur Dressers Corporation. In return for fees of as much as twenty thousand dollars annually, L and G promised to protect the interests of all fur dressers against undue competition. The government further charged that the L and G-sponsored trade organization did little else than harass those furriers who refused to join. L and G immediately appealed their conviction. Pending appeal, Judge Manton of the U.S. Circuit Court released the two on $10,000 bail. Since Dewey was then building an arsenal of facts against them and the prospect of yet another trial was very real, the two went into hiding in the spring of 1937.[33]

Though the gangsters remained fugitives, more indictments were issued against them. In August 1937, Dewey indicted L and G for conspiring to extort money from clothing manufacturers. When their demands were not met, they reportedly bombed the establishments of the recalcitrant owners or workers. A month later, in October, L and G were again the subject of great public interest as Dewey began prosecuting Harold and Max Silverman, Lepke's "tools," for extorting money from the bakery and flour industries. Nevertheless, the two remained in hiding, the object of an intense manhunt. New York State and the federal government vied with one another in their efforts to capture the racketeers, regularly issuing bulletins on their whereabouts and promising a large cash reward to anyone who found the two. After nearly a year of eluding authorities, who had been seeking him almost everywhere (including Palestine and Poland), Gurrah surrendered, and was tried and convicted of extortion in the bakery industry.[34]

The other half of "the most distinctive combination in the annals of modern crime" surrendered to the FBI on August 24, 1939. Earlier that month, the famous broadcaster Walter Winchell had received a tip that Lepke would surrender provided the federal government would not turn him over to New York State authorities. FBI director J. Edgar Hoover agreed, and Lepke surrendered to Winchell. Since the federal authorities had a prior claim to Lepke stemming from his earlier conviction in the fur racketeering case, he was placed in their custody and subsequently retried for and convicted of racketeering in the fur industry. The "terrorist of the garment manufacturing trade" was then sentenced to fourteen years in Leavenworth prison.[35]

A disappointed Dewey was not prepared to let Lepke off so easily; he applied to the U.S. Attorney General for permission to try the racketeer on extortion charges stemming from his involvement in the flour and bakery trucking business. Though several of Dewey's assistants preferred to try Lepke for his "piracy" in the garment center, Dewey felt his chances of "getting" Lepke were better if the racketeer were tried on the smaller, yet more solid, case of bakery extortion. Thus, after securing the Attorney General's permission, Dewey placed Lepke on trial in January 1940 for nineteen counts of extortion. Witnesses testified that bakers and flour truckers, many of them Jews, had paid Lepke and his associates sums totaling over $50,000 in 1935 alone for the purpose of settling potential labor problems with Locals 40 and 138 of the Teamsters Union. Through the "wrongful use of fear" Lepke and his lieutenant, Max Silverman, convinced Dugan Bakers to pay them $10,000 to avoid a clearly manufactured and artificial work stoppage; in another episode, the Flour Truckmen's Association, flour wholesalers, paid Silverman $15,000 to "protect" them from being physically harmed by a band of sluggers. After deliberating for more than thirteen hours, the jury found Lepke guilty as charged. Since he was by now a fourth-time offender, the racketeer was sentenced to life imprisonment. Yet, by a curious twist of events, neither the federal government nor Dewey could lay claim to ending Lepke's career. As we shall see in the next chapter, that distinction would go to Brooklyn District Attorney William O'Dwyer.[36]

"For the unesthetic pursuit it is," observed a student of the kosher poultry industry, "the simple buying and selling of poultry has a dramatic history." The kosher or live poultry business lent itself to the incursions of racketeers and, like the garment industry, had a stormy and long association with them. For one thing, the business was extremely profitable; experts estimated that between 1925 and 1935, annual sales exceeded fifty million dollars. For another thing, the industry was composed of distinct but interrelated operations and was therefore easily penetrated by gangsters; there were about fifteen discrete steps in the preparation of poultry before it reached the consumer. Chicken farmers shipped live poultry to New York where chicken pullers—"rough birds themselves"—unloaded the merchandise. Then workmen known as receivers weighed and fed the chickens and, based on weight, determined their market price. Truckers, in turn, transported the live chickens from the freight yards to slaughterhouses where *shochtim* or "kosher killers" slaughtered the birds in accordance with Jewish dietary laws. Finally, retailers purchased the freshly killed poultry directly from the slaughterhouse owners and sold it to the consumer. Since each phase of the business was built upon the next, he who seized control of one area could easily dominate the entire industry.[37]

As early as 1902, receivers had formed an association to control the wholesale price of poultry. By 1910, the price-fixing practices of this association were so pronounced that a New York City grand jury indicted eighty-seven members of the New York Live Poultry Commission Merchants Protective Association and ultimately, in 1911, convicted thirteen of them for restraint of trade. In November 1914, Bernard Baff, an independent poultry dealer, was killed in the Washington Street poultry market by unknown assailants who immediately escaped in a waiting getaway car. The press made much of the similarities between this murder and that of Herman Rosenthal two years earlier. One similarity was that Baff was gunned down in full view of many witnesses, all of whom later claimed not to have seen the shooting, another was that the murderers made use of an automobile in committing the crime. More important, Baff's murder "focused the microscope on the whole poultry trade" and revealed the extent to which businessmen like the New York Live Poultry Merchants Protective Association and gangsters conspired to control it.[38]

The murder victim, a German-Jewish immigrant who had entered the receiver business in 1908, was "cordially hated by everyone in the market," reported journalist Elias B. Goodman to Mayor John Purroy Mitchel in a twenty-page, specially commissioned memorandum on the murder. Upon entering the field, Baff had refused to become a member of the receivers' association. When that group then tried to prevent Baff from working, he sued. As a result, the District Attorney had ordered an investigation into the kosher poultry industry; it was this investigation that led to the 1911 conviction of thirteen leading poultry merchants. But that was not the only reason for Baff's unpopularity among his peers. By the time of his death, according to Goodman's account, he had singlehandedly threatened the economic well-being of most of his competitors. Baff had poultry farmers ship their product directly to him; he obtained his own fleet of trucks and his own slaughterhouses and was therefore able to eliminate the need for middlemen. He had also recognized and cooperated with a fledgling poultry workers' union before anyone else did and by so doing protected himself from potential work stoppages and other labor disturbances. Finally, because he had had access to such a large volume of poultry, Baff had frequently sold it directly to consumers, thereby undercutting the Association.[39]

After several years of probing into the circumstances of Baff's death, investigators found that a group of retail poultry men, angered by what they perceived to be Baff's unfair competition, had hired gunmen to do away with him. They also discovered that businessmen and leaders of the embryonic labor movement in the kosher poultry market increasingly turned to gangsters for assistance in eliminating competition or in helping to win support for kosher poultry labor unions. Jewish hoodlums, of the order of Dopey Benny, were only too willing to take advantage of the turmoil in the poultry market and soon dominated it. In September 1913, a new union composed of *shochtim* and low-level poultry workers was formed. Its organizers, among them a ne'er-do-well by the name of Jake Williams, hired the Sirocco gang to convince reluctant *shochtim* to join. The Italian gang also disrupted the business of poultry dealers opposed to unionization. In response, the wholesalers hired a rival group of thugs to break up the union. Observing the goings-on at the Washington Market, Goodman wrote, "It is a sad plight that the *Shochtim* attempting to uphold the Mosaic laws should be associated with . . . dangerous characters (white and colored) to do strong-arm work and calling them 'brethren.'" And: "It is a sad commentary that Jewish businessmen claiming to believe in the Mosaic Law and observe Kashrash [sic] should countenance the hiring of any gangs to break up an organization which ought to be brought into existence for the protection of the workingmen."[40]

By the 1920s, most New York poultry receivers and slaughterhouse owners were members of a "voluntary" trade association known as the New York Live Poultry Chamber of Commerce. It was voluntary, however, only in the sense that anyone in the kosher chicken business who wanted to earn a living had to belong to it. Headed by receivers Benjamin Simon and David Hirshorn, the association set prices and determined from whom a retailer could purchase his poultry. In return for these services, the Chamber levied a tax ranging from one to seven cents on each wholesale pound of poultry sold. Half of the money went to the Chamber; the other half to the "boys," a freely used euphemism for the gangsters hired by the Chamber to ensure compliance with its demands. Those who challenged the hegemony of the retail association would have "*tsuris*," reported one Yiddish newspaper. They would find *shochtim* walking off the job on the eve of a Jewish holiday when the demand for poultry was at its highest; retailers refusing to buy poultry from them; their offices wrecked; and sometimes their homes— and even persons—damaged.[41]

The real power in the kosher poultry business was not the Chamber but Arthur "Tootsie" Herbert, business agent of Local 167 of the International Brotherhood of Chauffeurs, Teamsters, Stablemen and Helpers of America. Born on the Lower East Side in 1899, the son of an immigrant kosher butcher, Herbert began his union career in 1914 by joining the Wagon-Driver and Porters Union and then by becoming a member of Local 167 several years later. By the mid-1920s, Herbert had succeeded in becoming the local's business agent, a position which he maintained through a combination of personal charm and force. A natty dresser with "hair combed in the style of a movie star," Tootsie, reported a poultry dealer, "has an engaging personality and is a likeable fellow despite his ruthlessness." Tootsie strengthened his hold over the poultry market by installing his brother Charles, a young man with a long string of arrests and convictions, as director of the Shochtim Union, Local 440. He also handpicked Joey Wiener, a Bronx-born smalltime racketeer with an equally long arrest record, as business agent of the local.[42]

Local 440, however, was a union in name only. "It has no meetings," explained the *Jewish Daily Forward*. "It never holds elections and it has no Executive Board or any other features which define a true union." The Shochtim Union, recalled an attorney familiar with the poultry market, "is not a labor organization . . . it is a private enterprise owned by a group of people who call themselves a union but are not more than merchants and contractors." "There is no connection whatsoever," said the *Jewish Forum*, a religious monthly, "between the Shochtim Union . . . and any of the organizations of rabbis to whom Kashruth is a vital religious issue." Contributing still further to the anomalousness of the Shochtim Union was its leadership. "One would expect," the *Jewish Daily Forward* wrote, "that the head of the union would himself be a *shohet* or at least a religious Jew . . . with a beard and side-locks [*payos*] able to *pasken* [render a judicial decision on Jewish ritual matters] on issues relating to kashrus. But Mr. Herbert hardly fits that description: he is far more interested in baseball than in ritual slaughtering." In fact, the reputation of the Shochtim Union was so bad, thanks to its connection with Charles Herbert, that in 1927 the UHT expelled it from membership. "So long as that man [Charles Herbert] was the representative of the union," recalled Morris Finestone, at the time UHT secretary-treasurer, "we warned the union that we would not take any responsibility upon ourselves. But the union insisted on having Herbert as its representative and we severed our connections. . . ."[43]

Largely Eastern European Jews, the members of the Shochtim Union insisted on retaining Herbert as their representative for several reasons. Some were intimidated into doing so; they felt they would lose their jobs or be physically harmed if they otherwise protested. Indeed, *shochtim* who refused to join the union were beaten up by Tootsie or his henchmen, while those who agreed "voluntarily" to become members of Local 440 "fear their bosses," as one poultryman put it. Some of the ritual slaughterers, though, were grateful to the Herberts for having raised their standard of living and were consequently willing to ignore the poultry czars' rapaciousness. Collectively, the two Herberts had succeeded in raising the income of the *shochtim* and in improving overall working conditions. Under their direction, working time was cut from twelve hours a day to a thirty-six-hour work week and salaries raised to sixty-five dollars a week in the wholesale market and to forty-five dollars a week in the retail market.[44]

As a result of the *shochtim*'s acceptance of the Herberts, born both out of fear and the need for economic security, Charles and Tootsie Herbert, together with Joey Wiener, controlled most aspects of the poultry industry. By imposing what one student of racketeering called a "vicious system of intimidation, enforced by violence," the three hired and fired the workmen at will, extorted huge sums of money as tribute from poultry dealers, and even went so far as to work with the Chamber in fixing the wholesale price of chicken. A ditty written at the time captures some of the atmosphere of fear in the kosher poultry market. Sung to the tune of "Sing a Song of Blackbirds," it went:

> Sing a song of shochtim, how we love to sing
> Four and twenty gangsters, done up in a sling
> When the markets opened, Tootsie came around
> And all the people ponied up one cent a pound.[45]

By 1928, some poultrymen were beginning to tire of the Herberts' exactions. In May of that year, B. Taits, a Brooklyn independent dealer, filed suit against the Chamber charging it with conspiring to violate the federal antitrust law. As a result of Taits's suit the U.S. Attorney's office began to look into the activities of kosher poultrymen. Months later, in January 1929, a federal grand jury charged eighty-eight members of the Chamber, the Herbert brothers, Joey Wiener, the Chamber itself, and Locals 167 and 440 with conspiring to violate the Sherman antitrust law by creating a "poultry trust." Members of this trust, the government argued, had created a "reign of terror" in the poultry market and had restrained persons from carrying out their business except under conditions dictated to them by the Chamber.[46]

The government's case, tried before Federal Judge John Knox in October 1929, was unusual in several respects. It was perhaps the first time the Sherman antitrust law had been used to fight racketeering, a practice which subsequently became rather common. In yet another departure from the judicial norm, all eighty-eight defendants were placed on trial at one time; "this is the largest number of defendants ever tried at one time before a federal judge," reported the *Times*. To seat all the defendants, the court built a special section of bleachers; this became known, appropriately enough, as the "chicken coop." Thanks in large measure to these unusual accommodations, the atmosphere in the courtroom often verged on the comic. Removed from the center of the court, the defendants squirmed in their uncomfortable wooden chairs, told jokes, and acted, one journalist observed, "more like an audience than like defendants." Unfamiliar with court procedure, some of those seated on the bleachers kept on their hats. "The shout 'Take off your hat,'" the papers related, "became almost a ritual chant of the courts." Giving "lessons" in Hebrew grammar and Jewish customs to the non-Jewish jury to help it comprehend the intricacies of the kosher poultry business, the prosecution, headed by Israel B. Oseas, himself Jewish, added still further to the amusement of both those on trial and those attending it. And yet, despite the lighthearted tone of the courtroom proceedings, there was surely nothing comic about religious Jews, indeed religious functionaries, on trial for wrongdoing and illicit activity in what was a wholly Jewish industry. "In a special sense," one dismayed Jewish reporter commented, "the trial concerned intimately the Jewish community . . . all the defendants were Jewish and were engaged in a Jewish business and . . . this business is rather closely connected with the Jewish religious ritual of kashruth." The trial, she concluded, "was a scandal . . . a disgrace."[47]

The trial lasted seven weeks, during which three defendants pleaded guilty, fifteen were dismissed, and four had their cases severed. Lawyers for the remaining sixty-six defendants opened their case by protesting the special seating arrangement. Calling it "un-American," Arthur Sager contended that the bleachers held the defendants up to ridicule. He also argued that the charges made were "reckless" and "as weird as the bleachers in which the defendants are seated." Far from terrorizing the poultrymen and ruling the market with an iron hand, the Chamber helped its members, many of them recent immigrants unfamiliar with "our institutions and language," to adjust to American life. "My clients," he explained, "are children of Israel groping in the darkness for a solution of their case." In presenting its case, the government produced a series of witnesses who told of being physically abused when they refused to abide by the Chamber's dictates. Morris and Anna Tether of Williamsburg testified that when they sold poultry several cents below the price set by the Chamber, men working for the Chamber disabled their car engines with emery. Abe Rosenthal, another kosher poultry retailer, informed the court that after refusing to pay his dues to the Chamber he was unable to find even one ritual slaughterer willing to service him. Max Harnett, a slaughterhouse owner, related that after he refused to cooperate with the Chamber, Tootsie beat him up.[48]

In mid-November 1929, the case went to the jury. After several days of deliberation, it found in favor of the government. All sixty-six defendants, among them the Herberts, were convicted for restraint of trade. Most were fined and given light prison sentences. Charles Herbert, for example, received a sentence of only two weeks, while his brother Tootsie received one of eight weeks. At the trial's conclusion, after learning of the jury's verdict, United States Attorney Charles Tuttle predicted that the conviction of all sixty-six defendants would bring "to an end one of the biggest rackets in this town." The jury's decision, he continued, "will particularly tend to benefit those members of the public whose religious beliefs require the observance of certain dietetic [sic] laws." Tuttle's optimism, however, was premature. Within days of serving their all too brief sentences, both Herbert brothers reentered the poultry business and resumed their former positions as business agents of Locals 167 and 440; so did Joey Wiener, who had escaped standing trial.[49]

Throughout the early 1930s, the Herberts and Wiener strengthened their hold on the industry. They entered into the manufacture of chicken coops and feed and, using their power as union leaders, compelled poultry dealers to buy these items exclusively from them. Recalcitrant merchants were forced by the unions into hiring additional workmen; frequently they suffered unexplained labor disturbances and were threatened with violence. On one such occasion, Joey Wiener allegedly said to the owner of the SS & B Poultry Market that if he did not purchase his feed from Wiener's company, he would "be found in a mudhole." When the dealer continued to resist, the racketeer sent three thugs to his office who, armed with sawed-off billiard cues, "wrecked all the office fixtures, the cash register, scales, windows, lights and everything else that had yielded to their clubs."[50]

This proved to be Wiener's undoing. Immediately upon learning of the attack, Bronx District Attorney Sam Foley issued a bench warrant for the arrest of the "ruthless dictator" Joseph Wiener, charging him with conspiracy to coerce. Wiener surrendered to the D.A. in June and was tried and convicted a month later. He was sentenced to an indeterminate sentence ranging from six months to three years. Following his conviction, the authorities declared war on the poultry extortionists. In August, just after Wiener's conviction, the government filed an information against Wiener, Tootsie Herbert, and Locals 167 and 440, charging them with ignoring an earlier court injunction which had warned them not to violate the antitrust law in future transactions. Both Wiener and Herbert were tried and convicted of the charge in 1934. Wiener was given an additional sentence of two years; Tootsie was given six months behind bars.[51]

Charles Herbert, the only member of the triumvirate not in jail, was eager to demonstrate his integrity as a union leader; to prove to himself and to the outside world that the *shochtim* respected and admired him, the union leader, in August 1935, put himself up for re-election as Local 440's manager. Much to his chagrin, the *shochtim* voted to oust him. This was too much for the poultry czar and he immediately applied to the AFL for a charter with which to establish a new *shochtim* union. To the utter dismay of some ritual slaughterers and the New York City Commissioner of Markets, William F. Morgan, Herbert received one. The AFL, reported one source, believed that Herbert was unjustly "being nailed to the cross" and therefore honored his request. It issued a brand-new charter for Local 370, a new *shochtim* union. Timid souls, "easily taken advantage of," most of the *shochtim* followed Herbert into the new union. Though they had voted to remove him, the racketeer's success at receiving immediate recognition from the AFL—despite his ouster—unnerved them; frightened of reprisal, they quickly joined the new union. A few *shochtim*, however, refused to join. "Better it would be," one explained, "that our hands should be cut off than we should use them to work under racketeers."[52]

Soon after Tootsie's release from jail in 1936, he and his brother Charles made new demands on the poultry industry. Employers were made to pay the salaries of the *shochtim* and other poultry workers directly to the union and not to the employees as they had done in the past; only the union could determine just how many workers were needed at the poultry markets; and, in what many poultrymen construed to be the most outrageous demand of all, the Herberts insisted that all business records were to be regularly subjected to their personal scrutiny. Poultry merchants and slaughterhouse owners were horrified by these new demands, an obvious test of the racketeers' strength. But faced with the alternative of costly strikes and violence, they reluctantly complied with them.[53]

Commissioner of Markets William Morgan felt no such constraints. In a July 1936 letter to then-Mayor La Guardia, he contended that the new regulations "would practically put the industry out of business" and urged the mayor to curtail the extortions of the Herberts. Shortly thereafter, Morgan suggested to Special Prosecutor Dewey that he look into the Herberts' affairs. The crime-fighter heeded Morgan's suggestion and, after six months of investigation, indicted Arthur Herbert, David Diamondstone, president of Local 167, and Harry Frankel, its secretary-treasurer and a well-known loan shark. The three were charged with embezzling close to $40,000 of union funds between 1933 and 1934.[54]

The press reported that more than five hundred members of the local stood solidly behind their leaders. "If they embezzled the money," shouted some of the Herberts' supporters, "we will raise more money for them to embezzle." Despite this curious show of support, perhaps orchestrated from above, the three leaders pleaded guilty to the charge. Tootsie was sentenced to a minimum of twenty years in jail.[55]

Early in 1915, when Dopey Benny's confessions first became public news, the *American Hebrew* decried the Jewish underworld's association with the garment industry as un-Jewish. "It is clear," the paper noted, "that there is nothing peculiarly Jewish" about Jewish labor racketeers like Dopey Benny and their methods. Admittedly Dopey's strongarm tactics probably struck many observers, accustomed to viewing the Jews as muscularly undeveloped, as uncharacteristic. That aside, however, Dopey and his successors Lepke Buchalter and Tootsie Herbert owed their respective success as racketeers precisely to their familiarity with the "peculiarly Jewish" aspects of New York life; attuned to the nuances of the New York Jewish experience, they effectively exploited them. Occasionally, Jewish labor racketeers ventured beyond the borders of the Jewish community, employing a heterogeneous mix of sluggers or blackmailing non-Jewish businesses. Still, they were anchored to the Jewish community and its economy; the two served as the context of much, if not most, of their activities. Commenting at the time on the inability of the police to suppress racketeering, Walter Lippmann observed that such efforts were "blunted" by the reciprocal relationship enjoyed by the underworld and the "upper-world." "The underworld," he explained, "performs many services which respectable members of society call for. . . ." The success of the Jewish labor racketeers illustrates Lippmann's point. Able to "read" the economic interests of the community and, by extension, the needs of the Jewish consumer, Jewish racketeers fueled the first and satisfied the second. By fixing prices and providing steady jobs, racketeers stabilized the volatile garment industry; Jewish poultry racketeers did much the same thing. They too regulated competition, fixed prices, provided jobs for poultry workmen, and thus steadied what was inherently an unsteady business. Furthermore, the insularity and self-contained quality of Jewish life in New York served as a cocoon for the racketeers, protecting them for many years against outside interference—in the form of Thomas E. Dewey. Jewish labor racketeering was an "in-house" affair. Both frightened by and in need of the Jewish racketeers, Jewish businessmen and workers kept silent about their relationship until the cost became far too onerous to bear.[56]

THE BUSINESS OF CRIME

Arnold Rothstein and Murder Inc.

On the evening of November 4, 1928, the police found
Arnold Rothstein, reputed "czar of the underworld" and well-
known "Broadway playboy and gambler," lying seriously
wounded at the servants' entrance to the posh Park Central
Hotel. Rothstein died several days later, at the age of forty-six, without
revealing the name of his murderer. The police suspected that Rothstein
had welshed on a gambling debt and was therefore killed by his angry
creditors, but were never able to find the murderer. Determined to
solve the case lest it reflect poorly on his administration, Jimmy Walker,
Tammany Hall "jazz mayor," personally supervised the police investigation, but to no avail. For over three years, amidst growing embarrassment on the part of the administration, the police delved unsucess-
fully into the circumstances of Rothstein's untimely demise; in 1932,
the District Attorney was compelled to dismiss the grand jury, which
had been sitting since 1928, for want of evidence. Who shot Rothstein
still remains an open question.[1]

The inability of the police to solve the case assumed a "political
bearing" as anti–Tammany Hall forces suggested that Walker and his
cronies deliberately quashed the investigation, fearing that it would
reveal their ties to the underworld figure. Broadly hinting that Walker
and other Tammany politicians not only socialized with Rothstein
but were indebted to him as well, the anti-Walker coalition hoped to
tarnish the mayor's reputation and thus defeat his chances for reelection. "Anti-administration forces," reported the *New York Herald
Tribune*, "are closely watching developments in the belief that the
Police Department will be the issue in the next election." True enough,
the following year the unsolved murder case came to the front as "the
leading issue in the municipal campaign," pitting young Fiorello

La Guardia, the Republican candidate for mayor, against the popular incumbent. Like the Rosenthal case sixteen years earlier, which had caused Tammany's defeat, the 1929 mayoral election menaced Walker's reelection. Political columnists and pundits predicted that the ramifications of the Rothstein case would "far outshadow those growing out of the Rosenthal killing."[2]

Walker, though, was reelected by a strikingly wide margin, a "Tammany tidal wave," one paper called it. Due to his "exceptional popularity" and with a well-oiled, "perfectly organized Tammany behind him," Walker was able to ignore La Guardia's charges that his administration was "shot through and through with graft and corruption." La Guardia, for his part, was hamstrung by the reluctance of many Republican party stalwarts to stand by their party's candidate. The Republican party, commented the *Times* in the aftermath of La Guardia's stunning defeat, "put forward a candidate who could neither hold the stalwarts nor attract the independents."[3]

Despite the outcome of the election, the reading public continued to be fascinated by Rothstein and his involvement with "that hidden section of life," the underworld. The politics of the case coupled with Rothstein's exploits made good copy. Rothstein's death, reported one paper, was a "thrilling mystery, full of subterranean implications"; his life, commented another daily, "reads like a sensational novel." Capitalizing on this fascination, the press featured full-page spreads on "Broadway's greatest chance maker" and in purple prose described the man and his underworld adventures. Thus, the *New York American* wrote of Rothstein:

> A lust for risk vibrated in every corpuscle of his blood, but he harnessed his emotions with nerves of steel wire. When others poured liquor down their throats, he sipped a glass of water. While others smoked a cigarette continuously, he did not even chew gum. And where they crashed into profanity, he clicked his teeth and uttered at most a monosyllable.

This sort of thing did nothing to lessen public interest in the case. Indeed, it was such a *cause célèbre* that humorist Will Rogers, starring in a Broadway musical at the time, could not resist capitalizing on it. Nightly he turned to his audience and suggested that, should Rothstein's murderer be among them, he stand up and take a bow![4]

Perhaps equally as fascinating or intriguing as the identity of Rothstein's murderer (or his motives for killing the well-known underworld figure) were the extent and variety of Rothstein's business interests. His financial dealings had been with a wide range of people: bootleggers, real estate developers, narcotics dealers, theatrical producers, socialites, and labor leaders—even common criminals. Rothstein possessed an "unbounded range of acquaintances," commented one contemporary, while another noted that Rothstein "carried on an existence with so many weird ramifications." With his good looks, polished manners, and "abundant personal charm," Rothstein moved easily in the upper echelons of New York's society. He was, one daily reported, "the pet of society people." He moved with equal fluency among the underworld; "Legs" Diamond and Waxy Gordon were among his associates. Then, too, Rothstein blurred the social and financial boundaries of the upper and underworlds through his business activities. He backed a number of highly profitable but perfectly legitimate real estate deals, and also one of the earliest attempts at rumrunning in the United States. Moreover, he was believed to be a power broker or, as the *Jewish Daily Forward* put it, a "shtadlan." "Wielding a power comparable to that of princes and potentates," Rothstein was sought out by politicians eager for reelection, theatrical producers in need of financial angels, garment manufacturers in trouble with the unions, and criminals in need of bail money.[5]

Rothstein's ability to move comfortably in both café society and the underworld distinguished him from most of his Jewish predecessors, tied to an exclusively Jewish environment. In many respects, Rothstein's career belongs more to the general history of American crime than to its particularly Jewish aspects. Rothstein was a "Jewish criminal" only by virtue of his origin. He neither derived his illicit income from the Jewish economy of New York nor for that matter were his business associates and friends largely Jewish. Unlike most contemporary Jewish members of the underworld, who lived among other Jews, Rothstein resided at 912 Fifth Avenue and had little, if any, connection with New York's organized Jewish life. It is one of the ironies of Rothstein's life that at the behest of his father, Abraham Rothstein, a leading Orthodox Jew, he was given a fully traditional Jewish burial. More telling still was that few people saw him as a Jewish criminal. "The typical East Side gangster," reported *Reflex* magazine shortly after Rothstein's death, "is a thing of the past." Unlike, say, a Rosenthal or a Zelig—two representative, typical East Side gangsters—Rothstein was seen as an American criminal, an heir to the tradition of gentlemen-gamblers and playboys like Jack Kelley and Dick Canfield. It was surely no coincidence that at the time of his death, the *New York Times* likened Rothstein to John Oakhurst, Bret Harte's fictional all-American gambler and man-about-town, "always a notable man in ten thousand." Commenting on the late gambler's career and, incidentally, on the mysterious way he had met his death, the paper wrote that Rothstein was very much in "the Oakhurst tradition."[6]

Rothstein's career marked the passing of one era of crime history and the beginning of another in other respects as well. As the *New York Herald Tribune* observed, he belonged to a new class of criminals, a "Brahmin caste," whose exploits were a far cry from those practiced a generation earlier. "He led crime into the business era," Rothstein's biographer notes; "he change[d] crime from petty larceny into big business." The underworld leader, observed still another student of the underworld, "coordinated the activities of criminals in almost every branch until crime became a 'big business.' " To be sure, Rothstein was not the first to have organized his followers along hierarchical lines, or to have made large and continuous profits from illegal enterprise. His contribution to the structure (and the history) of the underworld lay rather in his almost unparalleled ability to bring these, and other, trends into sharper focus. With a flair for business and business organization, Rothstein transformed criminal activity from a haphazard, often spontaneous, endeavor into one whose hallmarks—specialized expertise, administrative hierarchy, and organizational procedure—corresponded to the classic sociological model of a bureaucracy. Thus, Rothstein's illegal business had a definite administrative structure based on specific skills; competence and not ethnic pedigree determined one's rank and, of course, one's position, in his outfit. Though ethnically heterogeneous gangs predated Rothstein, one or another ethnic group stood out; Dopey's gang, for example, had a sprinkling of non-Jewish members but remained largely Jewish. Among Rothstein's followers, however, no particular ethnic group predominated. Furthermore, Rothstein's office, centrally located on West 57th Street, in the heart of the midtown business district, employed a staff comparable with that of any large (and legitimate) commercial firm, replete with secretaries, bookkeepers, and legal counsel. Decision making, too, attained a degree of rationality not much evidenced before in the underworld. A decision to enter some new illegal venture tended to be based not on personal motives of revenge or power but on strictly commercial considerations: the amount of profit to be made and the length of time it would take to make it. Finally, by investing the money he earned through illegal channels into legal enterprises such as real estate and the theater, Rothstein made it difficult to ascertain where the illegal enterprise left off and the legitimate one began. Rothstein himself, it is worth noting, was the very model of a bureaucrat. Affable yet distant, he subordinated his personal interests, sacrificing even his marriage, to build a vast business empire. Ultimately, Rothstein succeeded in professionalizing the underworld and thus laid the groundwork for what would become known as "organized crime."[7]

Rothstein was an unlikely candidate for one of New York's most stellar criminals. The son of wealthy and much respected New York Jews, pillars of the Upper West Side's Orthodox Jewish community, Rothstein, commented the *Times*, was "headed for a safe success in his father's dress business." Yet, "with the strange restlessness of the malcontent," he turned to crime. While a teenager at the turn of the century, Rothstein frequented the stuss parlors and poolrooms of the Lower East Side and was befriended by habitués Monk Eastman and Herman Rosenthal. Through them he became acquainted with Big Tim Sullivan, Tammany Hall leader and political boss of the Lower East Side, and soon was a regular at Big Tim's Second Avenue headquarters. Sullivan, it is alleged, was so impressed by Rothstein's mental agility that he took the well-groomed young man under his wing and personally trained him in the art of gambling. At first Rothstein served as a runner and collector of bets for several local bookmakers, but he quickly graduated to placing bets on his own. His gambling talents, or, as the *Tog* once put it, his *"ma'alehs,"* were so marked that in 1909, at the age of twenty-five, Rothstein opened a gambling casino on West 46th Street. Located in the heart of the Tenderloin area, a hitherto non-Jewish neighborhood and one commonly believed to be off limits to ambitious Jewish gamblers, Rothstein's establishment, virtually alone among the few Jewish casinos in the area, operated free from political and police interference until 1912.[8]

In the summer of that year, after Rothstein's less successful colleague Herman Rosenthal had been murdered, many of the city's gamblers, among them Rothstein, became fearful of reprisals and shut down their gaming establishments. Rothstein, though, quickly rebounded from what could have been a financial disaster by devising floating crap games as a substitute for the stationary gambling parlor. Later, after reform ardor had cooled, Rothstein returned to the covert operation of plush and remunerative gambling parlors. By attracting a sophisticated and worldly crowd and thanks to his own considerable personal charm and flair, Rothstein earned between three and four million dollars from his casino; he also earned himself the sobriquet of "king of the gamblers."[9]

Indeed Rothstein's expertise and fame as a gambler were so great that the mere use of his name was enough to convince eight disgruntled members of the Chicago White Sox baseball team to "throw" the 1919 World Series in return for a bonus of one hundred thousand dollars. Rothstein had been approached initially by agents of the ballplayers and asked to participate in the swindle, yet he had refused; why, we do not know. Undaunted, the professional gamblers masterminding the "Black Sox" scandal pretended they were working on Rothstein's behalf and therefore succeeded in convincing the ballplayers to proceed with the scheme. It was subsequently discovered. Despite Rothstein's repeated and heated denials of any complicity, the press charged him with "fixing the World Series," a charge picked up and embroidered upon by America's leading anti-Semite, Henry Ford. In articles with titles like "Jewish Gamblers Corrupt American Baseball" and "The Jewish Degradation of American Baseball," the inventor accused Rothstein of corrupting the quintessential, innocent, national pastime. "The Jews," he wrote in his *Dearborn Independent*, "are not sportsmen." Nevertheless, they were heavily involved in sports. "The Jew saw money where the sportsmen saw fun and skill. The Jew," he continued, alluding to Rothstein, "set out to capitalize rivalry and to commercialize contestant zeal."[10]

Discomfited by the unexpectedly negative play the press (and Ford) gave him in the wake of the 1919 World Series, Rothstein, in a rare public interview, announced his retirement from the world of gambling. "The unwarranted use of my name in this unfortunate baseball scandal," he explained, "was the last straw. It is not pleasant to be a social outcast . . . I am heartily sick and tired of having my name dragged in on the slightest provocation . . . and henceforth will devote myself to the real estate business and to my racing stable." Journalists intimated that Rothstein's retirement marked the end of his career as one of New York's most colorful and successful criminals. Yet during the next eight years, from 1920 until his death in 1928, Rothstein parlayed the vast revenues he had earned from gambling into real estate, insurance, and other numerous illegal ventures as well; these were his most lucrative years. Indeed, it was during the 1920s that Rothstein emerged as the "czar of the underworld."[11]

Rothstein's ability to "bankroll" or finance illegal business ventures requiring large amounts of capital was perhaps the major source of his power. Lloyd Morris called him the "Morgan of the underworld, its banker and master of economic strategy." Thus, shortly after Prohibition took effect, Waxy Gordon came to Rothstein with a plan for importing liquor from England. "Grasp[ing] the potentialities of Prohibition," Rothstein warmed to the idea and immediately arranged for associates in England to buy liquor for him. He then bought boats to transport the "liquid gold" from overseas and trucks to transport it inland, and finally distributed the liquor to restaurants and nightclubs in which he had a financial interest. Though this initial investment yielded large dividends, Rothstein soon decided to limit his bootlegging activity to financing others. Accordingly, Rothstein provided one of his former employees, Jack "Legs" Diamond, with capital to buy trucks, weapons, and personnel in return for a portion of the profits.[12]

At about this time, Rothstein reportedly realized that the narcotics business had even greater profit-making potential than bootlegging. Unlike the latter enterprise, which was highly competitive and which tied up large sums of capital over relatively long periods of time, trafficking in narcotics was thoroughly unorganized and yielded a quick return on one's investment. Thus, in the early 1920s, Rothstein began to buy and sell drugs. Much as he had organized the various stages of bootlegging into a well-coordinated operation, he consolidated the various phases of the narcotics trade, sending associates Yasha Katzenberg and "Dapper Dan" Collins overseas to Europe and Asia to buy the drugs, then hiring the young and ambitious Charles "Lucky" Luciano to sell them to retailers in New York, Chicago, St. Louis, and Kansas City. By 1927 United States Attorney Charles Tuttle could report that the "entire dope traffic in the United States is being directed from one source: Arnold Rothstein."[13]

Rothstein did not limit himself to providing Americans with illicit forms of pleasure. He was also involved with labor racketeering, especially in the needle trades: authorities believed he had supplied both the union and the bosses with their respective "balagoulas." After

Rothstein's demise, much more of his dealings, particularly with the Communists, became known. On November 17, 1928, in what must have been a journalistic scoop of the first order, the Socialist *Jewish Daily Forward* published a letter written by the erstwhile gambler in December 1927 to Julius Portnoy, a Communist party official and secretary of the Cloak, Suit, Dress, Skirt and Reefer Makers' Union. Portnoy had sent the underworld figure a check "for services rendered." Rothstein, who intensely disliked being in the limelight, wrote to Portnoy asking him to omit the phrase "for services rendered" in future communications. "It does not look very good for me," Rothstein is supposed to have said. The *Forward* gleefully pointed to this exchange as concrete proof that Rothstein had worked in tandem with the Communists in 1926, supplying them with goons and financing their activities as well.[14]

Its rival, the Jewish Communist newspaper *Freiheit*, glibly dismissed the accusation. "Only a yenta newspaper like the Jewish Daily Forward," it wrote, "would make political capital out of what is a kosher issue." Explaining that its ties with Rothstein were strictly financial, the paper described how, at the time of the internecine conflict, it was financially strapped and therefore turned to Rothstein for a loan. When pressed by the *Jewish Daily Forward* to explain why the Communists had sought Rothstein's assistance in the first place, rather than that of a legitimate lending institution, the paper breezily replied that Rothstein had given them the best terms. Day after day, for nearly two weeks, the *Jewish Daily Forward* taunted the Communists for their "moral bankruptcy." Insisting that "Rothstein was the dictator of the Communist faction," the Socialist paper demanded a full account of the Communists' dealings with the underworld figure. The Communists, however, refused to oblige, retorting that the newspaper's charges were "sour grapes," the result of having been bested by the Communists several years earlier in 1926.[15]

Though the exchange between the two factions became increasingly scurrilous, the charges and countercharges do not appear to have been mere fabrications forged in the heat of political passion. Reports substantiating Rothstein's collusion with the Communist-led ILGWU are widespread. Shortly after his death, the metropolitan press reported that the underworld czar had supplied the Communists with goon squads, even going so far as to buy police protection for them. The *New York World*, for instance, boldly suggested that the canny Rothstein had "played both sides against the middle," by supporting both the Communist-dominated ILGWU and the bosses in the hopes of ultimately neutralizing the two sides and thus gaining control of the entire industry. Moreover, at its 1928 convention, the General Executive Board of the ILGWU unhesitatingly charged Rothstein with having acted as "mediator" at the time of the 1926 strike. "Arnold Rothstein," the ILGWU leadership stated, "had been chosen by three men [among them Charles Zimmerman], without even consulting the advisory board of the General Strike Committee to whom they were responsible. This 'mediator,' Arnold Rothstein, so far as we knew, had at no time been identified with any movement of a public or labor nature. Certainly there was nothing in his career to resemble any of the previous mediators and arbitrators in our industry—Louis D. Brandeis, Hamilton Holt, Dr. Felix Adler. . . ." And yet, he had been acting for six entire weeks as a mediator between the opposing sides! Once again, the oral history reminiscences of Charles Zimmerman shed some light on this curious but by no means unimaginable episode. Whether acting independently or at the behest of his father, who had assumed an important role in effecting a rapprochement between management and labor, the younger Rothstein, it seems, "began interfering . . . to bring about a settlement," appearing at various negotiating sessions and using his considerable connections to end the enervating strike. "As I said," Zimmerman related, "we had these negotiations. It was most likely our stupidity in permitting Rothstein to come. . . . How it came about . . . I don't recall the details. . . . but I know everybody felt unpleasant. I found out afterwards."[16]

"In his own way," writes Irving Howe of Arnold Rothstein, "he was still another Jewish boy who had made good." Indeed, like so many of his Jewish contemporaries, Rothstein took advantage of the right business opportunities—in labor negotiations, in real estate, and in rumrunning—to make both a fortune and a name for himself. Yet if the czar of the underworld aspired to upward mobility with as much determination as his coreligionists, he did so, as Howe says, in his own way. Rothstein's vehicle of social ascent—crime—lay clearly outside the precincts of the New York Jewish community of the interwar years. Moreover, by coordinating and consolidating various aspects of the underworld, from gang life on its most elementary level to sophisticated and complicated business deals, Rothstein emerged as the "guiding hand" of the underworld, the person largely responsible for putting crime "on a corporate basis."[17]

Murder Inc. inherited many of Rothstein's legacies. A combination of second-generation Jews and Italians, the Brownsville gang for most of its history worked quietly and professionally behind the scenes, lending money, operating bookmaking establishments, and racketeering; the wholesale commission of murder that earned the gang its "indelicate name" was a much later development. Yet even when deliberately engaging in murder, Murder Inc. gang members proceeded along strictly defined and rational, indeed businesslike, lines, carefully orchestrating every detail of the effort. On the surface, though, Rothstein and the Murder Inc. gang members had little in common: Rothstein was as suave and polished as Murder Inc. was coarse and unfinished; Rothstein was soigné Manhattan, Murder Inc. lower-class Brooklyn. Despite these external differences, the two together represented a new cultural generation of American Jewish criminals, one with fewer ties to New York's Jewish community. Murder Inc. was composed of an ethnically heterogeneous band of followers; its illict activities had little to do either with the economy of the Jewish neighborhood in which it was headquartered or, for that matter, with its Jewish residents. It could have taken root anywhere; little bound it to the identifiably Jewish neighborhood of Brownsville, the "Jerusalem of New York." Murder Inc., explained Burton Turkus, the Brooklyn assistant district attorney responsible for prosecuting the group, "has been seen incorrectly as a Brooklyn group . . . Murder Inc. was about as peculiar to Brooklyn as the hot dog." Furthermore, neither Rothstein's activities nor those of Murder Inc. became modal Jewish behaviors; each, in its own way, represented the "tail end" of the Jewish underworld. Thanks to his considerable abilities, Rothstein was able to lay the foundation for many of the institutions that characterize organized crime today. Yet his unique combination of talents was such that the "Brain" (as Damon Runyan called him) had neither peers nor heirs; although many criminals, including the members of Murder Inc., learned a great deal from him, ultimately Rothstein must be seen as idiosyncratic. Similarly, while it is tempting to see Murder Inc. as the advance guard of a future generation of gun-toting Jewish criminals, criminality has all but disappeared as a Jewish social problem. Several Jewish gangsters like Meyer

Lansky and Bugsy Siegel were to play a significant part in the development of the post–World War II underworld, but they were soon
outnumbered by Italians who during the 1940s and 1950s came to
occupy leadership positions in the nation's criminal enterprise. Rothstein and Murder Inc., then, were anomalies, signifying the "last hur-
rahs" of the Jewish criminal experience.[18]

In January 1940, William O'Dwyer, a former Brooklyn county
court judge and policeman, took office as Kings County district attorney, vowing to rid the borough of its criminals. Singling out Brownsville as one of Brooklyn's more dangerous neighborhoods, which had
"spawned more gangsters and criminals than any other section of the
city," the Irishman embarked upon a cleanup campaign to rival that
of Tom Dewey's across the river. Before he began to "sweep" criminals
off Brooklyn's streets, however, O'Dwyer made sure to add that the
activities of Brownsville criminals were in no way a "reflection upon
the people as a whole."[19]

"The people"—the Brownsville citizens to whom the district attorney
referred—were largely working class and foreign-born Jews. A throw-
back to the immigrant enclaves of the prewar period, Brownsville,
writes Deborah Dash Moore, was a "miniature East Side." Both housed
a multiplicity of Jewish social, fraternal, and religious institutions; life
in that northeastern corner of Brooklyn, one of its residents recalled,
was akin to "living in a world all Jewish." It also resembled the Lower
East Side in possessing crowded tenements, a relatively unstable economic base, and a Jewish criminal element.[20]

As part of his cleanup campaign, O'Dwyer had his staff reopen
previously unsolved murder cases. While investigating the murder of
Red Alpert, a petty Brooklyn hoodlum, evidence was discovered that
Alpert had been murdered by Abe "Kid Twist" Reles and Martin
"Buggsy" Goldstein, allegedly "two of the most important leaders in
the city's underworld." Taking what he called a "wild chance," the
District Attorney presented his evidence to the grand jury, which
indicted Reles and Goldstein on first-degree murder charges. What
began as an investigation into a seemingly routine murder developed
into one of the most startling chapters in the history of American
crime. Turning state's witness, Reles described the activities of his
colleagues, the members of Murder Inc., over a ten-year period, accounting for as many as eighty previously unsolved murder cases in
Brooklyn, Manhattan, and Sullivan County. In testimony that filled

twenty-five stenographic notebooks, Reles linked leading racketeer Lepke Buchalter and waterfront czar Albert Anastasia to the Brownsville gang and through his testimony helped to convict Lepke of the murder of former garment trucker Joseph Rosen. Recalling the chain of events leading up to the execution of Lepke Buchalter, O'Dwyer noted that everything had moved so quickly his staff "didn't even have their feet under the desk."[21]

Given to "swaggering and bullying," to wearing flashy clothes and gaudy jewelry, Reles maintained an "air of importance" as the boss of the Brooklyn gang. With a decided penchant for carrying large amounts of cash and an equally pronounced penchant for displaying it, Reles liked to think of himself as a direct descendant of Kid Twist, a showy and tough prewar Jewish *shtarke*. Like his hero, Reles had had a long and busy criminal career. When indicted by O'Dwyer in 1940, he had previously been arrested forty-four times on charges ranging from burglary to homicide. After graduating from eighth grade in 1920, Reles became a delivery boy and worked at a succession of ill-paying jobs. While in his late teens, he became a pressman and worked for a printer. When his employer went bankrupt, Reles took to the streets and, as one law enforcement agent put it, "chose to pass his leisure time, of which he had plenty," in a Sutter Avenue poolroom. The poolroom or poolhall was the common meeting ground for Brooklyn youth and the fringe element of society. One former Brownsville resident, himself a frequent poolroom visitor while an adolescent, recalled that his favored haunt, Label's poolroom, was a surrogate home. There he would socialize and gossip with his friends; it was also a place to find "someone to break a head, beat up a guy, break a strike, buy junk, set a fire, plan a robbery or muscle a pedlar." It was in such a setting that the unemployed Reles met and became friendly with "Buggsy" Goldstein and Harry "Pittsburgh Phil" Strauss—men who, like himself, were in their early twenties, native-born American Jews, and out of work; in addition, all three possessed substantial arrest records, about which they often publicly boasted.[22]

In the spring of 1930, Reles and his chums, after discussing ways of making an "easy dollar," decided to go into the business of supplying candy stores and poolrooms with pinball machines. After installing the machines, Reles, Goldstein, and Strauss planned to charge a monthly rental fee and a small maintenance charge as well as to receive a share of the machines' earnings. Yet one factor stood in their way of financial

success: the pinball racket was controlled by the Shapiro brothers—
Irving, Meyer, and Willie—overlords of much of Brownsville's criminal
activity, including prostitution and bookmaking. Determined to wrest
at least part of the pinball operation from the Shapiros, Reles and
his partners joined together with a small group of Italian petty criminals
from the adjacent Ocean Hill section of Brooklyn whose leaders were
Happy Maione and Frank "The Dasher" Abbandando, and laid plans
to compete with the brothers Shapiro. There was an unexpected bonus
in the formation of the so-called Combination: the elder brother of
George DeFeo, one of the Maione gang members, was friendly with
the underworld's leading supplier of pinball machines. Interceding on
behalf of the Brownsville organization, William DeFeo, George's
brother, received permission from "Louis the Wop," reportedly the
person "in charge of the pinball department" of the underworld, to
enter the business. Furthermore, Louis supplied the pinball machines
on credit to the new partnership. "With these advantages," one police
official observed, "the partnership began to make inroads on the territory before monopolized by the Shapiros."[23]

Buoyed by their success, the Combination entered the loan-shark
business, also a former Shapiro stronghold, insisting that local Brooklyn
loan sharks place them on their payroll. One Brooklyn "shylock" related that, upon learning of the success of his business, the Combination
demanded a share of the profits. "They wanted to have a percentage
of the income," Seymour Magoon testified. "We had an understanding
with them, either 50–50 or 60–40 . . . and we hooked up with them."
As more and more loan sharks like Magoon and his partner "hooked up"
with the Combination, threatening the hegemony of the Shapiros, the
three brothers became increasingly angry. "Quite naturally," reported
the police, "friction arose between the rival gangs. The Shapiro's [sic]
resented the newcomers and their quick success." This resentment
grew so fierce that Irving Shapiro decided to end the growing competition between the two gangs by killing the members of the Combination. On June 11, 1930, Shapiro and several of his associates killed
George DeFeo and seriously wounded Reles and Goldstein. In retaliation, the Combination murdered first Meyer, then Irving, and
finally Willie Shapiro. By 1931, its domination of much of Brooklyn's
loan-shark, bookmaking, and extortion operations was complete; the
gang, commented the *Times*, "shot its way to the top." From its modest
headquarters at Midnight Rose's candy store, on the intersection of

Livonia and Saratoga Streets, Reles and his fellow gang members developed a sophisticated system of moneylending, receiving $6 for every $5 borrowed. With a "desirable" and ethnically mixed clientele of "doctors, lawyers, dentists, undertakers and other professional and business men of some account . . . ," the Combination earned thousands of dollars a week from its loan-shark activities; Magoon himself netted a substantial $500 a week "clear profit"! To qualify for a "loan," borrowers had to give Reles a series of post-dated checks totaling the amount borrowed plus interest to be paid out in installments. A delinquent borrower left himself open to the charge of passing worthless checks or, worse still, to a fierce beating.[24]

Following the death (killing?) in 1935 of a minor Jewish racketeer named Joey Amberg, Reles and his colleagues further developed their roster of enterprises, inheriting some of the "spoils" of the deceased racketeer and adding to them as well. "We had the book-making business and a couple of unions," Reles recalled. "We had the . . . dress end of the garment industry in Manhattan; we had the fruit market union on Osborne Street. We had the van movers and we had the painters for a while too, and the luncheonettes and the restaurant union, and part of Local 138 of the Truckmen's Union and the Retail Clerks and Plumbers Union." In each case, Reles followed the pattern of racketeering established years before by Lepke: strongarming and demanding "tribute."[25]

The gang's growing financial success cemented the ties between its Jewish and Italian members. Though Reles and his Jewish confreres continued to celebrate Jewish holidays like Passover—a particular favorite—and to mark rites of passage like the *bar mitzvah* with elaborate parties, they probably had far more contact with non-Jews than most of their coreligionists. For one thing, the Jewish and Italian members of the gang worked side by side on a daily basis, physically molesting tardy borrowers and stubborn union leaders. Moreover, the gang took its orders from Albert Anastasia, a leading Brooklyn underworld figure. Reles was the nominal head of the Combination, commanding the loyalty and directing the activities of the dozen or so "troops." Yet he himself deferred to Anastasia, proudly calling him "my boss." An illegal Italian immigrant who had smuggled himself into the United States in 1917, Anastasia began as a longshoreman on the Brooklyn waterfront, ultimately becoming its labor czar. At precisely what point he assumed control of the Combination's operations is not clear; by 1940, though, he was thought to be "the boss of the different mobs in Brooklyn." Together with Louis Capone, Anastasia's personal representative, Anastasia served as the "buffet man [sic] between the Italian Maione gang and Reles, keeping them in balance." His position, of course, was far more than just peacekeeper: he also planned many of the Combination's activities and shared in its considerable profits. For another thing, the Jewish and Italian members of the Brownsville gang both earned and broke bread together. The reports of the police and District Attorney's office surveilling the Murder Inc. members are replete with details of social get-togethers patronized by both Jews and Italians. Lucky Luciano, Albert Anastasia, Louis Capone, and other major underworld figures attended the *bar mitzvah* of Lepke's adopted son, Harold; Capone customarily celebrated New Year's Eve with Charles Workman and Allie Tannenbaum, two of the gang's premier "enforcers"; Workman invited many underworld personalities to the *bris* (circumcision ceremony) of his son. Enhancing the polyglot complexion of the Combination was its association with Lepke; the ties between the two gangs were fluid and many. In addition to socializing together, some members of Lepke's outfit worked as strongarm men for Reles; Workman and Tannenbaum, for example, were on both Lepke's and Reles's payrolls. Moreover, one gang would often assist the other in extorting money or beating up recalcitrant merchants, borrowers, or union leaders. "We did favors for them," Reles recalled, "and they, in turn, returned the favors."[26]

Indeed, it was through Lepke that the Combination became known as a gang whose members coolly murdered "for hire." Reles first met the garment racketeer in 1932 when he provided him with several "shtarkes." "There was some kind of dispute," Reles wrote, "and we had to go straighten it out." Apparently the two men did not meet again until 1937 when Lepke was in hiding from Thomas Dewey. The Combination then helped the fugitive in securing various houses of refuge. Louis Capone, according to one police report, "took the leading part" by arranging with a cousin, the owner of a Coney Island recreational facility—the Oriental Danceland—to hide Lepke. Furthermore, during the two years in which Lepke hid from federal and state authorities Reles visited him in his hideout on an average of twice a week, informing him of local political events and of potential dangers. By 1938, Reles had become Lepke's "contact man," the person "through whom Lepke's visitors came to see him." At these secret meetings,

Lepke and Reles, joined periodically by Anastasia, planned the murders of former Lepke employees and business associates who threatened to inform against the labor racketeer. Using guns provided by Anastasia and following carefully orchestrated plans, the members of the Combination killed anywhere between sixty and eighty persons at Lepke's behest. This "wholesale murder by contract" earned the gang its infamous nickname—Murder Inc.[27]

The invention of Harry Feeny, a reporter for the *New York World Telegram*, the name reflected the businesslike quality of the gang's murderous forays; there was nothing spontaneous or haphazard about them. When asked by O'Dwyer what business he was in, Reles replied matter-of-factly, "the murder business." The circumstances of the Albert "Plug" Shuman murder—the careful attention to detail on the part of the murderers and the professional manner in which the crime was executed—serve as a case study of Murder Inc. methods. Disturbed to learn, early in 1938, that Shuman, one of Lepke's strongarm men, had been talking to Dewey, Lepke ordered Reles to kill the disloyal gunman or, as Lepke put it, "to take him out." After receiving Anastasia's imprimatur, Reles set about mapping strategy. First he canvassed the city in search of a "good spot" for the murder. After finding one— on Rockaway Parkway near Linden Boulevard—Reles hired Irving "Knadles" Nitzberg, a Bronx bookmaker and occasional killer, who knew Shuman, for the job. Following dinner with Shuman at Dubrow's, Nitzberg suggested that the two go for a drive. As they drove down Rockaway Parkway, Nitzberg shot the unsuspecting Shuman, abandoned the body and the car (which had been stolen, of course), and waited for Reles to pick him up at a prearranged location. After Reles met Nitzberg, the two drove to a point overlooking Jamaica Bay where they disposed of the gun. It was not until years later that the crime was discovered.[28]

Reles's position as Lepke's "go-between" and his nearly infallible memory ultimately proved to be Lepke's undoing. On the basis of Reles's testimony, the labor racketeer was convicted in 1941 for the first-degree murder of Joseph Rosen. While interrogated by the police in the spring of 1940, Reles described how Lepke had paid him and several of his gang members to murder Rosen. Thanks to this testimony, the state successfully prosecuted Lepke and electrocuted him for this crime. Reles's testimony also provided the state with the evidence to sentence his two long-time partners, "Buggsy" Goldstein and Harry

"Pittsburgh Phil" Strauss, as well as Happy Maione and Frank Abbandando, to the electric chair; fifty others were given lengthy prison
sentences.[29]

Like his colleagues, Reles came to a sorry end. While under police
surveillance, Reles was found dead in November 1941 on a ledge of the
Half Moon Hotel in Coney Island. Some believed it was suicide, others
a failed escape attempt; still others contended that Reles had been
silenced by Anastasia lest he implicate the labor czar in criminal activities. Though theories abounded as to the cause of the gangster's
sudden demise, this murder, like the one a generation earlier, was
never solved.[30]

FROM BROOME STREET
TO FIFTH AVENUE

The Interwar Years

8

Despite the intense glare of publicity surrounding Arnold Rothstein and, later, Murder Inc., the general public refrained from branding New York Jewry as an underclass with collective and distinct criminal tendencies, as it had done a generation earlier; it seemed to be able to distinguish between the individual Jewish criminal and the Jewish community. Occasionally, detractors of the Jews like Henry Ford mistook the existence of a Rothstein as representative of a larger class of Jewish criminals. In his unabashedly anti-Semitic *Dearborn Independent*, Ford frequently published pictures of gangsters and labeled them "Jewish types." Yet most of the inventor's contemporaries failed to subscribe to the stereotype. Jewish criminality, they knew, was not the glaring social problem it had been prior to World War I. Rothstein, Waxy Gordon, and Murder Inc. notwithstanding, Jewish criminal activity had declined substantially in the aftermath of the Great War; formerly Jewish enclaves of crime like arson, horse-poisoning, pickpocketing, and prostitution had virtually withered away. Fewer and fewer Jews turned to crime as a vehicle of upward mobility during the interwar years; those few who elected to become (or to remain) criminals occupied select positions of power within the underworld but their influence was disproportionate to their numbers. "Within a comparatively few years," observed Ernest Coulter, a former court official, in 1931, "there has been a drop in delinquency and criminality among them [the Jews] almost beyond belief." The number of Jewish prisoners, he added, "is sinking to practically a negligible quantity."[1]

The percentage of Jews arrested during the interwar years was indeed "sinking." From constituting an all-time high of close to one-quarter of all persons charged with felonies in New York County on the eve of World War I, it dropped to 7.5 percent on the eve of World War II. Moreover, relative to their percentage of the general population, Jews continued to be decidedly underrepresented among those charged with felonies, with at least half as many arrests as their proportion of the population warranted. Figures on adult commitments to New York State prisons tell much the same story: where in 1921, for example, Jews constituted 14 percent of the New York State prison population, during the 1930s they accounted for approximately 7 percent. Similarly, where Jewish women imprisoned (largely on charges of prostitution) once comprised approximately 20 percent of all women so charged, by 1940, they accounted for less than 4 percent of all New York State women prisoners. The drop in the percentage of adult Jews either charged with or convicted of a felony offense during the interwar years paralleled the decrease in the percentage of Jewish juvenile delinquents. In 1928, the authors of the Jewish Communal Survey, an intensive study of contemporary Jewish trends in New York, forecast that Jewish juvenile delinquency would soon become a minor communal concern: "juvenile delinquency," the survey explained, "is a rapidly declining problem for the Jewish community of Greater New York." Their prediction turned out to be accurate: the number of Jewish children arraigned on juvenile delinquency charges citywide declined from slightly more than one-fifth of all juvenile delinquents in 1922 to 14.6 percent in the mid-1930s and to 8 percent by World War II.[2]

The embourgeoisment of New York Jewry during the interwar years had much to do with the dramatic reduction in criminal activity. The cessation of immigration from abroad; the impressive economic mobility of the second generation of Eastern European Jews; their relocation from the bleak tenements of the Lower East Side to the lavish apartment houses of the Grand Concourse; and the acquisition of a middle-class orientation militated against its continuation. The Jews of the 1920s and the 1930s, writes Deborah Dash Moore, "constructed a moral community with supports borrowed from American culture, middle-class values, urban lifestyles . . . fashioning an enduring structure." On the Grand Concourse, in Flatbush, Borough Park, and Pelham Parkway, she continues, "a middle-class way of Jewish living appeared." The acculturation of New York Jewry, then, spelled the ultimate disappearance of crime as a Jewish social problem: for New York Jews, crime was a one-generation phenomenon, a social and economic consequence of the immigrant experience. As they left the physical boundaries of that experience behind, second-generation Jews left as well its social pathologists and economic dislocations.[3]

The successful imposition of quotas limiting the number of Eastern Europeans able to emigrate from Europe guaranteed the imminent passing of the immigrant experience in the New World; it also dried up the potential pool of recruits to the Jewish underworld. The enactment, in 1921, of the temporary immigration act, followed a brief three years later by an even tougher quota, the Reed-Johnson Act of 1924, reduced the flow of immigrants to a trickle. Accordingly, between 1920 and 1940 the percentage of foreign-born persons in the Empire City declined; in New York County, for example, it dropped from 40.4 percent in 1920 to 28.6 percent twenty years later. The percentage of foreign-born persons arrested declined sharply as well: during this twenty-year period, the percentage of immigrants "held for trial" in the Magistrates Court dropped from one-half to one-fifth of all persons "held for trial" while the percentage of persons of foreign birth arraigned on felony charges dropped from close to 50 percent to under 20 percent. Where prior to World War I the troubled conditions associated with the immigrant experience fed the Jewish underworld, the subsequent cessation of immigration all but starved it. "The Jewish community seems to be getting over the worst phases of its readjustment process," observed the *American Hebrew* in 1930. "While we were in the midst of a period of unrestricted immigration both adults and children found it difficult to achieve a normal development in a strange, heterogeneous environment." But now, the paper concluded, "we have reached a more equitable condition . . . our old ideals are experiencing a rebirth."[4]

The impact of immigration restriction on the social fabric of New York Jewish life can be seen not only through the lens of crime statistics but in residential terms as well. Formerly the home of over one quarter of a million immigrant Jews and the *mise-en-scène* of the Jewish underworld, the Lower East Side during the prosperous 1920s housed fewer than one hundred thousand. During that decade, the map of New York Jewish life was "drawn anew": moving from the Lower East Side and Brownsville to new and modern neighborhoods in the Bronx and Brooklyn, second-generation Jews "acquired a middle-class American environment" and "left behind an immigrant, foreign world." For many, perhaps most, Jews of the interwar years, the immigrant experience, as defined by the Lower East Side, was a closed chapter, one they regarded with both nostalgia and relief. Capturing these sentiments, the *Jewish Forum*, an Anglo-Jewish monthly, early in 1923 published a retrospective on the Lower East Side of the preceding decades. Calling the area a "corridor to freedom," the magazine noted that the "East Side in 1922 is but a symbol of what it was three decades ago" and asked a number of the area's illustrious sons and daughters— "East Side alumni"—to reflect upon their experiences. Some wrote about the politics of Lower East Side residents, others about their health, while still others reflected on the cramped housing conditions of the Jewish neighborhood. No one so much as alluded to, let alone overtly discussed, that which a short time earlier had been such an oppressive burden on Lower East Side Jews: criminality. The absence of even a sentence on the Lower East Side and crime suggests that as early as the 1920s, second-generation Jews had begun, perhaps consciously, perhaps not, to "draw anew" not only the geography of New York Jewish life but its history as well. They had relegated the criminal experience to the shadows of American Jewish life.[5]

The distance many Jews put between themselves and their recent past was accelerated by the changes in their economic status. By the late 1920s, according to students of Jewish occupational mobility, Jews were solidly entrenched in middle-class occupations; close to half of them wore white collars. Contemporary surveys of New York Jews found that they "have a larger number of professional and clerical workers than the general population": nearly 12 percent of all New York Jews fell into the professional class; another two-thirds were to be found in the fields of manufacturing and trade or commerce. "A new middle class of Jews was emerging," writes one historian of the interwar Jewish experience, "fed by the profitable opportunities generated by World War I and nourished by the speculative prosperity of the 1920s." Not surprisingly, their economic well-being made them less likely to opt for crime as an alternative vehicle of upward mobility. In his classic essay, "Crime as an American Way of Life," Daniel Bell interprets the prevalence of minority groups within the underworld as proof that they regard crime as a form of upward mobility and economic advancement. Denied access to the more traditional sources of financial security and social status or, at the very least, finding such avenues temporarily blocked, many immigrants saw crime, Bell writes, "as a route of social ascent and place in American life." Crime, he adds, has a "functional role in society . . . illicit activity . . . is one of the queer ladders of social mobility in American life." In comparison to other ethnic groups like the Italians who, for example, found "the more obvious big-city paths from rags to riches pre-empted," Jews historically had greater latitude in climbing the ladder, as they soon controlled the garment industry and began to enter the professions in large numbers. Furthermore, Jews never regarded crime as a socially acceptable form of money-making; to them, it remained anathema. If this was true during the difficult years of the prewar period, it was much more so during the prosperous 1920s with the emergence of a rather widespread and successful Jewish middle class.

Even the Depression failed to shake the social and economic "supports" of New York Jewish life. Although its impact on American Jewry has not yet found its historian, the limited available evidence suggests that as a group Jews weathered the fiscal crisis more easily than others. "Relative to other groups, and especially the Italian group," explains Thomas Kessner, "[the Jews] survived with more modest losses." Concentrated in white-collar jobs, he adds, "relatively more Jews kept their jobs even in the midst of the economic crisis." Thus, one contemporary study found that a relatively scant 12 percent of Jewish heads of household were unemployed. "While the crisis struck a number of the members of our [family] circle," one New York Jew recalled, "its effect was not exactly catastrophic. Fine standards were considerably lowered, but they were not altogether subjected to hunger and privation." Nor was the effect of the Depression on Jewish criminality "exactly catastrophic"; from the outset of the Depression in 1930 to the outbreak of World War II, the percentage of New York Jewish prisoners remained roughly the same. No "sensational growth of crime, no 'crime wave'" characterized the years of economic hardship. Even at the worst moments, then, Jews did not turn to crime as a way out of their fiscal distress; alternative forms of livelihood on the one hand and strong cultural constraints against crime on the other were potent forces against its continued growth.[6]

The economic and social acculturation of New York Jews reduced the number of Jews turning to crime by providing them with the alternative of other, legitimate, opportunities, yet it also influenced Jewish crime rates in a second, rather subtle, fashion: the more acculturated the Jewish offender, the more sophisticated and less easily detected his offense. Thus, the Jew who committed a crime was less prone to arrest—detection—if his appearance was less distinctly "green"; one suspects the police would be more tempted to look the other way when they found an Americanized Jew breaking the law that made abortion, say, a crime than if the culprit had been an immigrant. By the same token, second-generation Jewish criminals probably knew enough about the American criminal justice system to concentrate on committing certain crimes (those with less risk of detection) and to avoid others. Even if caught, second-generation, acculturated Jews knew how "to work" with the system. By hiring clever legal talent to extricate them from their predicament, some Jews (we have no way of knowing just how many) were doubtless "deflected" from the courts. In a way, the decrease in Jewish criminality was probably more apparent than real.[7]

The efficacy of the postwar Jewish social service agencies in reducing the number of Jewish children coming before the courts is a good case in point. Organizations like the Jewish Protectory and Aid Society had undergone several changes during the interwar years, not the least of which was an increased emphasis on preventive care. Prior to World War I, the prevention of juvenile delinquency had been secondary to the JPAS's main activity of housing children committed by the Children's Court to the Hawthorne School or to the Cedar Knolls facility. After the war, largely in response to general changes in penology, preventive work replaced correctional work as the organization's main focus; commitments to Hawthorne became a "last resort." Housing over four hundred children prior to World War I, the Hawthorne School accommodated only 127 by 1930. The new orientation of the JPAS was reflected in the name it adopted in 1921, after several years of deliberation: the Jewish Board of Guardians. This new name symbolized the agency's shift in priorities: to act as a watchdog—a guardian—of Jewish communal interests rather than to serve as a "protectory" for those Jews already in trouble with the law. With a staff comprised largely of social workers (and correspondingly few volunteers), the Jewish Board of Guardians found "field work" to be its most effective remedy for juvenile delinquency. Going into the community, using the casework method, Jewish Board of Guardians (JBG) workers collected data about and interviewed those whom the public schools and the parents reported as disruptive. After ascertaining the social and psychological roots of the delinquent's behavior, JBG workers recommended family counseling or the participation in Big

Brothers' groups—anything but institutional care. "As a group," explained John Slawson, the JBG's executive director, "we take care of our behavior problems to a much greater extent than any other religious group by the case work method which implies non-court and non-institutional treatment." The gradual decrease in the number of Hawthorne's "boys" apparently reflected that policy.[8]

Whether artificial or real, whether measured in terms of actual arraignments or cases, Jewish criminal activity had declined substantially during the interwar years. In the long run, the reasons mattered little; what mattered was the decline per se. Eagerly, almost feverishly, the New York Jewish community of the interwar years monitored the decline. Keeping a close watch on the publications of the local and state courts and prisons, Jewish newspapers, whenever they could, seized the opportunity to broadcast news of the dip in Jewish criminal behavior. Time and again, the *American Hebrew* trotted out various statistics proving, happily, that the Jewish underworld was a thing of the past; hardly an issue of the *American Jewish Year Book* was published during the 1920s and 1930s without a reference to the Jews' underrepresentation among America's prison population. Though dry and colorless, these statistical enumerations proved what many Jews had passionately believed all along: that criminality had been a temporary form of backsliding, a result of the enervating and often confusing conditions of life in the New World. Vindicated and relieved by this turnabout in the collective fortunes of New York Jewry, the New York Jewish press widely publicized it. A defensive edge, however, was not altogether absent from the publication of crime statistics. While New York Jewry may have been fully aware of the decline in Jewish criminality, it worried lest others mistake the highly visible activities of a Rothstein, Lepke, or Murder Inc. as representative of a postwar class of Jewish criminals as large as its prewar predecessor and thus revive the notion of the Jew as criminal. Determined to prevent that association from getting off the ground, New York Jewish community leaders took the offensive by publishing statistics on Jewish criminal behavior. Statistical rebuttals had served the community well in the past; Jewish leaders hoped that they would continue to do so in the future—even if the need for such statistical arguments was less pressing.[9]

All these factors were present when, in 1921, the editors of the *American Hebrew* sought an interview with Richard Enright, the city's current police commissioner. In the interest of establishing publicly that Jews were, above all else, a law-abiding people and, perhaps less consciously, in the hope of replacing former Police Commissioner Bingham's unflattering remarks about the Jews with others far more congenial, the paper asked Enright "whether the Jew is actually a more flagrant violator of the law than his non-Jewish neighbor?" The police commissioner replied that as far as he could tell, Jews had an excellent record as law-abiding citizens and were to be commended on the success of their efforts in reducing Jewish crime. Jews, he noted, do not "figure to any great extent" in violent crimes and form "an insignificant part" of New York City's gangs. Enright also added that Jews were not reckless drivers because they were not given to intoxication. Pleased by the police official's comments, the Jewish press prominently displayed them and quoted at length from the interview. One suspects that, much as former Police Commissioner Bingham's remarks had once served as the benchmark of an earlier generation, Enright's comments were to serve as the benchmark of the current generation.[10]

A decade after the Enright interview, New York Jewry found further cause to celebrate its diminishing number of criminals. The occasion: the publication of an article entitled "Jews' War on Crime" in the popular *Outlook and Independent* magazine. Written by Ernest Coulter, a leading criminal justice authority and former clerk of the Children's Court, it was unstinting in its praise for New York Jewry's efforts at eliminating crime. Extolling the community's "silent but earnest and efficient campaign" to reduce Jewish criminality, Coulter observed that New Yorkers of all types were "rubbing their eyes at a tremendous social metamorphosis" as the number of Jewish malefactors rapidly declined over the years. The Jewish community's attempts at preventing the continued growth of its underworld, the court official added, have resulted in "amazing success." Greatly pleased by Coulter's remarks, the Jewish communal press widely reprinted them; the *American Hebrew* even went so far as to use the text of the *Outlook and Independent* article as the subject of several self-congratulatory editorials. Sensitive to innuendoes of Jewish wrongdoing, like those circulated by Henry Ford, and eager to dispel them, New York Jews were bolstered by Coulter's praise, coming as it did from an outsider. Heightening the community's pleasure in the Coulter article was the fact that its author had been among the *first* to decry publicly the outbreak of criminality among the Jews in the years preceding the

Great War. In a piece published in the *North American Review* earlier in the century, in 1904, the court clerk had baldly stated that New York's immigrant community, particularly its Jewish members, had greatly contributed to the city's juvenile delinquency problem. "Practically all of the material brought into the Children's Court," he had written, ". . . is a gift from Europe; . . . the vast majority of children in the Children's Court come from that one square mile area [the Lower East Side]." Now, several decades later, Coulter was reversing his original opinion of New York Jewry and publicly acknowledging that over the years it had been transformed. His article lent support to the community's own understanding of its history and, in turn, to its self-image. More important, by saying what he did Coulter underscored the substantial social changes wrought by the acculturation of New York Jews during the interwar years. "There are Jews in America," observed the *American Hebrew*, "who still recall with a shudder, the incident, almost a quarter of a century ago, when the then police commissioner Theodore A. Bingham informed Mayor McClellan that the Jews furnished more than fifty percent of the criminals of New York." Coulter's remarks, the paper went on to say, have demonstrated "to what a remarkable degree" crime has decreased among the Jews. "We can say that the scar left by Bingham is now ENTIRELY HEALED."[11]

With that metaphor in mind, the New York Jewish community of the interwar years reacted to any discussion of Jewish criminality with a marked absence of defensiveness. During the 1930s when the exploits of Jewish racketeers and of Murder Inc. made banner headlines in the city's press, it did not appear greatly disturbed by them, nor did its own newspapers treat these stories with the touchiness and discomfort one had come to expect. Though the Yiddish press scrupulously reported every detail of interwar Jewish criminal activity, from the improprieties in the kosher chicken industry to the murders committed by Abe Reles, accompanying editorials were few in number and mild, indeed cool, in tone. Prior to World War I, public discussions of Jewish criminality invariably sparked an internal review of the Jewish experience; the various elements of the community vied with one another in reciting their respective litanies of "*al chate*" (mea culpa) even as they jointly charged the outside world with anti-Semitism. Among second-generation New York Jews, though, the criminality of some of their coreligionists failed to occasion the outbursts to which an earlier generation had been so susceptible. The Yiddish newspapers, for example, closely followed the vagaries of Lepke's career for nearly a decade, yet at no time during that period did they issue broadsides against the racketeer or engage in any form of communal introspection. Editorials arguing that the New York Jewish community was responsible for creating a Lepke or that because of him the New York Jewish experience was less of a success than most Jews believed were conspicuously absent from the pages of the communal press throughout the 1920s and 1930s. Similarly, the exploits of Tootsie Herbert and his fellow "poultry czars" failed to touch off laments about the quality of Jewish life or about the participation of Jews in the criminal enterprise. At most, the press railed against the acquiescence of the *shochtim* to the Herberts' exactions. The religious press, like the *Jewish Forum*, were taken aback by the association of ritual slaughterers with unsavory characters like the Herberts. Racketeering in the kosher poultry industry, the monthly editorialized, "was bound to reflect on all of Jewry and to make it harder for the younger generation to maintain loyalty to Jewish tradition." The *Tog*, too, was disturbed by resigned acceptance by the *shochtim* of racketeering. Though not a religious paper as such, it was sensitive to the religious sensibilities of many of its readers and therefore chastised the ritual slaughterers for behaving in a manner inappropriate to their status as religious standard-bearers. "*K'lai Kodesh* [lit.: holy vessels or religious functionaries], the *shochtim*," argued the *Tog*, "are to conduct themselves in a certain, rigorous, fashion befitting their station." Racketeering in the kosher poultry industry, the paper seemed to suggest, occurred when the *shochtim* "forgot their worth and who they were." Yet, neither the sordid behavior of Lepke Buchalter nor that of Tootsie Herbert elicited wrenching sighs or worrisome expressions of doubt about the future of New York Jewish life.[12]

Even the brutal and shocking acts committed so casually by the members of Murder Inc.—crimes once denounced by the Jews as typically non-Jewish—failed to shake the community's equilibrium. The existence of Murder Inc. was, to be sure, an embarrassment, tarnishing the reputation of Brownsville and by extension, that of New York Jewry as a whole. "It is a great pity," said the *Tog*, "that Brownsville . . . which is known as the 'Jerusalem of New York' . . . should now be known as a nest of dangerous murder gangs. This gives Brownsville a bad name and . . . in turn the Jews a bad name as well."

Nevertheless, most New York Jews did not see the gang's existence as an indictment of or as cause for restructuring the social fabric of New York Jewish life. "Murder Inc.," one Yiddish newspaper commented pointedly, "is not a Jewish problem." Suggesting that New York Jews were in no way to feel responsible for the emergence of a group like Murder Inc., the paper dismissed it as an American product, the by-product of "American conditions, from American soil."[13]

New York Jews could well afford to be dispassionate and temperate in these discussions, for the numbers were on their side. Thanks to the constant policing of criminal justice records by the Jewish communal press and agencies like the American Jewish Committee, the community was kept abreast of the latest figures on Jewish criminal behavior; Jewish criminality, they knew, was noticeably on the decline and promised to decline even further. While the malefactions of Murder Inc. and other interwar Jewish criminals were unpleasant and somewhat embarrassing to a community which prided itself on its clean postwar, record, they in no way detracted from the overall picture; the statistics clearly revealed that the Jewish underworld lay at the very margins of New York Jewish life. Implying that the Brownsville gang was an anomaly, the *Tog* argued that criminality was not a "Jewish characteristic. . . . On the contrary [*punkt verkehrt*]: all statistics on American crime prove that Jews not only have a smaller proportion of criminals than their percentage of the population warrants but the quotient of Jewish criminals is also steadily declining. Despite the addition of these Brownsville criminals [to the roster of Jewish criminals]," the daily added, "the situation will continue as outlined."[14]

This decline in the number of Jewish criminals reinforced New York Jewry's growing sense of being, in Deborah Dash Moore's words, "at home" in America. While occasional outbursts of anti-Semitism and xenophobia marred the 1920s and 1930s, testing this sense of belongingness, New York Jews persisted in feeling very much a part of the American experience. The Jewish communal attitude toward crime in many ways reflects that interwar sense of rootedness. Earlier, the community's intense concern with its Jewish underworld was fed by anxiety that it would be used against them by nativists and anti-Semites. Such fears, though, were not so real to the postwar generation. Because of the victory of immigration restrictionists in imposing a ceiling on immigration, the relative merits of the Russian (and Italian) immigrants were no longer debated; for all intents and purposes, the alleged association between the foreign-born and crime was now a dead issue. By the same token, the criminality of the Jews figured hardly, if at all, in the anti-Semitic literature of the interwar years. Despite a recrudescence of anti-Jewish sentiment, most anti-Semites tended to focus on the Jews' seemingly superior economic status; organized crime was not an issue. "In New York City," writes Ronald Bayor, "ethnic conflict centered round the threat of economic or political competition." Admittedly, some Jews were disturbed lest Tom Dewey's energetic racket-busting kick up clouds of latent anti-Semitism. Dewey himself said that a group of prominent Jews, troubled by the frequency with which Jewish names appeared on the list of local racketeers sought by the special prosecutor, formed a citizens' group to demonstrate the moral probity of New York Jewry. "A number of Jewish citizens," he recalled, "were gravely concerned with the fact that a majority of these leading mobsters were Jewish . . . they wanted to have a citizens group with a Jewish chairman to sort of dramatize the fact that the Jewish community was on the side of good citizenship and law and order. . . ." Such a group, headed by Harry Guggenheim, was indeed formed; its overt purpose, though, was to give financial aid to those who had testified before Dewey and consequently lost their jobs. Yet most Jews, it seems, did not share Mr. Guggenheim's fears. Ever alert to the spectre of anti-Semitism, the Yiddish press, for example, failed to draw any connection between Dewey's racket-busting and anti-Semitism; not one editorial on Jewish racketeering even so much as hinted that the Special Prosecutor's crusade well served the cause of xenophobic or anti-Semitic Americans. Similarly, Dewey's Jewish assistants, as a group, recalled that few Jews to their knowledge actually feared that publicity surrounding Lepke or Tootsie or even Murder Inc. would engender hostility toward the community. Thus, Judge Charles Breitel commented that he "did not recall having heard anything [anti-Semitic slurs] though I would have been sensitive to them"; Victor Herwitz likewise remarked that he and his fellow Jewish lawyers on Dewey's staff "did not think prosecuting Lepke would cause anti-Semitism."[15]

As second-generation New York Jews found themselves more and more at ease within American society, they found the existence of a Jewish criminal element less threatening—less of a blow—to their collective self-esteem and sense of security. Then, as now, Jews were not (nor will they ever be) fully comfortable with their complement of wrong-doers; the pull of the Chosen People notion—whether in its traditional religious form or in its secularized version ("Jews don't have criminals")—is simply too strong. Yet over the years they had grown more relaxed, less disturbed about their quotient of criminals; their growing sense of security accommodated or allowed for some criminal coreligionists. The existence of a Jewish underworld, commented an astute Jewish writer in the 1920s, is "no longer received with that wide-eyed and staggering feeling of surprise and astonishment of the earlier days, but rather with a certain amount of complacent matter-of-factness and fatalism, though not with any less of reprobation. In brief, it is accepted now. . . ." The attitude of Dewey's Jewish staff members to Jewish criminality, once again, is a case in point. Largely second-generation Jews, many had grown up on and were familiar with the "Jewish street"; even those who had only a passing acquaintance with the Lower East Side or Brownsville defined themselves as "sensitive to their Judaism." At the same time, they were products of the Columbia and Harvard law schools and felt well-integrated into the mainstream of American life. Among this group, as several of its members later recalled, no one was shocked by the relative prominence of the Jewish racketeer, nor did anyone feel that the involvement of Jews with racketeering (or, for that matter, with any other crime) would cause anti-Semitism. As Jacob Grumet, then one of Dewey's trial lawyers, put it: "It was a fact of life that there were Jewish criminals; no one liked to see them but there they were."[16]

One cannot help but wonder to what extent the community's matter-of-fact acceptance of Jewish criminality was itself an index of acculturation: was it New York Jewry's sense that having a number of criminals was a part of the national experience; that it normalized their status as Americans? It is hard to say, since nothing in the public record conveyed such a message. All the same, it is worth noting that for some younger members of the New York Jewish community, Murder Inc. was a source of perverse pride. One former resident of East New York, then sixteen, remembers feeling, "Why should other groups have all the criminals; Jews need their fair share, too," while another Brooklyn inhabitant, an adolescent at the time, recalls being "secretly proud" that Jews were adept at using guns. Meyer Lansky, one of the post–World War II period's few leading Jewish underworld figures, relates in his memoirs that he became a criminal and often engaged in acts of violence in order to move into the mainstream of American life;

crime, as he saw it, normalized his status as an American. "When I was young," the gangster explained, "I thought Jews should be treated like other people. I remember that young soldier in Grodno [the Eastern European town where Lansky was born] who said Jews should stand up and fight. I guess you could say I've come a long way from Grodno . . . but I still believe him. I wouldn't have lived my life any other way."[17]

These sentiments notwithstanding, most interwar New York Jews had grown too emotionally distant from the Jewish criminal experience to pay it much mind; the community's growing social and economic acculturation militated against—instead of prolonging—the Jewish criminal enterprise. Furthermore, that emotional distance was abetted by the physical fabric of Jewish life during the interwar years. As the Jews of the 1920s and 1930s spread out beyond their original neighborhoods, peppering the geography of the city with dozens of new Jewish enclaves and rendering the division between "uptown" and "downtown" obsolete, the Jewish underworld was directly affected. Where, earlier, Jewish criminal activity had been highly visible—what with prostitutes plying their trade on Allen Street and strikebreakers loafing outside their Second Street headquarters—it had become far less visible to the Jewish residents of Borough Park or Pelham Parkway. But what of Murder Inc., whose members lived in Brownsville, the "East Side of Brooklyn"? That neighborhood was the proverbial exception that proved the rule: a lower-class, predominantly immigrant, neighborhood well into the interwar years, Brownsville straddled the residential fence, having more in common with the pre–World War I Jewish neighborhoods than it did with those of the interwar period. Fewer and fewer second-generation Jews lived in neighborhoods like Brownsville; Borough Park, Crotona Park, Pelham Parkway, the Grand Concourse, and Bensonhurst were more the norm. And in these middle-class, spanking-new areas with their tree-lined boulevards, solidly built housing, and American amenities, the underworld activities, if in fact they even existed, were not readily apparent. Somehow, a Jewish prostitute or a Jewish pimp did not fit in with the happily bourgeois mothers pushing their baby carriages on Ocean Parkway or with the dapper lawyers and garment manufacturers breaking bread at Garfield's, the "cafeteria of refinement."

Finally, there was little intrinsically "Jewish" about the crimes committed by the postwar Jewish criminal element. Unlike, say, Dopey

Benny or Big Jack Zelig, the Jewish criminals of the interwar years were truly "social isolates," living apart and earning their livelihood in ways altogether different from most second-generation Jews. Tied to a Jewish environment, the Jewish criminals of the prewar period had been "Jewish" in an economic, social, and cultural sense; their crimes reflected the particular qualities of the Jewish immigrant experience. Not so the postwar Jewish criminals. Whether symptom or cause, much of what passed for Jewish criminal activity during the interwar years took place in the impersonal, specialized arena of the marketplace, at some remove from the center of one's daily life. In its move from the distinctly Jewish neighborhoods of the prewar period where home and work were often soldered together to the blander, more anonymous, and highly specialized marketplace of the postwar era, the Jewish criminal element lost many of its salient characteristics. Describing the Jewish underworld and its participants of the interwar years, the *Tog* noted that with their fancy suits and smooth manners, the criminals resembled "lawyers or even professors." Furthermore, they no longer lived on Broome Street or haunted the cafés of Second Avenue; instead, Fifth Avenue and the cafés of Broadway were their milieu. To be sure, the growing independence of the postwar Jewish criminal element from its anchor, the larger Jewish community, was not a linear process in which one stage of development unfolded smoothly from another. It was more checkered: Rothstein and Murder Inc., for example, represented one stage; Jewish racketeers like Lepke another. In the first instance, both Rothstein and Murder Inc. transcended the limits of the New York Jewish community. Little of their income or power was derived from it; New York Jewish life was incidental to their activities. In the second instance, Jewish racketeers derived virtually all of their income and power by maintaining a viselike grip on much of New York Jewish life; the community was central to their activities. In the long run, though, the subsequent development of the underworld owed far more to Rothstein and Murder Inc. than to Lepke.[18]

Ultimately, as both the nature and the location of the Jewish criminal experience became less demonstrably Jewish, it aroused fewer fears and spawned less anxiety. New York Jewry's concern with instances of wrongdoing, previously fueled by nativism and anti-Semitism, lessened. That is not to say that the interwar years were free of tensions; after all, this was the period during which Henry Ford was loudly fulminating against America's Jews and thousands of German Jews, victims of Hitler's anti-Semitic activities, were fleeing to the United States. Still, New York Jews in no way felt that the existence of a Jewish underworld challenged their stake in American society. Where once they had regarded the Jewish underworld as an "extraordinary development," calling into question the viability of the American Jewish experience, they now regarded it as "something inherent . . . in this land of the free," arousing little alarm.[19]

Appendix:
A Note on the Sources
Used in This Study

The quantitative data used in this study were taken from the records of the New York City criminal courts and the New York County District Attorney's office. Until quite recently the lowest rung in New York's multi-tiered criminal justice system was the Magistrates Court. Established in the mid-nineteenth century and known at that time as the Police Court, it functioned as the court of first instance. A person arrested for committing any offense whatsoever would be brought first to the local police station, where his name and the charge would be recorded. After this preliminary booking, he would be taken to the Magistrates Court in his neighborhood; in New York County there were at least nine local Magistrates Courts. The magistrate would then determine the category into which the alleged offense fell—whether felony, misdemeanor, or a minor offense—and once that was ascertained, decide upon an appropriate judicial course of action. Misdemeanor cases were tried in the Court of Special Sessions, while the Magistrates Court had summary jurisdiction over instances of vagrancy, disorderly conduct, violations of the Sunday Blue Laws and of the sanitary and corporation ordinances. Felony cases were brought to the attention of the district attorney, who in turn prepared them for a grand jury hearing. If the grand jury saw fit to indict the defendant, his case would be tried in the Court of General Sessions.

Most of the statistical material used in this study is based on an examination of the docket books, case files, and pedigree sheets of those persons arrested for committing a felony in New York County and the docket books of the United States Attorney's Office for the Southern District. Like the manuscript census sheets, these records contain information in an unsummarized form. The docket books of the New York County District Attorney's office are ledger books in which the clerks of that office recorded the first encounter between the district attorney and a person charged with committing a felony. In them one finds the name, age, sex, and address of the several thousands of persons arrested annually for having allegedly committed a felony; their specific offense; the legal particulars of the case—when brought before the grand jury, the latter's decision—and other pertinent judicial details.

Each person charged with committing a felony was represented as well by a case file. A record of the grand jury's preliminary deliberations, this

173

file not only summarizes the judicial particulars of each case but also contains additional biographical information about the defendant such as his nationality, place of birth, occupation and, if an immigrant, length of residence in the United States. Sometimes, too, the case file also holds the records of the D.A.'s investigations. Thus, the case file documenting the indictment of racketeer Lepke Buchalter for extortion in the garment industry is replete with accounts of Thomas Dewey's inquiries into racketeering in the garment industry as a whole, while the case file on Abe Reles, Murder Inc. gunman, is full of material on the history and personalities of other gang members. Finally, the social characteristics of persons convicted of committing a felony were enumerated on a pedigree sheet. The clerks of the D.A.'s office recorded in ledgerlike fashion a wide range of biographical information about each convict, from his marital status to degree of literacy, drinking habits, and occupation. Taken together, the docket books, case files, and pedigree sheets represent a dossier on every individual charged with committing a felony in New York County between 1900 and 1940.

Accordingly, a sample of names from the D.A.'s docket books was drawn: after consulting with a variety of sociologists and statisticians it was decided to take one out of every twentieth name for every third year from 1900 through 1939 to create a (presumably bias-free) sample population of 1,905 persons. Each case was then followed through the various documentary levels of the criminal justice system: from the first encounter between D.A. and arrestee to the records of the grand jury hearing to the final disposition of the case. The data were then placed in machine-readable form and a series of calculations performed on them by means of a computer language known as SPSS.

Supplementing the unpublished materials are the published records of the New York City police department, the District Attorney's office, the New York State Department of Corrections and most importantly, the annual reports of the Magistrates Courts. These reports have material, in tabular form, on the nativity, age, sex, and occupation of all persons brought before the various judicial bodies in New York. They are statistical summations of the information contained in the docket books, case files, and pedigree sheets of the various criminal courts. Like census enumerations, the published materials are numeral, aggregative, and anonymous; they present an overall composite picture of criminal activity in New York City. From them one is able to ascertain the total number of persons arrested, tried, and convicted in New York and for what offenses.

Although varied and rich, these statistical materials are not without their shortcomings. The most obvious limitation in working with crime statistics is that all too often they do not reflect the reality of criminal activity so much as the internal workings of the police department or some other intervening variable. It is also possible that reliance on criminal court records distorts the reality of the criminal enterprise. In what has become a tenet of criminology, Thorsten Sellin has argued that crime records become less reliable the further they are from the original criminal act. Does the use of material two or possibly even three stops removed from the initial criminal act call the conclusions of this study into question? In this case at least, it seems that greater distance is not a liability. First, the closest records—

those containing reports of crimes known to the police—were not routinely used by the police until well into the 1930s. And even if they had been available earlier, they would have been of scant value since they say nothing about the *criminal*, only about the incidence of crime. Second, the next set of papers—those compiling police arrests—were unavailable; police historians in New York claim, moreover, that their office has only the barest of files prior to the 1940s. Yet this is not as grave a loss as it may first seem since all persons arrested were brought to the Magistrates Court for preliminary hearings; the census taken at step three is not more selective than that taken at step two. Records of the Magistrates Court also provide information which the station house could not provide, such as the judicial classification and disposition of each case.

It is also worth mentioning that sloppiness and inconsistency were common to both the clerks of the Magistrates Court and the District Attorney's office; accurate recordkeeping, it seems, was just not their suit. In some instances, clerks of the Magistrates Court varied their method of tabulating court business from one year to the next while at other times the figures published in the court's annual reports do not add up. Another familiar defect of the published annual reports is their failure to correlate different sets of statistics with one another. The clerks of the Magistrates Court would compile detailed tables on the age and sex of those brought before the court and even more detailed tables on the occupation of those arrested, but made no attempt to conjoin the two tables. The clerks of the D.A.'s office were also inefficient: missing case files or pedigree sheets were all too common as was the incomplete registration of data (missing answers to the D.A.'s query about length of residence was the most noticeable casualty of sloppy recordkeeping).

Nevertheless, for all their shortcomings, the published and unpublished records of the New York City criminal justice system enable the historian to describe and to analyze the history of crime in the nation's largest city over a forty-year period. In a word, this material allows the student of crime to take a fresh look at the history of the New York underworld "from the bottom up"—to explore the history of the *individual* criminal—and in the process to examine the underside of the New York Jewish experience.

Most of the qualitative sources used and consulted in examining the attitude of New York Jewry to crime are cited directly in the footnotes. What follows is a listing of those materials essential to any study of New York Jews and crime. Heading the list is the Jewish press. Both Anglo-Jewish newspapers like the *American Hebrew* and Yiddish ones like the *Jewish Daily Forward* or the *Tog* are indispensable. Useful too were such publications as *Jewish Charity*, *Jewish Charities*, the *Proceedings of the National Conference of Jewish Charities*, and the annual reports of the Jewish Board of Guardians, the Jewish Protectory and Aid Society, the National Conference of Jewish Women, and the United Hebrew Charities. Finally, the Magnes Archives of the Central Archives for the History of the Jewish People, containing what is perhaps the single largest collection of documents—including Abe Shoenfeld's unparalleled accounts—on the prewar Jewish underworld, is an invaluable source.

Notes

ABBREVIATIONS USED IN THE NOTES

AH   *American Hebrew*
AJYB   *American Jewish Year Book*
CCAR   Central Conference of American Rabbis
FR   *Federation Review*
HS   *Hebrew Standard*
JBG   Jewish Board of Guardians
JDB   *Jewish Daily Bulletin*
JDF   *Jewish Daily Forward*
JM   *Jewish Messenger*
JPAS   Jewish Protectory and Aid Society
JT   *Judisches Tageblatt*
MA   Magnes Archives
MJ   *Morgen Journal*
NYT   *New York Times*
W   *Wahrheit*

1. INTRODUCTION

1. A. E. Costello, *Our Police Protectors* (New York, 1885), pp. 237, 324; "The Jews as Citizens," *Washington Sentinel*, May 21, 1854, quoted in Morris Schappes, ed., *A Documentary History of the Jews in the United States, 1654–1875*, 3rd ed. (New York, 1971), p. 343; "The Jew as a Citizen," *Evening Telegram* (Philadelphia), October 19, 1872, quoted in Schappes, p. 558; "The Jews in New York," *Century*, Vol. 43 (January 1892):558; Michael Dobkowski, *The Tarnished Dream: The Basis of American Anti-Semitism* (Westport, 1979), p. 45. See also I. Markens, *The Hebrews in America* (New York, 1888), p. 1.

2. "The Jews as Citizens"; Frederick A. Bushee, "Ethnic Factors in the Population of Boston," *Publications*, American Economic Association, Vol. 4, Third Series (1903):110.

3. AH, April 27, 1900; AH, June 16, 1916; JM, September 9, 1887; AH, September 25, 1908. Published nineteenth-century crime statistics bear out the Jewish community's opinion of itself. In contrast to the frequently arrested Irish, Jews appeared so rarely that it was not until the end of the

177

century that "Hebrews" appeared as a distinct category. See for example *Annual Report of the Secretary of State on the Criminal Statistics of the State of New York* (Albany, 1860–1890). German Jews arrested for an infraction of the law were defined as German, thus making it extremely difficult to ascertain just how many of them were involved in crime; *Jewish Charities*, Vol. 6, No. 5 (December 1915):71.

4. John Higham, *Strangers in the Land: Patterns of American Nativism, 1860–1925* (New Brunswick, 1955); Barbara Miller Solomon, *Ancestors and Immigrants: A Changing New England Tradition* (Chicago, 1966); Allen Steinberg, "A History of Immigration and Crime," *Select Commission on Immigration and Refugee Policy* (Washington, D.C., 1981); F. W. Dewes, "Delinquent, Defective and Dependent Classes in the United States," *Outlook*, Vol. 53 (1896):430.

5. Donald R. Taft, "Does Immigration Increase Crime," *Social Forces*, Vol. 12 (1933):70; "Immigration and Crime," Report of Committee G of the American Institute of Criminal Law and Criminology, *Journal of the American Institute of Criminal Law and Criminology*, Vol. 6 (1915–16): 522–32; E. A. Ross, *The Old World in the New* (New York, 1914), pp. 150, 149, 154, 106; Higham, p. 39; Steinberg, pp. 66, 71–74.

6. U.S. Immigration Commission, *Immigration and Crime* (Washington, D.C., 1911), p. 1; Oscar Handlin, *Race and Nationality in American Life* (Boston, 1948), pp. 93–138.

7. *Report and Proceedings of the Senate Committee Appointed to Investigate the Police Department of the City of New York* (Albany, 1895), 5 vol. See for example Vol. 2, pp. 1258–59; Vol. 3, pp. 2968–69; 2972, 2975, 2989, 3008–13.

8. *Report of the Special Committee of the Assembly Appointed to Investigate the Public Offices and Departments of the City of New York and the Counties Therein Included* (Albany, 1900). See for example Vol. 1, pp. 1895, 2029; Frank Moss, *The American Metropolis* (New York, 1897), Vol. 3, ch. 9, especially pp. 200–203, 236–37; 170, 161 (emphasis mine).

9. JM, June 15, 29, 1894; Felix Adler, quoted in NYT, April 23, 1900; AH, April 27, 1900; AH, May 3, 1889; Rudolph Glanz, *Geschichte de niederen judisches Volkes in Deutschland* (New York, 1968); Todd Endelman, *The Jews of Georgian England, 1714–1830* (Philadelphia, 1979), ch. 6; Lulla Rosenfeld, *Bright Star of Exile: Jacob Adler and the Yiddish Theatre* (New York, 1977), pp. 4, 13–14.

10. Adolph Radin, *Aserai Oni Ve Barzel* (New York, 1893), pp. 16–17; JM, January 21, 23, 1891; February 16, 1893. So troubled was the young chaplain by the possibility of Jewish prisoners' converting to Christianity that he published a volume in 1893, first in Hebrew and later in Yiddish, to underscore the importance of missionary work among Jewish prisoners. *Aserai Oni Ve Barzel* (Prisoners of Poverty and Iron) was that work. A copy is in the New York Public Library.

11. NYT, March 22, 1893; *First Annual Report of the Society to Aid the Jewish Prisoner* (1896), pp. 5, 17. What follows is drawn from the Annual Reports and the Minute Books of the Society to Aid the Jewish Prisoner (SAJP). Both sources are currently located in the library of the Jewish Board of Children and Family Services, New York; *Annual Report of the New York State Superintendent of State Prisons* (Albany, 1895).

12. *Second Annual Report, SAJP* (1897), p. 11; Minutes of the SAJP, February 1903; December 1904.

13. AH, July 2, 1897; AH, March 22, 1897; *First Annual Report, SAJP* (1896), p. 5.

14. AH, December 28, 1899; Abe Shoenfeld to Judah Magnes, January 5, 1915, p. 6, MA 1768; Harry Newberger to Judah Magnes, April 7, 1916, p. 8, MA 1774.

15. Ben Halpern, "America Is Different" in Marshall Sklare, ed., *The Jews: Social Patterns of an American Group* (Glencoe, 1958), pp. 23–29. For a concise summary of the Emancipation, see Ismar Schorsch, *Jewish Reactions to German Anti-Semitism* (New York, 1972), Introduction; and Jacob Katz, *Out of the Ghetto* (Cambridge, 1973).

2. "A SPLENDID INSTITUTION"

1. HS, May 17, 1907; AH, May 10, 1907.

2. HS, May 17, 1907; AH, May 10, 1907; JM, February 20, 1891; AH, November 6, 1884; JM, February 15, 1884; Louis Marshall, quoted in AH, July 31, 1903; *Israelite Alliance Review*, Vol. 1, No. 4 (January 1905). See also AH, March 8, 1901; April 3, 1903; "The Big Brother Movement," *Jewish Charities*, Vol. 5, No. 7 (February 1915):147.

3. David Blaustein, "Preventive Work on the East Side," *Proceedings*, National Conference of Jewish Charities (1904), p. 116; AH, April 10, 1903; AH, February 4, 1905; *54th Annual Report of the New York Juvenile Asylum* (1905), p. 56; *81st Annual Report of the House of Refuge* (1905), p. 34; AH, April 25, 1902; March 6, 1903. The published annual reports of the New York Children's Court are useful for ascertaining the general and aggregate dimensions of juvenile delinquency; they are, however, less helpful than one might hope in ascertaining the particular ethnic dimensions of the phenomenon. For one thing, the religion of those brought before the court was not asked, thus making it extremely difficult to pinpoint the number of youthful Jewish offenders. Fortunately, the nationality of the offenders is recorded, thus enabling one to tabulate how many children of Russian birth appeared before the court. Yet even here, there are difficulties in interpreting the data. Clerks of the Children's Court failed to organize the material in a uniform manner: in some years, the nationality of those arraigned is recorded, in other years, the nationality of those convicted. Thus, for 1902 and 1903, one finds that 7.8% and 7.2% respectively of those "Held for Trial and Convicted" in the Children's Court were Russian-born. For the period 1904–1910, though, the clerks provided ethnic data only for those arraigned: during those years, Russian-born children accounted for anywhere between 4.8% and 7.8% of all children arraigned in the Children's Court. See *Annual Report of the Children's Court, New York* (1902–1910). Missing from these reports is any sense of how many native-born Jewish youngsters of Russian-born parents were either arraigned or convicted.

From other sources, however, it seems that Jewish youth accounted for at least one-quarter, and occasionally for as much as one-third, of the city's youthful offenders. Writing in the *American Hebrew* in 1903, for example, New York Attorney General Julius Mayer estimated that Jewish delinquents comprised between 25 and 27% of all those brought before the Children's Court; several years later Boris Bogen observed that Jewish delinquents comprised approximately one-third of all New York youthful offenders. AH, August 7, 1903; Julius Mayer, "The Problem of the Delinquent Child," *Jewish Charity*, Vol. 3, No. 4 (January 1904):89; Boris Bogen, "The Jewish Boy Criminal," *Jewish Charity*, Vol. 4, No. 1 (January 1905):126.

4. HS, May 17, 1907; AH, May 10, 1907. There is also reason to suspect that New York Jewry was shamed into building its own correctional facility; its absence amidst a welter of Jewish communal organizations ranging from orphan asylums to vocational schools was conspicuous, and, to some civic officials, scandalous. In April 1899, John Goff, a leading New York City judge, censured the SAJP board for its failure to build a Jewish reformatory. "The time is fast approaching," he noted, "when the generous hearts of the Jewish race in this city must recognize the necessity of providing some home for the youth that goes astray." In succeeding years officials of the Children's Court repeatedly chided the Jewish community for its lack of a Jewish correctional facility, calling it an "embarrassment." (One Jewish periodical later recalled that this criticism was "humiliating.") SAJP Minute Books, April 25, 1899; *4th Annual Report, SAJP* (1899), pp. 47–48; *Annual Report of the Children's Court, First Division* (1905), p. 9; *Annual Report of the Children's Court . . .* (1906), p. 11; *Annual Report of the Children's Court . . .* (1907), p. 17; *Federation Review*, Vol. 1, No. 4 (January 1905):3.

5. The following descriptions of the Hawthorne School are drawn from the HS, May 17, 1907; AH, May 10, 1907; AH, October 25, 1907; AH, June 5, 1908; *Annual Reports of the JPAS*, 1908–1912, especially *Third Annual Report, JPAS* (1910), p. 12; AH, February 12, 1904. For Hawthorne's similarities with other progressive correctional facilities, see David J. Rothman, *Conscience and Convenience: The Asylum and Its Alternatives in Progressive America* (Boston, 1980), ch. 8.

6. Mark Haller, *Eugenics: Hereditarian Attitudes in American Thought* (New Brunswick, 1963); Kenneth Ludmerer, *Genetics and American Thought* (Baltimore, 1972); Anthony Platt, *The Child Savers: The Invention of Delinquency* (Chicago, 1969); Christopher Hibbert, *The Roots of Evil* (Boston, 1963); Leon Radzinowicz, *Ideology and Crime* (New York, 1966); Rothman, ch. 8.

7. AH, October 2, 1908; Bogen, "The Jewish Boy Criminal," p. 126; Jacob A. Riis, "The Jews of New York," *American Review of Reviews*, Vol. 13 (1896):62; Charles Bernheimer, "The Immigrant Youth," *Jewish Charity*, Vol. 4, No. 7 (April 1905):202; Charles Bernheimer, *The Russian Jew in the United States* (Philadelphia, 1905), p. 73; AH, March 6, 1903; July 31, 1903.

8. Bernheimer, "The Immigrant Youth," p. 202; Lee K. Frankel, "The Problem of Dependent and Delinquent Jewish Children," *Jewish Charity*, Vol. 4, No. 2 (November 1904):31–33; "Vice Report," November 14, 1913, MA 1765, pp. 5–6.

9. Rabbi Samuel Koch, "The Immigrant and Crime in America with Special Reference to the Jews," *Proceedings*, American Prison Association (1909), p. 174; AH, May 10, 1907.

10. Bernheimer, *The Russian Jew in the United States*, p. 73; Morris

Raphael Cohen, *A Dreamer's Journey* (Boston, 1949), pp. 98–99; Rothman, *Conscience and Convenience*, pp. 52–53; Bernheimer, "The Immigrant Youth," p. 202; AH, September 19, 1913.

11. *First Annual Report, JPAS* (1908), p. 12; AH, October 25, 1907; Rothman, *Conscience and Convenience*, p. 264; AH, June 5, 1908; *First Annual Report, JPAS* (1908), p. 21; HS, May 17, 1907.

12. AH, April 3, 1903; Louis Marshall, quoted in AH, July 31, 1903; May 10, 1907; *Third Annual Report, JPAS* (1910), p. 35; AH, October 25, 1907.

13. *First Annual Report, JPAS* (1908), p. 12; *Second Annual Report, JPAS* (1909), p. 10; AH, June 5, 1908; May 17, 1907; HS, May 17, 1907. If Hawthorne's statistics are to be believed, the institution had an especially low rate of recidivism. Between 1908 and 1920, only 232 out of 2,089 boys had been recommitted to Hawthorne or to another institution. "In proportion to their numbers," Klein proudly noted, "there are fewer of our graduates in the penitentiaries and state prisons than are reported from any other reform school." See *Fourteenth Annual Report, JPAS* (1920), p. 11.

Several years after the Hawthorne School opened, its Board of Managers observed that "the same condition exists as to girls as existed in regard to boys before the building of the school at Hawthorne." Convening a meeting of leading Jewish women, among them Mrs. Louis Marshall, Mrs. Madeleine Borg, and Julia Richman, the Jewish Protectory and Aid Society decided to form a "Girl's Branch." Beginning slowly, the Girl's Branch first hired a probation officer to oversee the activities of Jewish girls under 16 years of age who had been placed on probation. It then secured a temporary home in Tuckahoe, New York, for rehabilitating a limited number of seemingly hardened female delinquents. In 1917 it completed the building of a permanent facility known, poetically enough, as Cedar Knolls. Located on the campus of the Hawthorne School, this facility attempted to do for the youthful female offender what the Hawthorne School did for her male counterpart. See for example *Fourth Annual Report, JPAS* (1910), p. 18; *Fifth Annual Report, JPAS* (1911), p. 12; *Seventh Annual Report, JPAS* (1914), pp. 16, 64.

3. THE LOWER EAST SIDE

1. *Second Annual Report, JPAS* (1909), p. 9; *Third Annual Report, JPAS* (1910), p. 30; *Federation Review*, Vol. 2, No. 8 (July 1908):16; Theodore A. Bingham, "Foreign Criminals in New York," *North American Review*, Vol. 187 (September 1908):383–94.

2. Bingham, pp. 383, 384, 395.

3. William McAdoo, *Guarding a Great City* (New York, 1906), pp. 146, 143, 145, 156; Hutchins Hapgood, "The Earnestness That Wins Wealth," *World's Work*, Vol. 6 (May 1903):3463–64; George Kibbe Turner, "Tammany's Control of New York by Professional Criminals," *McClure's Magazine*, Vol. 33, No. 2 (June 1909):122; "Vice Report," November 14, 1913, MA 1765; AH, June 19, 1913; "The Public Dance Halls of the Lower East Side," *15th Annual Report, University Settlement Society* (1901), p. 31.

4. Stories No. 5, 6, 53, 197. MA 1779–1793 contains 1,900 case histories or stories of Jewish criminals covering the period 1912–17; "Vice Report," p. 17; Jonah J. Goldstein Oral History Interview, American Jewish Committee, p. 6.

5. Eric Monkonnen, *The Dangerous Class: Crime and Poverty in Columbus, Ohio, 1860–1885* (Cambridge, Mass., 1975), p. 79; Stories No. 14, 113; Marcella Tow, "The Neighborhood Druggist," *Commentary*, Vol. 3, No. 2 (February 1947):168; "Table of Contents—Glossary, November 19, 1917," pp. 15–18, MA 1779; Stories No. 4, 2.

6. "Influences in Street Life," *14th Annual Report, University Settlement Society* (1900), p. 32; Bernheimer, "The Immigrant Youth," *Jewish Charity*, Vol. 4, No. 7 (April 1905):201; Irving Howe, *World of Our Fathers* (New York, 1976), p. 264; Samuel Chotzinoff, *A Lost Paradise* (New York, 1955), p. 85; Turner, pp. 122–23; *Tog*, May 15, 1915; Abe Shoenfeld, Oral History Interview, American Jewish Committee, p. 132; AH, August 8, 1913; Mandel quoted in *Report and Proceedings of the Senate Committee Appointed to Investigate the Police Department of the City of New York* (Albany, 1895), Vol. 3, p. 2975.

7. "A Study of the East Side Courts," *Yearbook, University Settlement Society* (1900), p. 25; Raymond Moley, *Tribunes of the People* (New York, 1932); Mary Roberts Smith, "The Social Aspect of New York Police Courts," *American Journal of Sociology*, Vol. 5, No. 2 (September 1899):154.

8. Statistics taken from the *Annual Report, Board of City Magistrates, First Division*, 1900–1914.

9. "A Study of the East Side Courts," pp. 25–26; 28–29; State of New York, *Report of the Commission of Immigration* (Albany, 1909), pp. 63–64; *Annual Report, Board of City Magistrates, First Division* (1908), p. 43.

10. *Annual Report, Superintendent of New York State Prisons* (1903), pp. 14–15; Belle Israels, "Crime among Jews," *Charities*, Vol. 20 (1908):702; Michael M. Davis, *Immigrant Health and the Community* (New York, 1921), p. 86.

11. Ray Allen Billington, *The Protestant Crusade* (Chicago, 1938), p. 339; "Report of the Legal Aid Bureau," *Yearbook, University Settlement Society* (1901), p. 59; McAdoo, pp. 160–61; Lincoln Steffens, *The Autobiography of Lincoln Steffens* (New York, 1931), p. 206; AH, February 13, 1903; September 27, 1907; Marcus Ravage, *An American in the Making* (New York, 1917), p. 90; Howe, p. 124.

12. *New York State Immigration Commission*, p. 54; "Vice Report," p. 51; Samuel Ornitz, *Haunch, Paunch and Jowl* (Garden City, 1923), pp. 84–85, 206.

13. Sample taken from the docket books of the New York County District Attorney's office, 1900–1915. For a full description of the D.A.'s collection and the methodology used in drawing a sample, see Appendix A; Cities Census Committee, ed. Walter Laidlaw. *Population of the City of New York, 1890–1930* (New York, 1932), p. 275.

14. Joseph Reid, "Because You Are a Jew," *Independent*, Vol. 65 (November 26, 1908):1214; McAdoo, pp. 156–57, 148, 155; Bingham, p. 385; E. A. Ross, *The Old World in the New* (New York, 1914), p. 155; quoted in Reid, p. 1214. Running through each of these comments was a kind of generalized distaste for the types of crimes Jews committed. Even in their criminality, Bingham et al. seemed to say, the Jews were deviant: not for them the heroic crimes of derring-do but the passionless, cerebral ones.

15. Harry Newberger to Judah Magnes, p. 1; D.A. docket sample. For

more details on the ethnic breakdown of crime in New York County see my "Dark Shadows: New York Jews and Crime, 1900–1940" (Ph.D. diss., Columbia University, 1981), ch. 2, especially p. 123.

16. Thomas Kessner, *The Golden Door: Italian and Jewish Immigrant Mobility in New York City, 1880–1915* (New York, 1977), p. 63; Howe, pp. 154–59; McAdoo, p. 156; D.A. Docket Numbers 25690, 27045 (1900); 74250 (1909); AH, July 3, 1908.

17. D.A. Docket Number 72229 (1909); George Walling, *Recollections of a New York Chief of Police* (New York, 1887), pp. 279–91, especially p. 291; Moss, p. 209; William McAdoo, "The East Side as a Police Problem," *Harper's Weekly*, Vol. 50 (May 5, 1906):641.

18. NYT, Index, 1875–1899; *Puck*, Vol. 48, No. 1239 (December 5, 1900):6; *Puck*, Vol. 36, No. 925 (November 28, 1894):275; JM, March 14, 1890; March 27, 1891 (my emphasis); Edward Steiner, "The Russian and Polish Jew in America," *Outlook*, Vol. 72, No. 9 (November 1902):539; Ruth Rosen, ed., *The Maimie Papers* (Old Westbury, N.Y., 1977), p. 202.

19. NYT, February 13, 1879; JM, January 31, 1879.

20. NYT, June 1, 5, 6; December 18, 24, 29, 30, 1895; "The Epidemic of Incendiarism," *Leslie's Illustrated Weekly*, Vol. 84, No. 2162 (February 18, 1897):102–103; Moss, pp. 192–196.

21. NYT Index, 1900–1910; NYT, January 1, 11, 12, 13, 17–21, 1913; February 20, 1913.

22. Story Number 40; Harry Newberger to Judah Magnes, November 11, 1913, MA 1765; "In the Matter of the Application of Max Swersky for a Commutation of Sentence," MA 1774; NYT, January 29, February 5, 16, 20, 24, March 16, 25, May 17, August 24, 1913.

23. "In the Matter . . . ," p. 5.

24. Harry Newberger to Judah Magnes, November 11, 1913; Morse Frankel to Jonah J. Goldstein, September 11, 1913, MA 1774; William Gaynor to Morse Frankel, April 4, 1913, Gaynor Papers, Location 103, New York City Municipal Archives; New York City District Attorney Letterbooks, 1912–1913, New York City Municipal Archives.

25. Story Number 2; "Vice Report," p. 25; Story Number 112; Howe, pp. 256–59, especially p. 258; "Influences in Street Life," pp. 30–31; "Vice Report," pp. 5–6; *Tog*, May 15, 1915; JM, May 1, 15, 1885; *New York Society for the Prevention of Cruelty to Children, 16th Annual Report* (1890), p. 23; *Jewish Charity*, Vol. 3, No. 6 (March 1904).

26. Frank Marshall White, "New York's Ten Thousand Thieves," *Harper's Weekly*, Vol. 50 (December 29, 1906):1892–93; McAdoo, *Guarding a Great City*, pp. 129, 157; Ernest Coulter, "Alien Colonies and Children's Court," *North American Review*, Vol. 179 (November 1904):731–40.

27. Albert Fried, *The Rise and Fall of the Jewish Gangster in America* (New York, 1980), p. 26; James Reynolds quoted in *Federation Review*, Vol. 2, No. 6 (May 1908):15; *Wahrheit*, August 1, 1912; AH November 29, 1912; Mark Zborowski and Elizabeth Herzog, *Life Is with People: The Culture of the Shtetl* (New York, 1952), pp. 149, 340–41, 357 (my emphasis); AH, July 3, 1908.

28. McAdoo, *Guarding a Great City*, pp. 148, 155; Ruppin, quoted in Maurice Fishberg, *The Jews: A Study of Race and Environment* (New York, 1911), p. 416.

29. *The Reminiscences of Jonah J. Goldstein* (1966), pp. 589–90, in the Oral History Collection of Columbia University; Story Number 14; NYT, October 6, 1912; Andy Logan, *Against the Evidence: The Becker-Rosenthal Affair* (New York, 1970), pp. 171–72.

30. Egal Feldman, "Prostitution, the Alien Woman and the Progressive Imagination, 1900–1915," *American Quarterly*, Vol. 19 (Summer 1967):192; George Kibbe Turner, pp. 117–134, especially p. 121; Ruth Rosen, *The Lost Sisterhood: Prostitution in America, 1900–1918* (Baltimore, 1982).

31. *Yearbook, University Settlement Society* (1899), p. 37; Harry Newberger to Judah Magnes, April 7, 1916, p. 6; New York State, *Report of the Special Committee of the Assembly Appointed to Investigate the Public Offices and Departments of the City of New York and the Counties Therein Included* (Albany, 1900), Vol. 2, p. 2028; AH, March 8, 1929; Benjamin Antin, *Gentleman from the Twenty Second* (New York, 1927), p. 30; "Vice Report," pp. 17–19; Story Number 6.

32. Story Number 113; Joseph E. Corrigan, "Magnates of Crime," *McClure's Magazine*, Vol. XL, No. 1 (November 1912):5.

33. United States Immigration Commission, *The Importation and Harboring of Women for Immoral Purposes* (Washington, D.C., 1911), pp. 62–63; Katherine Bement Davis, "A Study of Prostitutes Committed from New York City to the State Reformatory at Bedford Hills," in George Kneeland, *Commercialized Prostitution in New York City* (New York, 1917), pp. 173–262; Reports of the Probation Committee of the Sisterhood of the Spanish and Portuguese Synagogue, 1915–1916, Alice Davis Menken Papers, American Jewish Historical Society.

Rabbi Stephen S. Wise's response to the issue of just how many Jewish women were engaged in prostitution was typical of that of the Jewish community at large: ". . . I have no sympathy with such Jews as urge that the percentage of Jewish women in the ranks of prostitutes is not proportionate to the magnitude of the Jewish population of our State," he wrote. "However few Jewish women there are in the prostitution traffic, there are too many. . . ." Quoted in *Third Annual Report, New York Probation and Protective Association* (1911), p. 23.

Despite Rabbi Wise's proclaimed lack of interest in the actual size of the Jewish prostitute population, the fact remains that it is most difficult to ascertain accurately the extent of Jewish prostitution. Because the social evil was a subject so enveloped by sensationalism, disentangling fact from fiction poses many problems. Indeed, one historian has recently noted that "most students of the subject hesitate to rely on either contemporary estimates of the number of prostitutes or police statistics." Prior to the establishment of the Women's Night Court in 1910, the court where most prostitution offenders were tried, women arrested on charges of soliciting were brought before the Magistrates Court or the Court of Special Sessions and tried on a variety of charges ranging from violation of the Tenement House Act to incorrigibility. Watching local magistrates try prostitution cases, one contemporary remarked facetiously that the judges "acted as Supreme Court judges would in trying anti-trust cases." Furthermore, as the records of prostitution-related trials are scattered among so many different courts and as the methods of tabulating court data varied from one judicial body to another, determining the exact number of women arraigned as prostitutes is riddled with difficulty.

Nevertheless, the most recent study of prostitution in this country, Ruth Rosen's evocative *The Lost Sisterhood,* states that "Jews . . . were under-represented in the foreign-born prostitute population." When compared with their percentage of the population, Russian Jewish women had a very low index of representation of .28; an index of one would indicate proportional representation. Just how many Jewish women of Russian origins (that is, first-generation American-Jewish women of Russian parentage) became prostitutes though, remains unclear. See Estelle Freedman, "Their Sister's Keepers: The Origins of Female Corrections in America" (Ph.D. diss., Columbia University, 1975), p. 292; "Vice Report," p. 12; George E. Worthington and Ruth Topping, *Specialized Courts Dealing with Sex Delinquency* (New York, 1921); Rosen, pp. 140–41; pp. 203–204, fn. 12.

34. Clifford Roe, *Panderers and Their Slaves* (New York, 1910), p. 94; "The Slave Traffic in America," *Outlook,* Vol. 93 (November 6, 1909): 528–29; Ernest Bell, *Fighting the Traffic in Young Girls* (Philadelphia, 1910), pp. 188–89, 260–62; "The 'White Slave' Revelations," *Current Literature,* Vol. 47, No. 6 (December 1909):595–98; "White Slaves," *Outlook,* Vol. 93 (December 25, 1909):581A–582; Vern L. Bullough, *The History of Prostitution* (New York, 1964), ch. 14; *The Social Evil,* ed., E.R.A. Seligman (New York, 2nd ed., 1912), ch. 2; Roy Lubove, "The Progressives and the Prostitute," *Historian,* Vol. 24 (May 1962):308–30; Fried, p. 18; Story Number 197; JM, March 29, 1901; George Kibbe Turner, "The Daughters of the Poor," *McClure's Magazine,* Vol. 34, No. 1 (November 1909):45, 49; S. S. McClure, "The Tammanyizing of a Civilization," *McClure's Magazine,* Vol. 34, No. 1 (November 1909):118; Rosen, ch. 7.

35. Story Number 231, 807; George Kibbe Turner, "The Daughters of the Poor," pp. 48–52.

36. See also Sholom Asch, *The God of Vengeance,* trans. Isaac Goldberg (Boston, 1918); Reginald W. Kauffmann, *House of Bondage* (New York, 1910), p. 79.

37. U.S. Immigration Commission, *The Importation* . . . , pp. 67–68; Feldman, p. 203; Frances Kellor, "The Menace of Intelligence Offices," *Jewish Charity,* Vol. 3, No. 6 (March 1904):136–38; Frances Kellor, *Out of Work* (New York, 1906/7); Belle L. Israels, "The Way of the Girl," *Survey,* Vol. 22 (July 3, 1909):486–97, especially p. 494; George Kibbe Turner, "The Daughters of the Poor," p. 56; Polly Adler, *A House Is Not A Home* (New York, 1953), pp. 20–21.

38. Turner, "The Daughters of the Poor," p. 59; Committee of Fourteen, *The Social Evil* (New York, 1st ed., 1902), pp. 183–86.

39. Feldman, p. 194; Arthur Goren, *New York Jews and the Quest for Community* (New York, 1970), pp. 139–40; "Report of the London White Slave Traffic Conference," AH, April 22, 1910; Victor Mirelman, "The Jews in Argentina, 1890–1930" (Ph.D. diss., Columbia University, 1973), ch. 8; U.S. Immigration Commission, *The Importation* . . . , pp. 60–63; 76–77.

40. Isaac Hourwich, "The White Slavery," *Federation Review,* Vol. 4, No. 1 (December 1909):1. See also Maurice Fishberg, "The White Slave Traffic and the Jews," *Federation Review,* Vol. 4, No. 1 (December 1909):2–4.

41. Kate Claghorn, "Crime and Immigration: A Clinical Study of Two

Hundred and Thirteen Immigrants Admitted to Sing Sing Prison within a Period of Nine Months," *Journal of the American Institute of Criminal Law and Criminology*, Vol. 8 (1917–1918):675–76.

4. TWO "PARTICULAR OCCASIONS"

1. Irving Howe, *World of Our Fathers* (New York, 1976), p. 101; JDF, January 10, 1898; Story Number 6, MA 1779.

2. AH, March 31, 1922; Harry Newberger to Judah Magnes, April 7, 1916, p. 3, MA 1774; Story Number 124, 128; "Vice Report," November 14, 1913, MA 1765, p. 201; Winthrop S. Lane, "The Four Gunmen," *Survey*, Vol. 32, No. 1 (April 4, 1914):13–16; Howe, p. 96. Newberger to Judah Magnes, April 7, 1916, p. 3; AH, August 29, 1913.

3. Newberger to Judah Magnes, April 7, 1916, p. 5; Theodore A. Bingham, "Foreign Criminals in New York," *North American Review*, Vol. 187 (September 1908):383.

4. JDF, September 1, 1908; JT, September 1, 1908; Arthur Goren, *New York Jews and the Quest for Community* (New York, 1970), ch. 2; New York *Evening Journal*, September 2, 1908; AH, September 4, 1908; New York *American*, September 18, 1908.

5. See for example AH, September 11, 18, 1908; MJ, September 4, 1908; JDF, September 2, 1908; JT, September 2, 1908; HS, September 25, 1908; *Wahrheit*, September 1, 1908.

6. Goren, pp. 30–33; AH, September 11, 1908; New York *American*, September 5, 6, 7, 1908; NYT, September 7, 1908; JT, September 6, 7, 1908; W, September 3, 7, 1908; JDF, September 6, 1908; MJ, September 3, 8, 1908.

7. Robert H. Bremner, *From the Depths: The Discovery of Poverty in the United States* (New York, 1956), p. 157. See for example AJYB (1910–1911):22–36; "Address of Jacob Bellikopf," 62nd Annual Convention, District Grand Lodge No. 2, I.O.B.B., June 7, 1914, Bellikopf Papers, American Jewish Archives; "Statement of Cyrus Sulzberger," 61st Congress, *Hearings before the United States Committee on Immigration and Naturalization*, 1910, p. 286. Belief in the infallibility of numbers was so great among American Jews that often some would seek the authority of numbers without truly understanding them. Thus, in an attempt to undermine Bingham's credibility, *Wahrheit* published the court's calendar on an average September day. Noting that out of thirty-nine cases on the docket eight had Jewish names, the paper concluded unmistakably that Jews comprised less than 20% of Gotham's underworld—all this based on *one* statistic! W, September 3, 1908.

8. In the December 29, 1906, issue of *Harper's Weekly*, journalist Frank Marshall White wrote that "of the portraits added to the Rogues Gallery last year, more than sixty percentum were those of Russian Jews." Alarmed, Lauterbach wrote to Bingham a week later asking whether White's comment was accurate. Bingham replied that it was "substantially correct." Repeatedly throughout the course of the year, Lauterbach asked the police department to furnish him with "figures on criminality with reference to various classes and denominations." It was never done. On this exchange see "The Police Department's Correspondence with the League," *Federation Review*, Vol. 2, No. 2 (October 1907):7; Frank Marshall White, "New

York's Ten Thousand Thieves," *Harper's Weekly*, Vol. 50, No. 2610 (December 29, 1906):1892. See also *Federation Review* (hereafter FR), Vol. 2, No. 5 (April 1908):14; FR, Vol. 2, No. 7 (June 1908):1; FR, Vol. 2, No. 8 (July 1908):1–5; AH, September 11, 1908. For a more recent look at the origins of Bingham's figures see my "An Answer to Commissioner Bingham: A Case Study of New York Jews and Crime, 1907," *Yivo Annual of Jewish Social Science*, Vol. 18 (1982).

9. AH, September 11, 1908; NYT, September 17, 1908.

10. E. A. Ross, *The Old World in the New* (New York, 1914), p. 155; JDF, September 17, 1908; JT, September 14, 1908; NYT, April 23, 1900.

11. George B. McClellan, *The Gentleman and the Tiger*, ed., Harold Syrett (New York, 1956), p. 295; NYT, September 7, 1934; *Annual Report of the New York Police Department* (1906), p. 23; quoted in AH, September 11, 1908. See also "Because You Are a Jew," *Independent*, Vol. 65 (November 26, 1908):1214.

12. AH, September 25, 1908; JT, September 8, 1908.

13. The following account is drawn from Andy Logan, *Against the Evidence: The Becker-Rosenthal Affair* (New York, 1970); Henry H. Klein, *Sacrificed: The Story of Police Lieutenant Becker* (New York, 1927); NYT, July–December 1912; Joseph Corrigan, "Magnates of Crime," *McClure's Magazine*, Vol. XL, No. 1 (November 1912):1–11.

14. New York *World*, July 30, 17, 1912; New York *Herald Tribune*, July 30, 1915; NYT, August 15, 1912; "Barbarism in New York," *Outlook*, Vol. 101, No. 651 (July 27, 1912):651.

15. New York *American*, July 28, 1912. The New York *Herald* and its sister paper the *Evening Telegram* were two exceptions to this general policy. At various times, both newspapers called Rosenthal "an undersized Jew . . . malignant, greedy and coldblooded"; the alleged murderers "East Side Thugs," and the Jewish owners of gambling parlors "Jew Gamblers." See New York *Herald*, July 18, 19, 30, 1912; New York *Evening Telegram*, July 17, 1912. See also JT, July 28, 1912.

16. W, July 17, 1912; "Jewish Disclaimer of Gambling Profanation," *Literary Digest*, Vol. 45, No. 2 (August 24, 1912):305; JT, July 28, 1912; MJ, July 23, August 1, 1912; Marcella Tow, "The Neighborhood Druggist," *Commentary*, Vol. 3, No. 2 (February 1947) 168; Lane, pp. 13–16; James Forbes, "Where the Gunmen Come From," *Outlook*, Vol. 104 (November 30, 1912):719–22; AH, August 2, 1912; Stories Number 122–129, especially Number 124; W, August 4, 1912; Cyrus L. Sulzberger quoted in AH, November 29, 1912; AH, September 16, 1912.

17. JT, July 21, 28, 1912; MJ, July 22, 1912; AH, August 9, 1912; W, July 18, 27, 1912; JDF, July 23, 27, 1912.

18. W, July 22, August 3, 1912; AH, September 6, 1912; December 12, 1912.

19. W, August 5, 1912; AH, December 12, 1912; Cyrus Sulzberger to Judah Magnes, August 11, 1912; Cyrus Sulzberger to Judah Magnes, September 14, 1912, MA 1749; Goren, p. 159; W, July 18, 25, 1912; "Minutes of the Executive Board of the Kehillah," August 1912, MA 1753; AH, August 23, August 2, 1912.

20. AH, August 23, 1912; MJ, July 30, August 1, 1912.

21. W, August 5, 1912; Goren, pp. 162–63, 170; "Vice Report," pp. 12,

30; Jonah J. Goldstein, Oral History Interview, American Jewish Committee, p. 59.

22. Abe Shoenfeld, Oral History Interview, American Jewish Committee, pp. 125, 215; Letter sent by Judah Magnes to Kehillah supporters, January 12, 1914, MA 1765; *4th Annual Report, Jewish Community of New York (1913)*, pp. 16–17.

23. Abe Shoenfeld to Judah Magnes, January 5, 1915, pp. 5–6, MA 1768; Goren, pp. 177–78; 180–81. See also Judah Magnes to Felix Warburg, January 12, 1913, Warburg Papers, Box 165, American Jewish Archives.

24. W, August 3, 1912; Goren, p. 154; AH, December 12, 1913.

5. FROM SANCTUARY TO MARKETPLACE

1. AH, August 9, 1912; Albert Fried, *The Rise and Fall of the Jewish Gangster in America* (New York, 1980), p. 93; Cornelius Willemse, *Behind the Green Lights* (New York, 1931), p. 284.

2. Quoted in Herbert Asbury, *The Great Illusion* (New York, 1950), p. 151. See also Thomas Coffey, *The Long Thirst* (New York, 1975), ch. 1; Charles Merz, *The Dry Decade* (New York, 1930), ch. 7; Joseph Gusfeld, *Symbolic Crusade* (Urbana, 1966).

3. NYT, January 29, 1917; Louis Marshall to Emanuel Celler, May 24, 1924 in Charles Reznikoff, ed., *Champion of Liberty* (Philadelphia, 1957), Vol. 2, p. 1006; Louis Wolsey to Morris Lazaron, May 20, 1926, CCAR Archives, Box 2375mm, American Jewish Archives.

4. Charles Bernheimer, *The Russian Jew in the United States* (Philadelphia, 1905), pp. 222, 327; AH, quoted in "Religious Press on the Prohibition Amendment," *Literary Digest*, Vol. 60, No. 32 (February 15, 1919):33; Fishberg quoted in Bernheimer, pp. 222, 290–91; Donald Davison Glad, "Attitudes and Experiences of American-Jewish and American-Irish Male Youth as Related to Differences in Adult Rates of Inebriety," *Quarterly Journal of Studies on Alcohol*, Vol. 8, No. 3 (December 1947):409; Maurice Fishberg, "Health and Sanitation of the Immigrant Jewish Population," *Menorah*, Vol. 33, No. 2 (August 1902):79. See also Charles R. Snyder, *Alcohol and the Jews: A Cultural Study of Drinking and Sobriety* (Glencoe, 1958), p. 3.

Then, too, the liquor business had for centuries been a major part of European Jewish economic life; the production and distribution of spirits was one of the chief occupations of Russian and Polish Jews. In the villages and small towns of the Russian and Polish countryside, the Jewish tavern was a common feature of the landscape and a major source of revenue for the Jews of both countries. See for example Simon Dubnow, *The History of the Jews in Russia and Poland* (New York, 1975), Vol. 2, pp. 72, 265; Vol. 3, p. 17.

5. JDF, February 1, 1920; July 28, 1920; AH, January 23, 1920; *Masekhet Prohibition* (New York, 1929), p. 1.

6. AH, December 26, 1919; Cover letter to CCAR Members Sent by Rabbi Edward Calish, January 2, 1922, CCAR Archives, Box 1410; CCAR Yearbook, Vol. 32 (1922):106–110; Stephen S. Wise, quoted in NYT, January 29, 1917; AH, January 6, 1922.

7. "Regulation Number Sixty Relative to the Manufacture, Sale, Barter,

Transportation, Importation, Exportation, Delivery, Furnishing, Purchase, Possession and Use of Intoxicating Liquor under the National Prohibition Act of October 28, 1919," *United States Treasury Decisions*, Number 2985, Vol. 22, January 16, 1920 (Washington, D.C., 1921), pp. 65–126, especially pp. 88–89; *United States Treasury Decisions*, Number 2881, Vol. 21, July 3, 1919. It is, of course, conceivable that Treasury officials met informally with clergymen to discuss this aspect of Prohibition but I have not come across any official references to such a meeting. The *Congressional Record* between 1917 and 1920 (65th and 66th Congress), for example, reports no discussions of this sort.

8. "To the Members of the CCAR," March 19, 1920, CCAR Archives, Box 2375. See also "Report of the Committee on Responsa—Prohibition and Sacramental Wine among the Jews," *CCAR Yearbook*, Vol. 30 (1920):108–12; NYT, January 23–26, 1922; Louis Ginzberg, "Whether Unfermented Wine May Be Used in Jewish Ceremonies," AJYB, Vol. 25 (1923–24):400; MJ, Jaunary 24, 1922. Another responsum on this subject, drawing a similar conclusion, is that of Reverend Dr. Moses Hyamson. Entitled "The Jewish Concept of Wine and Its Use," the responsum was read before the New York Board of Jewish Ministers on February 19, 1920. A copy is in the New York Public Library.

9. Louis Marshall to Rabbi Moses Z. Margolies, March 20, 1920, in Reznikoff, Vol. 2, p. 933 (my emphasis); NYT, May 2, 1925; *Jewish Daily Bulletin* (JDB), September 3, 1925; NYT, October 28, 1927; *Jewish Forum*, Vol. 6, No. 4 (May 1923):267.

10. Louis Marshall to D. H. Blair, quoted in AJYB, Vol. 25 (1923–24): 379; Ben Halpern, "America Is Different," in Marshall Sklare, ed., *The Jews: Social Patterns of an American Group* (Glencoe, 1958), p. 70; Louis Marshall to Albert Lasker, June 7, 1932 in Reznikoff, Vol. 2, p. 935; *Tog*, December 23, 1921; Leo Franklin to Felix Levy, December 5, 1919, CCAR Archives, Box 2375ee. Other religious groups also viewed the abuse of the sacramental wine privilege as a Jewish issue. In 1922, after learning of Marshall's efforts at convincing American Jewry to refrain from availing itself of the sacramental wine privilege, the National Catholic Welfare Council, afraid that the privilege was "in danger," inquired of the New York State Prohibition Director as to its status. He assured the council that he had no intention of abolishing the privilege, only to regulate more effectively its use at home among the Jews. This story was later played up in the pages of the *Catholic News*, the official paper of the New York Archdiocese, as proof that violations of the sacramental wine privilege were committed by Jews. See *Catholic News*, January 7, 1922.

11. Louis Marshall to D. H. Blair, AJYB, Vol. 25 (1923–24):379.

12. Burton Hendricks, "The Jew in America: The 'Menace' of the Polish Jew," *World's Work*, Vol. 45 (February 1923):371; Imogen Oakley, "The American People versus the Alien Bootlegger," *Outlook*, Vol. 143 (May 5, 1926):18; Martha Bruere, *Does Prohibition Work?* (New York, 1927), pp. 253, 257 (my emphasis); Mark Haller, "Bootleggers and American Gambling, 1920–50," in Commission on the Review of National Policy towards Gambling, *Gambling in America* (Washington, D.C., 1976), p. 109. I would like to thank Professor Haller for bringing this article to my attention.

Author's sample drawn from the docket books of the U.S. Attorney's Office, Southern District, 1924, 1928, 1932. Every twentieth name from the dockets was taken over a period of three years to create a sample population of 1,200 persons with information on the name, offense and disposition of each case; unfortunately, the defendant's "nativity" was not provided. Despite this limitation, the docket books provide a useful index to the number of persons arraigned on charges of violating the Volstead Act during the late 1920s and early 1930s. The docket books are currently housed in the Federal Archives and Records Center, Bayonne, New Jersey. See also Constantine Panunzio, "The Foreign Born and Prohibition," *Annals of the American Academy of Political and Social Science*, Vol. 163 (September 1932):151.

13. Leo Katcher, *The Big Bankroll* (New York, 1958), p. 232; Larry L. May and Elaine Tyler May, "Why Jewish Movie Moguls: An Exploration in American Culture," *American Jewish History*, Vol. LXXII, No. 1 (September 1982):6–25; Irving Howe, *World of Our Fathers* (New York, 1976), p. 165; Haller, pp. 117, 109; John Landesco, "Prohibition and Crime," *Annals of the American Academy of Political and Social Science*, Vol. 163 (September 1932):125.

14. Bruere, p. 225.

15. The following account is drawn from Elmer Irey, *Tax Dodgers* (New York, 1948), pp. 134–53; "Breweries Operated by the Jewish Syndicate, 1928–1933," Report found in the William O'Dwyer Papers, New York City Municipal Archives, Box 9244, n.d.; NYT, September 25, 1925; April 28, May 26, November 22, November 24, December 2, 1933; Joseph Driscoll, "Men of Action," *The New Outlook*, Vol. 162, No. 5 (November 1933): 27; Fried, p. 92.

16. "Breweries Operated . . .", pp. 3–4; NYT, November 24, 1933; Merz, p. 66; Irey, pp. 142–43; "Report on Abner 'Longy' Zwillman," Report found in the William O'Dwyer Papers, Box 9244, n.d. This document noted that Seagram Distillers, soon to become one of the nation's largest legitimate distributors of liquor, had been one of Longy's major clients during Prohibition. At that time, Longy's gang had not only provided the Canadian liquor concern with the illegal alcohol to "cut" its whiskey but had also smuggled liquor on Seagram's behalf into the United States.

17. This account is drawn from NYT, March 30, November 7, December 23, 1921; January 4, 28, February 2, September 13, October 13, 16, 17, November 11, 1922; April 28, May 16, October 2, 1926; February 8, 1927; Izzy Einstein, *Prohibition Agent Number One* (New York, 1932); Leo R. Sack, "The Sacramental Wine Scandal," AH, March 20, March 27, 1925; June 17, 1927; JDF, December 7, 1926; Rudolph Coffee, "Stamping out Wine Congregations," *Survey*, Vol. 49 (December 14, 1922):366–67.

18. It stands to reason that at least some of those violating the sacramental wine provision were non-Jews. Since the docket books of the U.S. Attorney's Office, however, do not record the religion of those arraigned before it, there is no surefire way of ascertaining the religious complexion of Prohibition violators; United States Congress, Senate. 68th Congress, First Session. *Hearings before the Select Committee on the Investigation of the Bureau of Internal Revenue* (Washington, D.C., 1925), p. 2184.

19. United States Department of the Treasury. Bureau of Industrial

Alcohol. *Statistics Concerning Intoxicating Liquor* (Washington, D.C., 1931), pp. 58–59.

20. AH, March 27, 1925. "Testimony of Roy Haynes," United States Congress. Senate. 68th Congress, First Session. *Hearings before the Select Committee on the Investigation of the Bureau of Internal Revenue* (Washington, D.C., 1925), pp. 2184–85.

21. Coffey, pp. 170–71.

22. NYT, February 2, April 9, 1921; *Tog*, March 31, 1921; NYT, September 15, November 12, 1922; AH, November 24, 1922; JDF, March 25, 1925; *Washington Post*, November 23, 1925; JDB, January 29, 1926. For its part, the Catholic press firmly emphasized that Andrews's regulations were intended to correct the abuses associated "with the distribution of Jewish sacramental wine." "This is supported by the fact," *Catholic News* observed, "that General Andrews . . . conferred with several prominent Jewish leaders. Absolutely no changes are contemplated," stressed the weekly, "which will in any way affect the procedure of distributing sacramental wine for the use of Catholic priests," *Catholic News*, November 7, 1925.

23. NYT, November 23, 1925; JDF, December 2, 1925; Moshe Davis, "Jewish Religious Life and Institutions in America (A Historical Study)" in Louis Finkelstein, ed., *The Jews: Their History, Culture and Religion* (New York, 1960), Vol. 1, pp. 488–587; AH, December 24, 1922.

24. AH, June 17, 1927; MJ, December 3, 1925; *Washington Post*, November 23, 1925; *Tog*, December 5, 1925.

25. NYT, August 27, 1926. Facetiously, the *Morgen Journal* regarded the large number of withdrawals differently: as proof that American Jews had not weakened in their attachment to Jewish ritual. MJ, March 29, 1926; NYT, August 27, 1926; JDF, August 27, 1926; *Tog*, August 27, 1926; MJ, August 27, 1926; JT, August 27, 1926; NYT, August 28, 1926; JDF, August 29, 1926; "Closing Jewish Wine Shops," *Outlook*, Vol. 144 (September 8, 1926):39–40.

26. NYT, August 29, 1926; JT, August 28, 1926; MJ, August 29, 1926; *Tog*, August 29, 1926; JDF, August 30, 1926.

27. NYT, September 28, October 5, 1926; *Tog*, October 5, 6, 1926; JT, October 5, 1926; MJ, October 6, 1926.

28. *Tog*, October 6, 12, 1926; AH, November 29, 1926; JDF, October 6, 1926.

29. NYT, December 9, 1926; U.S. Congress, House of Representatives, Committee on Appropriations, 69th Congress, First Session, *Hearings before a Subcommittee of the House Committee on Appropriations*. Vol. 18, pp. 254–55 (my emphasis).

30. Fiorello La Guardia to General Andrews, December 8, 1926, La Guardia Papers, Box 2742, New York City Municipal Archives; NYT, December 10, 1926.

31. NYT, January 8, February 3, 1927; La Guardia to Andrews, May 2, 1927; Andrews to La Guardia, May 6, 1927, La Guardia Papers, Box 2742; NYT, February 8, 1927; U.S. Treasury, Bureau of Industrial Alcohol, *Statistics Concerning Intoxicating Liquor* (Washington, D.C., 1932), pp. 53–54.

32. Louis Marshall to Albert Lasker, June 7, 1932 in Reznikoff, p. 935.

6. UNSAVORY CONNECTIONS

1. Louis Adamic, "Racketeers," *New Republic*, Vol. LXV, No. 840 (January 7, 1931):210. What follows is drawn from Thomas E. Dewey, *Twenty against the Underworld* (New York, 1974); Murray Gurfein, "Racketeering," *Encyclopedia of Social Sciences* (New York, 1937), pp. 45–50, especially p. 47; John Hutchinson, *The Imperfect Union: A History of Corruption in American Trade Unions* (New York, 1972); Harold Seidman, *Labor Czars: A History of Labor Racketeering* (New York, 1938); Craig Thompson, *Gang Rule in New York* (New York, 1940); Donald Cresey, *Theft of a Nation* (New York, 1969), pp. 95–99; interview with Judge Charles Breitel.

2. NYT, June 29, 1935.

3. U.S. Congress, Senate, 73rd Congress, Second Session. *Hearings before a Subcommittee of the Committee on Commerce.* Investigation of So-Called "Rackets," p. 101; Gurfein, p. 44; Herbert Asbury, *The Gangs of New York* (New York, 1928), pp. 361–63; "Vice Report," November 14, 1913, p. 13, MA 1765.

4. NYT, May 16, 1915; Asbury, pp. 362–63; Cornelius Willemse, *Behind the Green Lights* (New York, 1931), pp. 289–302; Story Number 719, 871; New York *World*, May 13, 1916; NYT, January 12, 1914; May 13, 16, 1915; *Tog*, May 15, 1915; "Gunmen's Crimes in New York," *Independent*, Vol. 82, No. 3468 (May 24, 1915):316; Louis Adamic, "Racketeers and Organized Labor," *Harper's Magazine*, Vol. 161 (1930):407; Adamic, "Racketeers," pp. 46–51.

5. Story Number 719, 443, 762, 852, 871; Charles Zimmerman's unpublished rebuttal of Benjamin Stolberg's *Tailor's Progress*, 1944 in the Charles Zimmerman Collection, ILGWU Archives, Box 114, Folder 34, p. 1; George Kibbe Turner, "Tammany's Control of New York by Professional Criminals," *McClure's Magazine*, Vol. 33, No. 2 (June 1909):123; Grand Jury of the County of New York, Court of General Sessions, *The People of the State of New York vs. John Doe*, March 15, 1915 (hereafter Grand Jury). Testimony of Benjamin Fine, pp. 14, 33.

6. Asbury, p. 362; NYT, May 13, 16, 1915; Story Number 745, 871; Testimony of Benjamin Fine, Grand Jury, p. 40; Testimony of Jacob Fine, March 18, 1915, Grand Jury, pp. 103–104.

7. Asbury, p. 363; NYT, May 13, 1915; Story Number 1, 282; "Using Gangs in Labor's Wars," *Literary Digest*, Vol. 50 (May 29, 1915):1260; Benjamin Schlesinger to Arthur Woods, July 2, 1915, Schlesinger Collection, ILGWU Archives, Box 2, Folder 5, p. 2; Testimony of Benjamin Fine, p. 19.

8. New York *World*, May 13, 1915; Asbury, p. 361; "Vice Report," p. 26; Story Number 871.

9. Story Number 871; NYT, May 30, 1915; JDF, May 12, 1915; MJ, May 12, 1915. Writing in 1931, police official Cornelius Willemse related that "Dopey Benny . . . is on the level now." Willemse, p. 302.

10. New York *World*, May 13, 1915; NYT, January 24, May 12, 1915; New York *Evening Post*, May 12, 1915; Testimony of Benjamin Fine, pp. 18, 33, 37, 68, 77; New York Supreme Court, Criminal Branch, Trial Term, Part One, *The People of the State of New York vs. Morris Stupnicker, Max Sigman, Julius Woolf, Solomon Metz, John Auspitz, John Wedinger*

and Max Singer, Vol. 1, September 23, 1915 (hereafter Court Transcript), pp. 9, 49, 117, 186–90. Portions of this document can be found in the ILGWU Archives, Collection 11. See also Kenneth Wolpin, "Gangsters and Union Officials: Attitudes toward Crime in the Jewish Immigrant Community" (M.A. thesis, Columbia University, 1977).

11. JDF, May 12, 13, 18, 19, 1915; W, May 18, 1915; "To the Executive Board, Local # _____, August 14, 1915"; "To the Executive Board, Local # _____, March 1, 1915," Schlesinger Collection, ILGWU Archives, Box 3, Folder 3. Mass meetings were often staged in support of the seven defendants. Thus, in June, 1915, the "Baltimore Defence [sic] Conference" wrote to Benjamin Schlesinger, the ILGWU's president, asking him "to send us two prominent speakers one in English and one in jewish [sic] . . . to create a sentiment amongst the public in general and especially our local English press. . . ." H. Gold to Benjamin Schlesinger, June 7, 1915, Schlesinger Collection, Box 1, Folder 9.

12. Morris Hillquit, *Loose Leaves from a Busy Life* (New York, 1934), pp. 132–33; Story Number 282; JDF, May 19, 1915; Benjamin Schlesinger to Samuel Gompers, May 22, 1915, Schlesinger Collection, Box 2, Folder 7, p. 1.

13. W, May 15, 1915; *Tog*, May 15, 1915; MJ, May 16, 1915.

14. MJ, October 11, 1915; W, September 26, 1915.

15. Court Transcript, pp. 407, 457, 458, 459; JDF, September 24, 1915; Story Number 871; Hillquit, pp. 137–40; JDF, October 1, 1915; *Tog*, October 1, 1915; W, October 1, 1915; Wolpin, p. 8. See also correspondence of Lillian Wald with Simon Hirdansky, May 13, 17, 1915, Wald Collection, Columbia University Manuscript Collections, Box 19. There, the social worker described Sulkes's organization as a "scab union." On Isaac Levine, see Court Transcript, pp. 186–90. When asked why Sulkes' union chose to call itself the ILGWU of the World, Levine replied: "I don't know . . . I was not asked anything and I did not know anything." Hearing this, the defense asked incredulously, "You know what you are president of?" Court Transcript, pp. 454–55.

16. Hillquit, p. 140; JDF, October 9, 10, 1915; W, October 9, 10, 1915; MJ, October 11, 1915; *Tog*, October 10, 1915; W, October 10, 1915.

17. Benjamin Stolberg, *Tailor's Progress* (New York, 1944), p. 253, ch. 7; J. B. S. Hardman, "The Inter-Relationship of the Jewish and General American Labor Movement," *Yivo Annual of Jewish Social Science*, Vol. 9 (1954):373; Irving Howe, *World of Our Fathers* (New York, 1976), pp. 331–38; General Executive Board of the ILGWU to Executive Council, AFL, January 10, 1927, Sigman Collection, ILGWU Archives, Box 2, Folder 1, p. 1; Statement by Morris Sigman, President of the ILGWU, June 1925, Sigman Collection, ILGWU Archives, Box 6, Folder 13, p. 1; Morris Sigman to Chief Inspector John Lahey, June 17, 1925, Sigman Collection, ILGWU Archives, Box 4, Folder 1, p. 3. "The great problem," writes labor historian John Hutchinson with regard to researching the history of labor racketeering, "is evidence. Private records of unsavory episodes are seldom available and definitive public documentation is rare." Available information is also highly partisan, with both the right and left wings accusing one another of having invited the participation of gangsters in the first place. The account that follows is drawn from the (hitherto unexamined) records of Thomas E. Dewey's administration first as New York County

Special Prosecutor and then as New York County District Attorney. Currently located in the New York City Municipal Archives, this collection includes reports issued by Dewey's staff of private investigators; transcripts of their interviews with the victims of racketeering and, in many instances, with racketeers themselves; internal office memoranda and random staff notes. Additionally, several of the surviving members of Dewey's staff—Judges Charles Breitel, Stanley Fuld, Jacob Grumet and Mr. Victor Herwitz—were interviewed at length; sadly, Judge Murry Gurfein died before I had an opportunity to meet with him.

18. Stolberg, p. 143, ch. 7; NYT, November 12, December 17, 22, 1926; Howe, pp. 331–38; Open letter to ILGWU Workers from Morris Sigman, September 21, 1926, Sigman Collection, Box 1, Folder 20, p. 1; General Executive Board of the ILGWU to Executive Council, AFL, p. 2; ILGWU Oral History Interview with Charles S. Zimmerman, November 8, 1976, pp. 384–85, 386. Selected portions of that interview were made available to me by Henoch Mendelsund, Director of the ILGWU Archives, and with the kind permission of Charles Zimmerman. Interestingly enough, as late as 1944 Zimmerman persisted in denying that the Communist-dominated ILGWU had used the services of Little Augie in 1926. In his unpublished rebuttal to Stolberg, Zimmerman wrote (pp. 1–2), "It is not true . . . that the Joint Board employed professional gangsters. . . . Neither Little Augie nor any other professional gangster ever worked for the Joint Board during the strike. . . . The facts are very different. . . . The only connection the Joint Board or the cloakmakers ever had with gorillas consisted of the blows they received on the picket lines from the gangsters."

19. Stolberg, p. 143; NYT, November 12, 1926; November 21, 1931; Meyer Berger, "Lepke: The Shy Boss of Bloody Murder, Inc. Awaits Death in the Electric Chair," Life, Vol. 16 (February 28, 1944):88.

20. Interviews with Victor Herwitz, Judge Jacob Grumet; Howe, p. 337; Matthew Josephson, Sidney Hillman: Statesman of American Labor (New York, 1952), pp. 327–51; J. B. S. Hardman, "The Needle Trade Unions: A Labor Movement at Fifty," Social Research (1950):345–46.

21. NYT, July 16, 25, November 21, 1930; January 1, March 8, 1931; Thomas Crain to Benjamin Schlesinger, November 15, 1930, Schlesinger Collection, Box 1, Folder 3. Several months after convening this conference, Max Zaritsky, president of the Cap and Millinery Workers' Union, charged that Crain's war on racketeering was nothing more than "window dressing."

22. Howe, p. 337; NYT, June 26, 27, 29, July 1, 20, 30, 1931; November 21, 1931; JDF, July 29, 1931; Tog, July 29, 30, 1931; Albert Fried, The Rise and Fall of the Jewish Gangster in America (New York, 1980), pp. 232–40; George Soule, Sidney Hillman: Labor Statesman (New York, 1939); Josephson, pp. 327–40; Howe, p. 338.

23. Josephson, pp. 338–40; Joel Seidman, The Needle Trades (New York, 1924), pp. 191–94.

24. The Reminiscences of William O'Dwyer (1965), p. 417, in the Oral History Collection of Columbia University; NYT, October 16, 1935; "Louis Buchalter: Notice of Criminal Record, March 29, 1940" in William O'Dwyer Papers, Box 2500; Louis Valentine, Night Stick (New York, 1947), pp. 131–

41; Berger, pp. 86–88; Andrew Tully, *Treasury Agent* (New York, 1958), p. 51; Dewey, ch. 14.

25. NYT, October 16, 17, 26, 30, November 5, 1927. Morris Drabner, a former member of the Pocketbook Makers' Union, told Dewey that he was "quite certain that . . . Gurrah himself killed Little Augie." Drabner Testimony, n.d., Thomas E. Dewey Collection, New York City Municipal Archives, Box 2465; Valentine, p. 135; interview with Mr. Victor Herwitz.

26. Moses Rischin, *The Promised City: New York Jews, 1870–1914* (New York, 1970), p. 60; *Real Estate Record and Builders' Guide,* December 6, 1919, pp. 559–62.

27. Interview with Mr. Victor Herwitz; Judges Charles Breitel and Stanley Fuld; Dewey, p. 305.

28. To protect the identity of those who testified before Dewey and may still be alive today, I have used their initials instead of their full names. "Testimony of I. R., September 18, 1939," Dewey Collection, Box 2842; "Testimony of I. F., October 9, 1939," Dewey Collection, Box 2842.

29. "Testimony of M. B., September 8, 1929," Dewey Collection, Box 2842; "Testimony of J. G., June 13, 1938," Dewey Collection, Box 2842; "Memorandum Re: Benny Levine from Abraham Poretz to Frank Hogan, December 1, 1942," Dewey Collection, Box 2500.

30. Josephson, p. 339; "Danny Fields, February 14, 1938," Dewey Collection, Box 2842.

31. Interview with Mr. Victor Herwitz.

32. NYT, September 14, 15, 1938; O'Dwyer Reminiscences, Vol. 8, pp. 236–39; "Statement of Sylvia Rosen, October 16, 1936," William O'Dwyer Collection, New York City Municipal Archives, Box 9243; "Statement of Morris Blustein, June 27, 1941," William O'Dwyer Collection, Box 9248; "Statement of Harold Rosen, October 16, 1936," William O'Dwyer Collection, Box 9243; "Statement of Mrs. Joseph Rosen, September 23, 1936," William O'Dwyer Collection, Box 9243.

33. NYT, October 16, 1935; October 27, 29, November 6, 9, 10, 17, 30, 1936; Foner, pp. 396–414.

34. NYT, August 10, 13, October 2–4, 1937. See also Thomas E. Dewey Collection, Boxes 2456 and 2472 for information on the bakery and flour trucking rackets; NYT, April 15, 26, June 18, 1939; Federal Writers Project. WPA. Jews of New York. "Jews in Rackets." Municipal Archives, Box 2633.

35. NYT, April 15, 1938; August 10, 1937; August 24–26, 1939; January 3, 1940.

36. NYT, January 5, 11, February 16, 17, March 1, 1940; interview with Judge Jacob Grumet; Indictment Number 22174, October 31, 1939, Dewey Collection, Box 2465.

37. Philip Reister, "The Live Poultry Industry of Metropolitan New York," unpublished mimeographed report, 1935. Commissioned by the New York City Commissioner of Markets who was alarmed at what he perceived to be the growing control of the industry by racketeers, the Reister study is an invaluable source of information on New York's poultry trade. A copy is in the Business School Library of Columbia University. See also Harold P. Gastwirt, *Fraud, Corruption and Holiness: The Controversy over the Supervision of the Jewish Dietary Practice in New York*

(Port Washington, 1974); Gordon Sprague, *An Economic Survey of the Live Poultry Industry in New York* (Washington, D.C., 1933); Elias B. Goodman, "The Baff Murder, January 1915," p. 12, John P. Mitchel Papers, New York City Municipal Archives, Box 196.

38. NYT, March 2, 23, 24, April 5, 1910; May 30, July 28, August 16, 18, 1911; November 24–27, December 3, 16, 21, 31, 1914; JDF, November 25, 26, 1914; Sarah Shane, "Chronicles: The Kosher Chicken Racket," *Menorah Journal*, Vol. 18, No. 2 (February 1930):152.

39. Goodman, pp. 2, 4–10.

40. NYT, December 10, 1916; July 20, 1917; Reister, pp. 24–25; Elias B. Goodman, "In re: Poultry Situation—The Rule of Gangsters, September 1913," pp. 1, 8, Mitchel Papers, Box 196.

41. Reister, pp. 124–26; NYT, November 24–27, December 3, 16, 21, 31, 1914; JDF, December 17, 22, 28, 1914.

42. Reister, pp. 16, 20–22, 81–85, 88–93; George Solosky, "Rackets and Labor," *Atlantic Monthly*, Vol. 162 (1938):393–402; "The Twenty Million Dollar Chicken Stealers," *Saturday Evening Post*, Vol. 210, No. 25 (December 18, 1937):82; Seidman, ch. 11; Dewey, ch. 15; Isidor Feinstein, "Racketeering in the AFL, Part One: The Poultry Racket," *Nation*, Vol. 141, No. 2662 (September 11, 1935):288–91; JDF, November 21, 1929.

43. JDF, November 21, 1929; "Are You Eating Kosher Food?" *Jewish Forum*, Vol. 11, No. 12 (December 1928):605–606; "Minutes of Meeting of Fact-Finding Commission Appointed by the Mayor to Ascertain Facts Existing in the Kosher Poultry Industry, February 6, 1939 through June 19, 1939," pp. 75, 223–24," Yivo Archives.

44. "Minutes of Meeting . . . ," p. 226; Gastwirt, p. 50.

45. Reister, pp. 16, 21.

46. NYT, May 6, August 15, 21, September 11, 21, 23, 30, November 8, 1928; January 18, 29, 1929; JDF, January 18, 1929; *USA vs. Greater New York Live Poultry Chamber of Commerce*, Information, Indictment No. 61-284, August 20, 1928"; *USA vs. Greater New York Live Poultry Chamber of Commerce*, Special Plea, September 10, 1928"; *USA vs. Greater New York Live Poultry Chamber of Commerce*, Defendants' Motion, September 6, 1928; *USA vs. Greater New York Live Poultry Chamber of Commerce*, Nolle Prosequi, June 10, 1931." These court documents are housed in the Federal Archives and Records Center, Bayonne, New Jersey.

47. Interview with Israel B. Oseas; NYT, October 6, 8, 9, 10, 16, 19, 24, November 15, 19, 22, 1929; *Tog*, October 8, 9, November 22, 24, 1929; JDF, October 7, 9, 10, November 21–23, 1929; Shane, p. 148.

48. NYT, October 9, 10, 19, 24, November 19, 1929.

49. NYT, October 22, November 19, 1929.

50. Reister, pp. 50–52.

51. Reister, p. 32; NYT, April 7, 24, 25, May 13, June 2, 11, 1933; January 20, June 6, 1934.

52. NYT, August 6, 7, 14, 28, September 19, 1935; David Brody, *The Butcher Workmen: A Study of Unionization* (Cambridge, 1964), p. 119; writing in the *Nation*, Isidore Feinstein suggested that the release of the Reister study had prompted Charles Herbert to submit his resignation. The wily racketeer had, of course, expected an unequivocal vote of confidence. Feinstein, p. 290; NYT, August 28, 1935.

53. "Minutes of Meeting . . . ," pp. 224–27; NYT, July 9, 1936.

54. William Morgan to Mayor La Guardia, July 6, 1936, La Guardia Papers, Box 2628, File 80; NYT, January 8, 9, July 20, 28, August 3, 4, 1937; Saturday Evening Post, p. 86. For some unexplained reason, Thomas E. Dewey's files on the brothers Herbert are marked "destroyed" and are missing from the Municipal Archives!

55. NYT, July 20, 1937.

56. "The Problem of the Gangster," AH, January 15, 1915; Walter Lippmann, "The Underworld: A Stultified Conscience," *Forum*, Vol. 85 (February 1931):65–69; Walter Lippmann, "The Underworld: Our Secret Servant," *Forum*, Vol. 85 (January 1931):1–5.

7. THE BUSINESS OF CRIME

1. NYT, November 5, 1928; February 3, 1932; New York *Herald Tribune*, November 5, 1928; New York *World*, November 5, 1928; New York *American*, November 5, 1928. Although Rothstein was reported to have left a sizable body of private papers at the time of his death, they were impounded by the District Attorney's office and as of this writing cannot be located. There are, however, scattered papers relating to Rothstein in the mayoral and police collections of the New York City Municipal Archives but, for the most part, they are thin. Interestingly enough, the New York City Police Department says it may still have some data pertaining to Rothstein's death but unfortunately this material, if indeed it exists, is closed to researchers. Most of what follows, therefore, is drawn from the city's major newspapers—the New York *American*, the New York *Herald Tribune*, the New York *Times*, and the New York *World*—between 1928 and 1932. The extant secondary literature, especially Leo Katcher's *The Big Bankroll* (New York, 1958), proved useful as well.

2. *Herald Tribune*, November 13, 1928; NYT, September 25, 28, 1929; *American*, November 21, 1928.

3. NYT, November 4, 5, 6, 1929.

4. *Herald Tribune*, November 11, 1928; JDF, November 13, 1928; *American*, November 6, 1928; Russell Crouse, *Murder Won't Out* (New York, 1932), p. 237; *World*, November 11, 1928.

5. *Herald Tribune*, November 6, 7, 1928; Crouse, pp. 219–20; NYT, October 6, 1929; *American*, November 7, 1928.

6. Joel Slonim, "The Jewish Gangster," *Reflex*, Vol. 3, No. 1 (July 1928):36–41; "In the Oakhurst Tradition," NYT, November 9, 1928; Bret Harte, "A Passage in the Life of Mr. John Oakhurst," in *The Best of Bret Harte*, eds., Wilhelmina Harper and Aimee Peters (Boston, 1947), p. 288; *Herald Tribune*, November 8, 1928; JDF, November 17, 1928.

7. *Herald Tribune*, November 9, 1928; Katcher, p. 351; Crouse, p. 227. See for example Max Weber's theory of bureaucracy in H. H. Gerth and C. Wright Mills, eds., *From Max Weber: Essays in Sociology* (New York, 1958).

8. NYT, November 18, 1928; *World*, November 11, 1928; Katcher, pp. 20–51; Crouse, p. 221; *Tog*, November 18, 1928.

9. NYT, October 2, 1920; *Herald Tribune*, November 7, 1928.

10. NYT, September 25–27, October 16, 17, November 7, 1920; Katcher,

pp. 139–43; "Jewish Gamblers Corrupt American Baseball" and "Jewish Degradation of American Baseball," in *Jewish Influences in American Life* (Dearborn, 1921), Vol. 3, pp. 38–39, 51–63.

11. NYT, October 2, 1920; *World*, October 1, 1920.

12. Lloyd Morris, *Incredible New York* (New York, 1951), p. 345; Katcher, pp. 232–36.

13. Katcher, p. 297; *Herald Tribune*, November 24, 27, 1928; *World*, November 15, 1928; NYT, December 18, 19, 1928; October 12, 1932.

14. JDF, November 17–24, 1928. How the paper got hold of Rothstein's correspondence with the Cloak, Suit, Dress, Skirt and Reefer Makers' Union is not known.

15. *Freiheit*, November 18, 19, 1928; *Daily Worker*, November 23, December 6, 1928.

16. JDF, November 24, 28, 1928; *Freiheit*, November 19, 20, 1928. See also *World*, November 22, 27, 1928; *Herald Tribune*, November 28, 1928; Irving Howe, *World of Our Fathers* (New York, 1976), pp. 331–38, especially p. 337; *Report and Proceedings of the Nineteenth Convention of the ILGWU*, May 7–17, 1928, pp. 75–77; ILGWU Oral History Interview with Charles Zimmerman, November 8, 1976, pp. 338–39, 395.

17. Howe, p. 384; Crouse, p. 227; Katcher, p. 232.

18. "The Story of Murder, Inc.," NYT, April 1, 1951; Burton Turkus and Sid Feder, *Murder, Inc.* (New York, 1951), p. 8; NYT, April 24, 1941; much of what follows is drawn from the William O'Dwyer Collection, New York City Municipal Archives, Boxes 9244–51.

19. NYT, February 3, 4, 1940; Norton Mockridge and Robert Prall, *The Big Fix* (New York, 1954).

20. Deborah Dash Moore, *At Home in America: Second Generation New York Jews* (New York, 1981), pp. 69–71, 61.

21. NYT, February 3, 1940; *The Reminiscences of William O'Dwyer* (1965), pp. 403, 893, in the Oral History Collection of Columbia University; "The Testimony of Harry Rudolph," n.d., O'Dwyer Collection, Box 9244; "Memorandum Re: Red Alpert, April 3, 1940," O'Dwyer Collection, Box 9249.

22. NYT, March 24, May 16, 1940; O'Dwyer Reminiscences, p. 414; "Memorandum of Information Received Re: The Killing of George DeFeo," n.d., O'Dwyer Collection, Box 9247; "Criminal History of Harry Strauss," n.d., O'Dwyer Collection, Box 9247; "Memorandum of Information Given by Reles on April 24, 1941 Re: Shuman Killing," O'Dwyer Collection, Box 9245; Turkus and Feder, ch. 3; Sammy Aaronson, *As High as My Heart* (New York, 1959), pp. 30, 37, 43.

23. "Memorandum of Information Re: The Killing of George DeFeo," pp. 1, 3; NYT, July 12, 13, September 7, 10, 1931.

24. "Memorandum of Information . . . ," p. 3; NYT, July 12, 13–20, 1931; Turkus and Feder, p. 119; Mark Haller and John Alviti, "Loan Sharking in American Cities: Historical Analysis of a Marginal Enterprise," *American Journal of Legal History*, Vol. 21, No. 2 (April 1977):146–47; "Memorandum of Information Given by Seymour Magoon in Re: Killing of Irving (Puggy) Feinstein," n.d., pp. 3, 9, O'Dwyer Collection, Box 17. See also "Questioning of Louis Benson, Investigation in Re: Killing of "Puggy" Feinstein, June 12, 1940," p. 7, O'Dwyer Collection, Box 17.

25. "Background of Buggsy Goldstein and Harry Strauss as Furnished by Abe Reles," n.d., O'Dwyer Collection, Box 9251; "Re: Louis Capone," n.d., O'Dwyer Collection, Box 9247; "Memorandum of Information Received from Reles on the Killing of Albert 'Plug' Shuman," n.d., p. 3, O'Dwyer Collection, Box 9249.

26. "Testimony of Abe Reles," Transcript of People vs. Nitzberg, May 16, 1941," pp. 62–63, O'Dwyer Collection, Box 9245; NYT, October 26, 1956; "Memorandum of Information Furnished by Seymour Magoon in re Jimmy Abbatamaro," n.d., O'Dwyer Collection, Box 9251; Turkus and Feder, pp. 459–63, 479; "The Criminal Activities of Louis Capone, December 1, 1941," O'Dwyer Collection, Box 9251; "Re: Louis Capone"; "Memorandum of Information Given by Allie Tannenbaum on April 29, 1941 re: Charles 'The Bug' Workman," O'Dwyer Collection, Box 9247; "Testimony of George Stanley Ungar, November 28, 1940," O'Dwyer Collection, Box 9247.

27. "Transcript of People vs. Nitzberg, May 16, 1941," pp. 63, 150; "Memorandum of Information Received from Reles on the Killing of Albert 'Plug' Shuman," p. 2.

28. "Transcript of People vs. Nitzberg," pp. 147, 73; "Memorandum of Information Received from Reles . . . ,"; "Re: Albert Shuman," n.d., O'Dwyer Collection, Box 9244; Handwritten notes on Abe Reles relating to the Nitzberg trial, n.d., O'Dwyer Collection, Box 9244.

29. NYT, March 5, November 13, 1944; O'Dwyer Reminiscences, pp. 435–36.

30. The failure of the Brooklyn District Attorney and the Brooklyn police department to prevent Reles's death or to solve the crime became a heated political issue, the subject of a grand jury investigation and one of the major concerns of the Senate Crime Committee (the Kefauver Committee) of 1950–51. Boxes 9248 and 9250 of the O'Dwyer Collection contain numerous material on the grand jury investigation and the Kefauver Committee. See also William Howard Moore, *The Kefauver Committee and the Politics of Crime* (Columbia, 1974), pp. 195–200.

8. FROM BROOME STREET TO FIFTH AVENUE

1. Ernest Coulter, "The Jews' War on Crime," *Outlook and Independent,* Vol. 158 (August 12, 1931):55–56, 478.

2. Sample drawn from the docket books of the New York County District Attorney's Office, 1918–39. For details see Appendix A; "Jewish Juvenile and Adult Delinquency by Years," *Annual Report, Jewish Board of Guardians* (1932–33), p. 31; F. N. Trager to Morris Fine, July 30, 1940, American Jewish Committee Archives; Jewish Communal Survey of Greater New York. *Report of Executive Committee.* October 1929, p. 31; AH, March 26, 1926.

3. Deborah Dash Moore, *At Home in America: Second Generation New York Jews* (New York, 1981), p. 76.

4. Computed from the *Fourteenth United States Census, Population,* 1920; *Fifteenth United States Census, Population,* 1930; *Sixteenth United States Census, Population,* 1940; "Nativity of All Persons Arraigned," *Annual Report, City Magistrates Courts,* 1920–1940; AH, January 24, 1930.

5. Moore, pp. 30, 22; "East Side Number," *Jewish Forum*, Vol. 6, No. 1 (January 1923):12–13.

6. Nathan Goldberg, "Occupational Patterns of American Jews," *Jewish Review*, Vol. 3, No. 3 (October–December 1945):161–86; Nathan Goldberg, "Occupational Patterns of American Jews," *Jewish Review*, Vol. 3, No. 4 (January 1946):262–90; Thomas Kessner, "Jobs, Ghettoes and the Urban Economy, 1880–1934," *American Jewish History*, Vol. LXXI, No. 2 (December 1981):218–38, especially pp. 234–37; Moore, p. 22; Daniel Bell, "Crime as an American Way of Life," *The End of Ideology* (Glencoe, 1962), pp. 129, 133, 125; Lillian Zahn, "The Economic Status of the Family Circle," p. 10, WPA Collection, New York City Municipal Archives, File 3631—Jews in New York City; *Annual Report of the New York State Commission of Correction*, 1930, 1935, 1940; Clarence J. Enzler, *Some Social Aspects of the Depression, 1930–35* (Washington, D.C., 1939), ch. 6; James M. Williams, *Human Aspects of Unemployment Relief* (Chapel Hill, 1933), ch. 8; Caroline Bird, *The Invisible Scar* (New York, 1966), pp. 285, 63.

7. Sophia Robison, "The Apparent Effects of the Factors of Race and Nationality on the Registration of Behavior as Delinquent in New York City in 1930," *Publications of the American Sociological Society*, Vol. 28 (May 1934):40; Julius Maller, "Juvenile Delinquency among the Jews of New York," *Social Forces*, Vol. 10 (1932):544. Perhaps additional proof can be found in the relatively small number of white-collar cases documented in the D.A. docket books sample between 1918 and 1939. Of a sample of close to one thousand units, fewer than fifty related to the alleged commission of a white collar crime. Jews, however, were disproportionately represented among those charged with committing such offenses, accounting for more than half of that population. See my "Dark Shadows: New York Jews and Crime, 1900–1940" (Ph.D. diss., Columbia University, 1981), pp. 304–306.

8. Report of the Executive Director of the Jewish Board of Guardians, September 21, 1932, p. 3, Archives of the Jewish Board of Children and Family Services (hereafter JBCFS); Minutes of the Committee on Outside Activities of the Jewish Protectory and Aid Society, 1919, Archives of the JBCFS; Minutes of the Board of Managers of the Jewish Protectory and Aid Society, January 30, June 17, 1921, Archives of the JBCFS; *14th Annual Report, Jewish Protectory and Aid Society* (1920), p. 11; Minutes of the Executive Committee Meeting, Jewish Board of Guardians, November 1, 1939, p. 1, Archives of the JBCFS; Address of Mrs. Sidney Borg at the Annual Meeting of the Jewish Board of Guardians, 1932–33, p. 12, Archives of the JBCFS; Report of the Executive Director of the Jewish Board of Guardians, September 21, 1932, p. 2, Archives of the JBCFS.

9. AJYB, Vol. 29 (1926–27):54; AJYB, Vol. 33 (1931–32):203–211; *Digest of Events of Jewish Interest*, Vol. 1, No. 9 (December 30, 1932); *Digest of Events of Jewish Interest*, Vol. 2, No. 35 (September 25, 1933); Harry S. Linfield, "Report of the Statistical Department of the American Jewish Committee for the Year Ending September 30, 1930," American Jewish Committee Archives; H. S. Linfield to Max Kohler, February 5, 1930, American Jewish Committee Archives.

Indeed, the statistics compiled by the New York Jewish community proved useful on various occasions; though published for a general audience, they were kept handy, as AJC President Cyrus Adler put it, "so that we may be ready for outbursts." One such "outburst" occurred late in December 1929 when Nathan Cayton, a Washington, D.C., municipal judge, publicly accused American Jewry of having created a "Jewish crime wave." Published in both local and national newspapers, Cayton's remarks caused a "wave of indignation," leading Washington Jewish leaders to ask the American Jewish Committee's help in drafting a rebuttal. See *Jewish Daily Bulletin*, January 2, 6, 1930; AH, January 10, 1930; Cyrus Adler to Morris Waldman, January 6, 1930, American Jewish Committee Archives; Harry Schneiderman to Louis Marshall, December 9, 1927, American Jewish Committee Archives; Morris Waldman to Cyrus Adler, January 2, 1930, American Jewish Committee Archives.

10. AH, September 7, 1921.

11. Coulter, pp. 55–58; "Why Crimes among Jews Decrease," *Jewish Sentinel* (1931), pp. 10, 29, 39 in Scrapbook Number 3, Alice Davis Menken Papers, American Jewish Historical Society; AH, August 14, 1931; Ernest Coulter, "Alien Colonies and Children's Court," *North American Review*, Vol. 179 (November 1904):731, 733; AH, August 21, October 9, 1931; *Tog*, August 16, 1931.

12. "Scandals within Orthodoxy," *Jewish Forum*, Vol. 11, No. 9 (September 1929):428–30, especially p. 430; *Tog*, November 24, 1929.

13. *Tog*, March 19, 1940.

14. *Tog*, April 26, 1940; JDF, February 18, 1940; November 13, 1942.

15. Ronald Bayor, *Neighbors in Conflict: The Irish, Germans, Jews, and Italians of New York City, 1929–41* (Baltimore, 1978), p. 164; Charles Stember, *Jews in the Mind of America* (New York, 1966); *The Reminiscences of Thomas E. Dewey* (1959), p. 364, in the Oral History Collection of Columbia University; interviews with Judges Stanley Fuld, Charles Breitel, and Jacob Grumet; Victor Herwitz; and Mrs. William B. Herlands.

16. Norman Mirsky, "Toward a Theory of Modern Jewish Social Control," *Judaism*, Vol. 30, No. 4 (Fall 1981):444–52, especially pp. 448, 452; Harold Berman, "Criminality among the Jewish Youth," *Open Court*, Vol. 38, No. 1 (January 1924):48; interviews with Judges Breitel, Fuld, Grumet, and Mr. Victor Herwitz.

17. Interview with Dr. Norman Snyder and Irving Weissman; Dennis Eisenberg, Uri Dan, and Eli Landau, *Meyer Lansky: Mogul of the Mob* (New York, 1979), p. 323; David Singer, "The Jewish Gangster: Crime as 'Unzer Shtik,'" *Judaism*, Vol. 23, No. 1 (Winter 1974):70–77; David Brion Davis, *Homicide in American Fiction: A Study in Social Values, 1796–1860* (Ithaca, 1957), p. viii. "America," he writes, "has ranked hardened killers with the greatest of folk heroes."

18. Eric Monkonnen, *The Dangerous Class: Crime and Poverty in Columbus, Ohio, 1860–1885* (Cambridge, Mass., 1975), p. 79; *Tog*, November 21, 1928.

19. AH, November 29, 1912; Harold Berman, "Criminality among the Jewish Youth," *Open Court*, Vol. 38, No. 1 (January 1924):46.

Index